Researching Student Learning

SRHE and Open University Press Imprint
General Editor: Heather Eggins

Researching Student Learning

Approaches to Studying in Campus-based and Distance Education

John T. E. Richardson

The Society for Research into Higher Education
& Open University Press

Published by SRHE and
Open University Press
Celtic Court
22 Ballmoor
Buckingham
MK18 1XW

email: enquiries@openup.co.uk
world wide web: http://www.openup.co.uk

and
325 Chestnut Street
Philadelphia, PA 19106, USA

First published 2000

A catalogue record of this book is available from the British Library

ISBN   0 335 20515–1   (hbk)

Library of Congress Cataloging-in-Publication Data
Richardson, John T.E.
    Researching student learning: approaches to studying in campus-based and
distance education / John T.E. Richardson.
        p.   cm.
    Includes bibliographical references and indexes.
    ISBN 0–335–20515–1
    1. Distance education.   2. Learning.   3. Open learning.   4. Study skills.
5. Education, Higher.   I. Title.

LC5803.L43 R53 2000
378.1'75—dc21   99–088223

Typeset by Graphicraft Limited, Hong Kong
Printed in Great Britain by St Edmundsbury Press, Bury St Edmunds, Suffolk

Contents

Preface

An unprecedented expansion of higher education has taken place in the vast majority of industrialized and developing countries since the early 1960s. In most cases, this expansion has occurred through campus-based universities offering conventional forms of degree programme. More recently, however, many countries have found it difficult to sustain even the current level of provision in economic terms, and yet world-wide there are increasing numbers of people seeking access to higher education. Daniel (1996) recently argued that this crisis of resources and access could be resolved by the development of 'mega-universities': institutions with over 100,000 students delivering courses by distance-teaching methods using the latest computer and telecommunications technologies. According to Daniel, 11 such institutions already exist:

- Anadolu University (Turkey)
- Centre National d'Enseignement à Distance (France)
- China TV University System
- Indira Gandhi National Open University (India)
- Korea National Open University
- The Open University (United Kingdom)
- Payame Noor University (Iran)
- Sukhothai Thammathirat Open University (Thailand)
- Universidad Nacional de Educación a Distancia (Spain)
- Universitas Terbuka (Indonesia)
- University of South Africa.

To date, of course, the majority of students in higher education around the world have studied in campus-based institutions, and it is therefore not particularly surprising that the mainstream research literature on higher education has invariably taken this traditional setting for granted. Conversely, mainstream researchers into higher education have in the past paid little attention to the possibility of course delivery by distance education. A research literature concerned with distance education (or 'correspondence education' as it was previously known) does exist, although, historically, this was not concerned in the main with degree-level studies and thus it developed in parallel with, but essentially in isolation from, the mainstream literature on higher education. However, the advent of institutions to provide mass higher education through distance learning has rendered this separation between the two research communities wholly inappropriate.

A particular focus of interest in both research communities has been the approaches to learning that are exhibited by students on the relevant programmes. Several books provide good summaries of the relevant research carried out in campus-based institutions of higher education (for example, Richardson *et al.* 1987; Marton *et al.* 1997; Prosser and Trigwell 1999), although in this book I shall endeavour to provide a more detailed and critical account of that research than has previously been available. There are, in contrast, fewer publications that cover the research carried out in distance-learning institutions and these are often much less widely available (for example, Morgan 1991; Kember 1995). What is lacking is an integrated account and comparison of the research findings obtained in both kinds of institution, and this book aims to fill this gap. A central question from this point of view is whether students who are following courses by distance education set about their academic studies in different ways from students on similar courses in campus-based institutions of higher education.

In Chapter 1, I shall consider possible definitions of 'distance education' and discuss whether and how it is different from campus-based higher education. I shall also discuss the conceptual differences between 'distance learning', 'open learning', 'independent learning' and 'flexible learning'. In Chapters 2–4, I shall consider the results of qualitative investigations based upon the use of structured interviews with students about how they go about their learning in higher education. I shall conclude that these investigations have found broadly the same approaches, conceptions and orientations towards studying in distance-learning and campus-based students. The only apparent exception to this pattern is that distance-learning students – not surprisingly – are unlikely to be motivated by a 'social' orientation towards studying in higher education.

In Chapters 5–10, I shall discuss the findings of quantitative investigations based on the use of formal inventories or questionnaires. Here, I shall conclude that these investigations have found broadly the same factors underlying the responses given by distance-learning and campus-based students when filling out these instruments. Some researchers have identified differences in the scores obtained by distance-learning and campus-based students, but it needs to be remembered that students pursuing courses in distance education tend to be demographically quite different from students in campus-based institutions of higher education. More specifically, I shall argue that differences of this sort can be readily attributed to confounded differences in their ages, academic disciplines or response rates. In other words, students in distance education show no intrinsic differences in their approaches to studying attributable to the mode of course delivery.

This should mean that a productive *rapprochement* can be achieved between the two previously separate research communities. On the one hand, findings in the mainstream research literature concerned with approaches to studying in campus-based higher education will be broadly valid for understanding approaches to studying in distance education and thus can be fully exploited by academics in distance education in seeking new ways to develop and evaluate their courses. On the other hand, it also means that the distinct literature that is concerned with approaches to studying in distance education can be used to illuminate the processes at work in campus-based higher education. For instance, the student population in distance education tends to be far more heterogeneous than the student population in campus-based institutions, partly (although not exclusively) because of the use of more selective entrance criteria in the latter institutions. As a consequence, the effects of demographic characteristics such as age or educational background upon students' approaches to learning may be more apparent in research carried out in distance education. However, the more fundamental point is that research on distance education should not remain marginal but should be of interest to all involved in mainstream higher education.

Acknowledgements

I began the research that was eventually to result in this book during 1996–7, when I was able to spend a year's study leave from my position in the Department of Human Sciences at Brunel University as a Visiting Research Professor in the Institute of Educational Technology at the Open University. The research was originally intended by way of background work to the main purpose of my visit, which was to investigate approaches to studying in students with a hearing loss who were studying with the Open University. In the event, the background work took on a life of its own in parallel with my project on students with a hearing loss. I was able to retain my appointment as a Visiting Research Professor on a part-time basis after my return to Brunel University and I am grateful to both these institutions for their support over the last four years.

Particularly in the first of those four years, I was very grateful to Thaiquan Lieu, who was then the Project Officer in the International Centre for Distance Learning at the Open University, for his invaluable assistance in locating many of the sources mentioned in this book. Subsequently, I benefited greatly from many helpful discussions with Alison Ashby, Alan Woodley and their colleagues in the Student Research Centre at the Open University. The debates and discussions that I had with the late Alistair Morgan were particularly instrumental in bringing the present work to fruition, and his critical viewpoint and kind support are both greatly missed. Finally, I am also very grateful to David Kember, Diana Laurillard, Erik Meyer, Jan Vermunt and David Watkins for their comments on an earlier working paper that formed the basis for this book.

John T.E. Richardson
Brunel University

Abbreviations

ASI	Approaches to Studying Inventory (Entwistle)
CLEV	Checklist of Educational Views (Perry)
CLSI	Learning Style Inventory (Canfield)
CPQ	Course Perceptions Questionnaire (Ramsden)
DESP	Distance Education Student Progress [inventory] (Kember)
EPI	Eysenck Personality Inventory (Eysenck)
ILP	Inventory of Learning Processes (Schmeck)
ILP-R	Revised Inventory of Learning Processes (Schmeck)
ILS	Inventory of Learning Styles (Vermunt)
LASSI	Learning and Study Strategies Inventory (Weinstein)
LSI	Learning Style Inventory (Kolb)
LSQ-HM	Learning Styles Questionnaire (Honey and Mumford)
LSQ-MM	Learning Style Questionnaire (Marshall and Merritt)
QCI	Qualitative Context Inventory (Meyer)
RASI	Revised Approaches to Studying Inventory (Entwistle)
SAQ	Student Attitudes Questionnaire (Entwistle)
SBQ	Study Behaviour Questionnaire (Biggs)
SPQ	Study Process Questionnaire (Biggs)

1

Campus-based and Distance Education

Higher education has traditionally been conceived as an arrangement whereby students attend particular institutions for the purposes of receiving teaching through immediate contact with the members of academic staff and support in their learning from libraries and other services. There is unfortunately no convenient expression to refer to this means of delivering higher education. Kaye and Rumble (1982: 242) used the term 'conventional' to refer to 'formal classroom-based instruction in a school, college or university setting where teacher and students are physically present at the same time at the same place'. This is far from satisfactory, because it carries the implication that the teachers and institutions being referred to are not open to change, and it is an easy matter to find counterexamples to this idea (see, for instance, Gibbs 1992, 1994, 1995).

Some writers have used the phrase 'contiguous education', in the sense of being adjacent to, in close proximity to or in actual contact (see Rumble 1989), but this is an ugly expression that fails to capture the wide range of activities that go on in institutions of higher education. It also begs the question: 'contiguous to what?' If it means 'contiguous to the teacher', the students in question are often required to work by themselves or in small groups without any immediate supervision. If it means 'contiguous to the institution', they might also be required to carry out fieldwork or research elsewhere. In this book, I shall use the phrase 'campus-based education' instead, in the sense that the teaching and learning activities originate within the grounds of the institution in question. (I recognize, of course, that institutions in deprived city-centre locations might hesitate to describe their setting as a 'campus', given the mental images that this evokes.)

Many alternative means of delivering higher education have been proposed, and many of these have been implemented to a greater or lesser extent at different times and in different countries. Nevertheless, I am going to be concerned in this book specifically with the idea of 'distance education' and with comparing how students set about their academic studies in campus-based and distance-learning institutions of higher education.

Unfortunately, the definition of 'distance education' is not entirely straight-forward. I therefore need to spend this introductory chapter considering what 'distance education' involves and how it relates to a number of other concepts discussed in the contemporary literature on teaching and learning in higher education, such as 'open learning', 'independent learning' and 'flexible learning'.

Distance education

One early definition of 'distance teaching' was put forward by Moore (1973):

> Distance teaching may be defined as the family of instructional methods in which the teaching behaviors are executed apart from the learning behaviors, including those that in a contiguous situation would be performed in the learner's presence, so that communication between the teacher and the learner must be facilitated by print, electronics, mechanical or other devices.
>
> (Moore 1973: 664)

Of course, this definition focuses on the activities of the teacher in distance education and it largely leaves out the learner's side of the relationship (Keegan 1988, 1996: 37). It also implies a somewhat narrow conception of campus-based education, as it equates contiguous teaching with face-to-face instruction. Even so, it does serve to highlight the key element of a physical or geographical separation between teachers and students: whatever else it is, distance education is based upon 'non-contiguous' communication (Holmberg 1981: 11).

The physical separation between teachers and students in distance education often also implies a separation in time: that is, their communication is 'asynchronous' (see Threlkeld and Brzoska 1994). At a more fundamental level, the separation is often not simply geographical or temporal in nature, but social and personal as well (Keegan 1990). To capture these different aspects of the relationship between teachers and learners in distance education, Moore (1980, 1983) used the term 'transactional distance', which he defined as a function of two variables, 'dialogue' and 'structure':

> Dialogue describes the extent to which, in any educational programme, learner and educator are able to respond to each other. This is determined by the content or subject matter which is studied, by the educational philosophy of the educator, by the personalities of educator and learner, and by environmental factors, the most important of which is the medium of communication . . .
>
> Structure is a measure of an educational programme's responsiveness to learners' individual needs. It expresses the extent to which educational objectives, teaching strategies and evaluation methods are prepared

for, or can be adapted to, the objectives, strategies and evaluation methods of the learner.

(Moore 1983: 157)

In fact, many institutions running programmes by distance education exploit different devices to try to narrow the transactional distance between the teachers and the students. These include tutorials or self-help groups arranged on a local basis, induction courses and residential schools, audio teleconferencing or computer conferencing, and other forms of personal support. Saba (1988) showed how Moore's notion of transactional distance could be elaborated in order to accommodate the new forms of telecommunications technology that were being adopted in distance education. In particular, Moore (1994) himself argued that these forms of technology could be employed to harness the 'interdependence' of geographically separated students through self-help groups. Since the early 1980s, there have been many experiments to investigate the possibility of collaborative learning and teaching using new technology, and the Internet has been exploited as a channel for both course delivery and student support in many programmes.

In general, as Moore's (1973) original definition of 'distance teaching' implied, and as Garrison and Shale (1987) subsequently made explicit, learning at a distance will still necessitate some kind of communication between teachers and students, and institutions responsible for distance education will exploit whatever technology is available to facilitate that communication. It is, for example, possible for teachers and learners who are physically separated from each other to interact in a simultaneous or 'synchronous' manner by means of modern telecommunications technologies. It therefore may be useful to distinguish between distance education that is based on traditional correspondence techniques (possibly supplemented by material recorded on audio or video cassettes) and distance education that is based on telecommunications that permit a simultaneous link between the teachers and the students (Barker *et al.* 1989). Such technologies can also, of course, be used to facilitate links among the students themselves (Keegan 1988).

To deal with these and other issues, Keegan (1988, 1996) presented an elaborated definition. On this account, distance education is a form of education that is characterized by:

- the quasi-permanent separation of teacher and learner throughout the length of the learning process (this distinguishes it from conventional face-to-face education);
- the influence of an educational organization both in the planning and preparation of learning materials and in the provision of student support services (this distinguishes it from private study and teach-yourself programmes);
- the use of technical media – print, audio, video or computer – to unite teacher and learner and carry the content of the course;

- the provision of two-way communication so that the student may benefit from or even initiate dialogue (this distinguishes it from other uses of technology in education); and
- the quasi-permanent absence of the learning group throughout the length of the learning process so that people are usually taught as individuals rather than in groups, with the possibility of occasional meetings, either face-to-face or by electronic means, for both didactic and socialization purposes.

(Keegan 1996: 50)

At the same time, it is fair to question precisely how 'contiguous' campus-based programmes of study really are. Although students are normally expected to attend at a physical institution for access to teaching and learning facilities, they are also usually expected to engage in periods of independent study. Indeed, in the humanities and social sciences it is common for students to spend the majority of their notional learning time in activities other than face-to-face education. Many of these activities need not take place on campus, especially if students live elsewhere. In practice, then, as Rumble (1989) pointed out, educational programmes lie along a continuum from the highly contiguous to the purely distance-based. Even so, at a purely conceptual level, the distinction between campus-based and distance education is relatively unambiguous. To try to accommodate these various points, Bell and Tight proposed a more general definition:

'Distance education' refers to those forms of organized learning which are based on, and seek to overcome, the physical separation of learners and those (other than the learners themselves) involved in the organization of their learning. This separation may apply to the whole learning process or only to certain stages or elements of it. Some face-to-face contact may occur, but its function will be to supplement or reinforce the predominantly distant interaction . . .

(Bell and Tight 1993: 7–8)

Two models of distance education

At an institutional level, a wide variety of arrangements have been adopted for the delivery of distance education in different countries (see Keegan and Rumble 1982). Nevertheless, one can make a basic distinction between two different models (see Mugridge 1992). In the 'dual-mode' model, the same courses are delivered to campus-based students and distance-learning students by the same departments within the same institution. In this case, the intention is to replicate the experiences of campus-based students as far as possible within the context of distance learning, in order to ensure uniformity of educational provision, parity of academic standards and parity of external status between the two forms of course delivery. This model is exemplified in the Australian system of higher education, for instance, where certain academic institutions have a constitutional responsibility to provide courses both in an 'internal' or campus-based mode and in an 'external' or distance-learning mode. The relevant lectures and tutorials are replaced by written course materials and teleconferences, but distance-learning students are usually subject to the same assessments and academic schedules as campus-based students (see Arger 1993).

The disadvantage of a system such as that which pertains in Australia is that distance-learning students usually constitute the minority, not only across the system of higher education as a whole, but also within most individual institutions of higher education. For example, external students constitute merely 10.6 per cent of all enrolments and only 8.6 per cent of all graduates at Australian institutions, and more than half of all external courses are taken by fewer than ten students (see Department of Employment, Education and Training 1993; Johnson *et al.* 1996). Consequently, distance education is of relatively minor importance in the allocation of resources to individual institutions, and teaching external students may come to be regarded as a peripheral and inferior responsibility, even by those members of academic staff who are actually involved in delivering their courses (see Teather 1987: chapter 3; Chick 1992).

The other model for delivering higher education through distance learning is the 'single mode' model: this model is based on a distinct organization that has no involvement in the delivery of campus-based courses. The organization in question might be a separate institution of higher education that is responsible for its own academic programmes and awards or it might be a separate faculty within a campus-based institution of higher education. It is fairly common for the form of education that is being provided to be described as 'open learning', as in the case of the Open Universities of the UK, the Netherlands, British Columbia, India and Pakistan. (Under this heading, one might also include the Open Education Faculty of Anadolu University in Turkey, although this is strictly a dual-mode institution that comprises 15,000 campus-based students but more than 500,000 distance-learning students.)

Consider, by way of example, the Open University in the UK. This was founded in 1969 to provide degree programmes by distance education throughout the UK. Originally, nearly all its courses were delivered by specially prepared correspondence materials, combined with television and radio broadcasts, video and audio recordings, tutorial support at a local level and (in some cases) week-long residential schools. Nevertheless, the Open University has made increasing use of computer-based support, including CD-ROMs and computer-mediated conferencing. It accepts all applicants over the normal minimum age of 18 onto its courses without imposing any formal entrance requirements, subject only to limitations of numbers on specific courses. Most courses are assessed by a combination of coursework (submitted by post or in some cases by electronic mail) and traditional unseen examinations (taken at regional assessment centres).

Within the single-mode model, the delivery of distance education is the central responsibility (indeed, the *raison d'être*) of the institution in question, and so there is no question of its being assigned a prime importance. However, the main disadvantage is that it may be difficult for the institution to attain parity of status and to demonstrate parity of academic standards with other, campus-based institutions of higher education. This will be a particular problem if the distance-learning institution is perceived to be offering courses in innovative (and hence non-traditional) ways to students who might not meet the standard admissions requirements of campus-based institutions. In the UK, the introduction of a national system for the assessment of teaching quality in higher education has, whatever its demerits, served to remedy this problem, in so far as the Open University regularly receives extremely positive assessments from panels of external assessors for the quality of its provision in different academic disciplines.

From the perspective of a researcher, the advantage in considering the dual-mode model is that it is possible to compare campus-based students and distance-learning students who are taking the same courses and are subject to the same assessments and academic schedules. In contrast, when examining the impact of a single-mode model on student learning, it may well be difficult or impossible to find an appropriate group of students taking campus-based courses with whom it would be sensible to compare the target group of distance-learning students. Nevertheless, the converse difficulty is that in the dual-mode model the need to ensure comparability of standards and experience between campus-based and distance-learning students tends to limit those staff responsible for developing the academic curriculum to conventional forms of course design and inhibits them from exploring the full potential of distance education. In the single-mode model, these constraints are typically much weaker and curriculum developers are accordingly freer to develop distinctive forms of course design. In the UK, for instance, it is apparent that Open University courses differ from other university courses in their content and design, and not simply in their mode of delivery (Brew and McCormick 1979; Shaw and Taylor 1984).

Distance learning and open learning

In principle, then, it is possible to distinguish between distance education as external study (the dual-mode model) and distance education as open learning (the single-mode model). However, this apparently straightforward distinction is often obscured because in many countries there is an increasing tendency for administrative units responsible for distance-learning programmes in dual-mode institutions to refer to themselves as centres for 'open learning' or 'flexible learning' (see Keegan 1996: 29, 36). What do the latter concepts have to do with distance education?

The notion of 'open learning' has been very fashionable in further and higher education since the 1960s, although Bell and Tight (1993) argued that it had a much older history in British higher education. However, in practice, this expression has been used in a wide variety of ways and for a wide variety of purposes. As MacKenzie *et al.* (1975) commented:

> Open Learning is an imprecise phrase to which a range of meanings can be, and is, attached. It eludes definition. But as an inscription to be carried in procession on a banner, gathering adherents and enthusiasms, it has great potential. For its very imprecision enables it to accommodate many different ideas and aims.
>
> (MacKenzie *et al.* 1975: 15)

Rumble and Keegan (1982: 12) noted that the Open University in the UK was set up to be 'open' in respect of '(1) people, since it would not debar applicants on account of their lack of educational qualifications; (2) place, in the sense that learning would be home based and not restricted to classrooms or a campus; (3) the use of new methods of teaching and (4) ideas'. However, they acknowledged that not all of these features were to be found at other supposedly 'open' universities.

It is, in fact, common to find all distance education portrayed as a variety of open learning (see, for instance, Lewis and Spencer 1986: 17; Thorpe and Grugeon 1987: 2; Bell and Tight 1993: 3–4; Race 1994: 23). However, other writers have argued that there is no direct relationship between open education and distance learning (Keegan 1980). For example, Rumble (1989) proposed that 'distance learning' referred to a distinctive means or method of education (which could be either 'open' or 'closed'), whereas 'open learning' referred to the nature of the education being delivered (whether contiguously or at a distance) and more specifically to the objectives and the character of the educational process. To elaborate, Rumble gave the following quotation (from a writer who was describing the process of setting up 'open universities' in Latin America):

> *Open education* is particularly characterized by the removal of restrictions, exclusions and privileges; by the accreditation of students' previous experience; by the flexibility of the management of the time variable; and by substantial changes in the traditional relationship between professors and students. On the other hand, *distance education* is a modality which permits the delivery of a group of didactic media without the necessity of regular class participation, where the individual is responsible for his own learning.
>
> (Escotet 1980: 264)

Lewis and Spencer (1986: 37–42; see also Lewis 1986) suggested that particular programmes could be assessed as falling along a continuum from 'closed' to 'open' in terms of the extent to which learners have freedom and choice on a number of different aspects of their studying:

- who can learn
- why they learn

- what they learn
- how they learn
- where they learn
- when they learn
- how their learning is measured
- who can help them learn
- what they do afterwards.

Kember and Murphy (1990; see also Kember 1995: 11–12, 15–17) noted that some of these criteria of 'openness' were related to social or political trends that were concerned with the removal of restrictions on participation in higher education, whereas others were related to educational trends that were concerned with the promotion of student-centred learning in higher education. Kember and Murphy argued that only the former set of criteria should be used to define 'open learning'. They suggested that distance-education courses could be regarded as 'open learning' courses even if they showed no evidence whatever of being student-centred. Conversely, they suggested that activities in a typical primary school classroom, for example, might be highly student-centred but would not normally be characterized as examples of 'open learning'. However, even on the more restricted criteria, Kember and Murphy suggested that the external programmes operated by many Australian universities exhibited at best only a moderate level of openness.

In practice, institutional constraints, combined with the need to award externally recognized qualifications, often make it difficult to implement a genuinely student-centred approach to course design and course delivery in distance education (Farnes 1975; Thorpe and Grugeon 1987; Keegan 1988; Bell and Tight 1993: 152–7; Holmberg 1993). Indeed, Harris and Holmes (1976; see also Harris 1987) argued that institutional factors tend to militate against 'openness' in distance education, even when this concept is defined in terms of social and political criteria. As a consequence, the concept of open learning nowadays has a rather confused and contested status in distance education (Bell and Tight 1993: 4, 139). Moreover, there will be additional problems in seeking to transfer the concept of openness from industrialized countries in which distance-learning programmes are supported by a rich variety of communication technologies to developing societies that are more dependent upon traditional written media (Escotet, 1980).

Distance learning and independent learning

Another expression that is used to capture the idea of students learning how, when and where they wish is 'independent learning'. In discussing how this was used in the literature, Moore (1972, 1973) proposed that it consisted of two different aspects or 'dimensions'. The first dimension was the separation of teachers at the time of teaching from learners at the time of learning. The second dimension was the promotion of increased responsibility or autonomy on the part of the learners. Moore hypothesized that it was this latter dimension that differentiated distance education from campus-based activities involving programmed learning or computer-assisted instruction, which might otherwise be regarded as examples of independent learning.

Moore went on to argue that there was a positive relationship between distance education and student autonomy. On the one hand, he claimed, learning at a distance should encourage student autonomy by forcing learners to function in a self-directed way. On the other hand, autonomous learners should find distance teaching more amenable or congenial than traditional constrained learning situations. Indeed, in the subsequent research literature on distance education, student autonomy has tended to be characterized in two different ways, as Schuemer (1993: 5–6) noted: first, as a prerequisite for successful academic attainment in the face of transactional distance; second, as a goal or ideal that distance educators should strive to inculcate in their students.

Moore suggested that distance-learning institutions should try to design programmes that were more attractive to autonomous learners and, in a subsequent article (Moore 1986), he discussed the implications of this account for course design and academic staff development in distance education. Nevertheless, he also acknowledged that the promotion of learner autonomy was becoming widely accepted as a fundamental goal in the education of children and adolescents. Moore inferred from this that methods of distance teaching would provide the most appropriate means of delivering programmes in further and higher education for the forthcoming generation of autonomous adult learners.

As was implied earlier, at the time when Moore first proposed that distance learning required students to function in a self-directed or autonomous manner, the most common examples of independent learning in campus-based institutions were programmed learning and computer-assisted instruction. However, since that time, it has become increasingly recognized that the students' control of the learning process is a desirable – if not essential – ingredient of effective learning in all forms of secondary and tertiary education (see, for instance, Perry 1991; Taylor and Burgess 1995; Bandura 1997: chapter 6). As a consequence, it is becoming widely accepted that campus-based courses can and should involve independent learning.

No educational programme can be wholly autonomous because it has to be accredited by some relevant institution (Keegan 1996: 36). However, in principle, campus-based activities might be just as independent as distance learning, as is clear in the following quotation from Wedemeyer (1971), who was responsible for promoting the idea of independent study in the US:

Independent study consists of various forms of teaching–learning arrangements in which teachers and learners carry out their essential tasks and responsibilities apart from one another, communicating in a variety of ways for the purposes of freeing internal learners from inappropriate class pacings or patterns, of providing external learners with opportunities to continue learning in their own environments, and of developing in all learners the capacity to carry on self-directed learning.

(Wedemeyer 1971: 550)

Thus, distance learning and independent learning are in principle independent of one another. However, in practice, course designers in distance education may specifically aim to promote independent learning in their students. Indeed, in the US, all distance education has traditionally been characterized as a form of independent study (see, for example, Wedemeyer 1971; Moore 1980; Markowitz 1983).

Distance learning and flexible learning

During the 1990s, another approach to student-centred learning emerged under the heading of 'flexible learning'. Wade (1994: 12) defined this as 'an approach to university education which provides students with the opportunity to take greater responsibility for their learning and to be engaged in learning activities and opportunities that meet their own individual needs'. Flexible learning can be readily justified from a pedagogical perspective, on the grounds that it 'offers the learner a more actively constructive role by providing a framework in which learning goals can be more independently pursued' (Fleming 1993: 322). Nevertheless, in practice, the interest in flexible learning has been fostered by institutions of higher education as a response to economic constraints and other external challenges (Kirkpatrick 1997). As a consequence, examples of flexible learning may in fact turn out to be teacher-centred or institution-centred rather than student-centred (see Hudson *et al.* 1997: 3).

Whatever the underlying motivation, flexible learning usually has the goal of promoting student autonomy but, in order to achieve this, it has to combine the provision of learning packages that students can follow at their own pace with support and guidance at both an individual level and an institutional level. Laurillard (1993) examined the ways in which educational technology can be exploited for both these purposes. Indeed, flexible learning often amounts to a reorganization of institutional resources so as to bring about gains in economic efficiency through the use of new technology instead of face-to-face teaching (Kirkpatrick 1997). Moreover, for educational technologists, 'flexibility' often lies in the technology designed to support student learning and is not a feature of the learning itself (for a number of examples, see Hazemi *et al.* 1998).

The proponents of flexible learning often borrow techniques of course design and delivery from distance education. In fact, flexible learning is often referred to as a 'mixed-mode' form of course delivery that combines features of campus-based and distance education. Hudson *et al.* (1997: 191) concluded that the introduction of more flexible delivery methods was resulting in a blurring of the distinction between campus-based learners and distance learners. Nevertheless, most of the case studies described in their book are unequivocally examples of campus-based education (where flexible learning may be used to develop the generic skills of an increasingly diverse student population) or of distance education (where flexible learning may be used to develop the skills of specific professional groups) (see also Wade *et al.* 1994).

In short, flexible learning can be applied in campus-based education or in distance education. This is made explicit in the definition of 'flexible learning' given by Van den Brande (1993):

> *Flexible learning is enabling learners to learn when they want (frequency, timing, duration), how they want (modes of learning), and what they want (that is learners can define what constitutes learning to them).* These flexible learning principles may be applied at a distance. If so then the term 'distance learning' is used. In such cases the learners can *choose where they want to learn (at home, at an institution or company, at a training centre, etc.).*
>
> (Van den Brande 1993: 2; italics in original)

Once again, distance learning and flexible learning are in principle independent of one another. Or, as Keegan (1996: 29) put it, distance education is neither flexible nor inflexible *per se.*

Approaches to studying in campus-based and distance education

To return to the main theme that I elaborated earlier in this chapter, there is a physical, temporal and transactional separation between students who are taking courses by distance learning and their teachers. There is a similar separation with the teaching institution itself and, often, with other students taking the same courses. All this clearly implies that the experience of distance education is likely to be different from the experience of campus-based education. As Marland (1989: 178) spelt this out: 'Distance learners constitute a sub-group of tertiary students whose instructional programmes and materials, learning contexts and problems differ markedly from those of their on-campus peers'. What is far less clear, however, is whether the different mode of course delivery has an impact upon how students go about their academic studies. For instance, if distance education either demands or fosters learner autonomy, students taking programmes by distance learning should be more likely to engage with their studies in an active manner than students taking equivalent courses in campus-based institutions.

In attempting to investigate whether the different mode of course delivery has an impact upon how students in distance education go about their academic studies, there are several important practical considerations to be borne in mind. Kember (1989b) identified three of these. First, the process of data collection is rendered more difficult when the student participants are external to their teaching institution. Unless contact can be made at residential schools or tutorials, they will need to be visited for the purpose of carrying out interviews, while questionnaire surveys may suffer from inadequate address lists or poor response rates. Second, a much wider range of contextual variables needs to be taken into account, because distance-learning students will be working in a wide variety of physical and social contexts. (In the dual-mode model of distance education, it is at least possible to compare internal and external students who are following the same courses, but even this is not possible in the single-mode model.) Third, the population of students in distance education is usually more heterogeneous in terms of demographic variables than the population of campus-based students; in particular, students in distance education often show a much wider distribution of age, social background, previous educational experience and academic qualifications.

Nevertheless, my aim in this book is to evaluate the hypothesis that approaches to studying in distance-learning students are different from those in campus-based students. Many of the key concepts originated in qualitative, interview-based research, and I shall consider the evidence from this research in the following three chapters. Subsequently, different attempts were made to operationalize these concepts in formal inventories and questionnaires that could be used to generate quantitative data from large numbers of participants, and the main part of this book will describe the development and application of these various instruments. My justification for this approach is the social constructionist position that concepts and theories in social research are constituted in specific social encounters between researchers and their participants (Gergen 1994). It does not therefore make sense to describe research on approaches to studying without providing a detailed account of the nature of those encounters, the research methods by which they are regulated and the analytic techniques that are used to make sense of the results.

In short, I shall describe the concepts and methods used in qualitative and quantitative research concerned with approaches to studying in higher education, and in each case I shall provide a critical review of the main findings, with particular regard to those that bear upon the central hypothesis that the approaches to studying of distance-learning students are different from the approaches to studying of campus-based students. I will also consider whether any differences that are found between the approaches to studying of distance-learning students and campus-based students are produced by the different modes of course delivery or by differences in background variables such as age and previous academic experience. Finally, I shall discuss the main issues that emerge from this research, as well as its implications for future research and for course development in both campus-based and distance education.

Concluding summary

- For the purposes of this book, 'campus-based education' refers to the traditional arrangement whereby students attend particular institutions to receive teaching through immediate contact with academic staff and support in their learning from libraries and other services.
- In contrast, 'distance education' refers to arrangements whereby students engage in learning at a physical distance from their teachers and their institution (and, often, from one another) and typically at a temporal, social and personal distance as well.
- Campus-based education and distance education may be delivered by the same institution (in the dual-mode model) or different institutions (in the single-mode model). Distance learning is often described as 'external study' in the former case and as 'open learning' in the latter.
- Nevertheless, the expressions 'open learning', 'independent learning' and 'flexible learning' all refer to the nature of the educational process and, conceptually at least, they are strictly independent of whether the education is being delivered contiguously or at a distance.
- This book is concerned with whether approaches to studying in distance-learning students are different from approaches to studying in campus-based students, and whether any differences that arise are due to the different modes of course delivery and not simply to differences in background variables such as their age or their previous academic experience.

2
Approaches to Studying

Research on approaches to studying in higher education began in the 1970s with a programme of experimental investigations that was carried out at the University of Göteborg (Gothenburg) in Sweden. In this chapter, I shall describe the key findings of this research with regard to both the outcome and the process of learning. I shall then go on to discuss the results of subsequent, more naturalistic investigations that were carried out to explore the relevance of those original findings for how students actually go about learning both in campus-based institutions and in distance education.

A precursor to the kind of investigation to be discussed in this chapter was an experiment on the role of organization in human learning and memory that was reported by Marton (1970). In this study, the experimenter asked each of 30 paid volunteers (who were male students taking an introductory course in education) to learn a list containing the names of 48 well-known public figures. The list of names was presented on a recorded audio tape a total of 16 times in different randomized orders. After each presentation of the list, the participants were asked to recall as many of the names as they could remember in any order they liked. When the experiment itself had been completed, the participants received an informal, semi-structured interview in which they were asked about their experience of carrying out the learning task.

The experimental methodology in this study was not particularly original and the quantitative results were similar to those of previous experiments on which it had been explicitly modelled (for instance, Tulving 1962). In particular, as the participants learned the list of famous names, they tended increasingly to recall particular groups of names together on successive trials. This phenomenon was (and still is) generally taken to reflect the participants' imposing organization and structure upon the inherently random and constantly changing sequence of items (Baddeley 1996: 131). What was novel about Marton's study was the use of interviews to obtain accounts from the participants themselves of what they had been doing during the learning task. These accounts confirmed what had been inferred from the pattern of recall, in so far as the participants were duly able to describe the process of imposing a hierarchical structure on the list of names.

Although Marton was concerned to emphasize the limitations of this study, especially in terms of the generality of its findings and conclusions, it provided a clear basis for a heuristic strategy that might well illuminate the nature of learning in more naturalistic situations:

* the outcome of learning could be studied by a careful analysis of recall performance
* the process of learning could be studied by means of retrospective interviews
* the relationship between process and outcome could be compared across individual learners.

In his subsequent work, Marton criticized the simplistic, quantitative view of learning on which experimental investigations of this sort had been based: that what is learned can be reduced to a number of logically independent and personally neutral pieces of knowledge (see, for instance, Marton 1976c). Instead, he focused on 'non-verbatim' learning in the form of students' memory for the broad gist of academic texts. Nevertheless, in a series of studies carried out in the 1970s, Marton and his colleagues at the University of Göteborg employed the same heuristic strategy to make qualitative comparisons in the outcome and process of learning in individual students.

Levels of outcome in student learning

The first study of this nature was reported by Marton (1975; see also Marton and Säljö 1976a). This involved 30 paid volunteers (5 men and 25 women, all aged between 19 and 23 years) who had just enrolled on a programme in educational psychology at a campus-based institution of higher education. They were each asked to read through a newspaper article of roughly 1400 words concerned with impending curriculum reform in Swedish universities. There was no time limit, but it was suggested to the participants that about 15 minutes should be long enough for them to carry out the task. Immediately afterwards, they were asked to say what the article was about, and they were then given a structured interview concerning how they had set about the task of reading the article and their general approach to academic studies. Finally, the participants were unexpectedly invited to attend another session about 5 weeks later, when they were again asked to recall the gist of the article and to answer questions both about their approach to the task of reading the article and their approach to academic studies in general.

With the assistance of two independent judges, Marton found that it was fairly straightforward to classify the students' attempts to recall the article at each of the two sessions into different categories of learning outcome that reflected qualitatively different ways of understanding the article. The relevant curriculum reforms had been proposed as a response to poor examination pass rates in some institutions of higher education; the author of the article had argued that pass rates varied between different groups of students and that, instead of blanket reforms, it would be more effective to introduce selective measures that were aimed at groups with low pass rates. The students' summaries implied four different conceptions of the article's intended meaning:

> *Level A: Selective Measures.* (Meaning that measures were to be taken only for those groups of students that did not fulfil the necessary requirements.)
> *Level B: Differential Measures.* (Measures to be taken which allow for differences between the various groups.)
> *Level C: Measures.* (Measures to be taken only.)
> *Level D: Differences.* (Differences between groups only.)
>
> (Marton and Säljö 1976a: 8)

Marton noted that the entailment relations among these categories defined a partial ordering in which each category logically subsumed the categories below it: in other words, the categories defined a hierarchy in terms of the depth of the learning outcome. (In this example, A implies B, which implies both C and D, but the relationship between C and D is indeterminate.) For a particular text, Marton argued that the different categories of outcome and the logical relations among them defined an 'outcome space'. Particular outcomes could be regarded as being more appropriate or desirable than others, in so far as they bore a closer relationship to the author's original conception of the phenomenon in question (Marton, 1976c).

This general pattern was replicated in a number of other studies involving students at the same campus-based institution (Säljö 1975; Marton and Säljö 1976a, 1976b; Svensson 1976, 1977; Fransson 1977). To take one further example, Marton and Wenestam (1978) used four different texts, each of which described a certain principle and illustrated it by reference to some detailed example. For instance, one text (which was taken from a textbook on the philosophy of science) was concerned with the principle that hypotheses about causal factors are tested by comparing two otherwise identical situations, one in which the presumptive causal factor is present and one in which it is absent. This principle was illustrated by reference to an account of an Austro-Hungarian physician investigating the cause of childbed fever in the nineteenth century. Marton and Wenestam identified the following levels of outcome for each of the four texts:

(A) The principle and the example as well as the relationship between them is understood.
(B) The principle and the example are understood (separately) but not sufficiently to understand the relationship between them.
(C) The principle is not understood but constructed on the basis of the fragments retained.

(D) The example in itself is seen as the main point of the text.

(Marton and Wenestam 1978: 641)

Even so, these descriptions reflect only the structural similarities between the levels of outcome obtained from the four different texts, which were obviously different in terms of their actual content. In general, the number of levels of outcome (usually four), the levels themselves and the precise relations between them were dictated by the content of the text and were specific to that text.

A basic research question is whether the procedures for identifying different levels of outcome are a reliable means of classifying individual students. Marton (1975) found that 16 out of his 30 participants were assigned to the same level of outcome according to their performance at the first session and at the follow-up session after 5 weeks. None of the 14 participants who had been assigned to two different levels of outcome showed a superior quality of outcome at the follow-up session, and this suggests that these discrepancies were due to forgetting during the intervening interval and not to unreliability on the part of the classification procedure. Marton and Wenestam (1978) retested their participants after different follow-up intervals. They found that 14 out of 15 participants were assigned to the same level of outcome after 1 day; that 12 out of 14 participants were assigned to the same level of outcome after 1 week; but that only seven out of 14 participants were assigned to the same level of outcome after 1 month. Of the ten participants who were assigned to two different levels of outcome, only one person (who had been retested after just 1 day) showed a higher level of outcome at the follow-up session.

In contrast, Marton and Säljö (1976a, b) described two (otherwise similar) studies in which the participants were given feedback and correction after the first session if they had not given a 'Level A' account of what the text was about. Not surprisingly, under these conditions, a few of the participants did show a higher level of outcome at subsequent follow-up sessions. Svensson (1976, 1977) described results along similar lines from Marton's (1975) original investigation. After Marton's participants had been interviewed at the follow-up session, they had been asked to read an elaborated version of the article about curriculum reform in Swedish universities that was roughly three times the length of the first version. They were then tested and interviewed as before, and they were retested and re-interviewed at a third session roughly 5 weeks later. Four out of the 30 participants showed a higher level of outcome as a result of reading the elaborated text, but, as Svensson noted, the dominant feature of the results was the remarkable consistency shown by the other participants in their understanding of the two different versions of the text. Similar results were obtained by Marton *et al.* (1992) when they asked 60 children at secondary schools in Hungary and Sweden to read a story by Kafka on four successive occasions.

Dahlgren (1975) attempted to determine whether a similar analysis could be applied to students acquiring a coherent body of knowledge: in this case, some basic concepts in economic theory (see also Marton and Dahlgren 1976). He employed 38 paid volunteers (14 men and 24 women) who were sociology students at a campus-based university. He asked them to read the first two chapters of a textbook on economics and then interviewed them on the main topics. They were retested at a follow-up session about 45 days later. Each of the topics demonstrated an obvious 'outcome space', in that there were qualitative variations in the levels of outcome generated by different participants. Dahlgren and Marton (1978) went on to ask whether studying economics in higher education changed students' understanding of everyday economic phenomena. They interviewed 20 students who were taking an introductory course in economics and asked them questions such as, 'Why does a bun cost 50 öre?' Their responses fell into four categories:

A:1 The price of the bun is determined by the market price of its constituents: in other words, the price depends on the supply and demand situations for e.g. wheat, flour and transport services.
A:2 The price of the bun is determined by the supply of and demand for buns . . .
B:1 The price of the bun is the sum of the 'value' of its constituents . . .
B:2 The price of the bun is equal to its 'value' . . .

(Dahlgren and Marton 1978: 34)

The first two levels of outcome reflected what was taught in the economics course, whereas the last two levels of outcome reflected lay conceptions of 'price'. However, Dahlgren and Marton remarked that the latter were found even in students who had completed the economics course.

Levels of processing in student learning

The main objective of Marton's (1975) research was not simply to describe qualitative differences among individual learners in terms of different levels of outcome, but also to derive a parallel or 'commensurable' description of the levels of processing employed in non-verbatim learning. This was based upon a suggestion made by two experimental psychologists, Craik and Lockhart (1972), that remembering was a consequence of the learner's information-processing activities at the time of learning, so that differences in retention should be analysed in terms of the aspects of the material to be learned upon which the attention of different learners had been focused. A similar proposal had been made in the context of educational research by Anderson (1970), whom Marton also cited. However, Craik and Lockhart proposed more specifically that memory could be regarded as a hierarchical system of representations or 'levels of processing'. For instance, remembering a list of words printed on a page might involve any of the following:

• an orthographic representation (the visual appearance of each word on the page)

- a phonological representation (how each word would sound if it were spoken aloud)
- a semantic representation (the meaning of each word)
- an associative representation (the semantic relationships among different words).

In their account, Craik and Lockhart made the key assumption that the use of 'deeper' or more abstract levels of processing would lead to better retention than the use of shallow processing.

Craik and Lockhart's analysis attracted a good deal of interest and led to some novel kinds of experiments on human memory. As Marton (1975) pointed out, in these experiments different levels of processing were experimentally induced by manipulating the conditions of learning. For instance, the participants might be instructed to go about learning in particular ways (such as by making up mental images of the things described by the words to be remembered), they might be given tasks designed to focus their attention on particular aspects of the material (such as deciding whether a word was printed in upper-case letters or in lower-case letters), or they might be encouraged to use particular levels of processing by virtue of how the items had been presented (such as learning an arbitrary sequence of letters or digits presented very quickly one after another, which might be expected to inhibit the use of semantic processing).

In contrast, Marton's aim was to characterize qualitative differences in the process of learning under constant conditions of learning. To achieve this, he referred to the accounts that had been given by the participants in his study to the interview questions concerning how they had gone about the task of reading the academic text on curriculum reform in Swedish universities. Again with the help of two independent judges, Marton found that the 30 students could be classified in terms of whether or not they exhibited various 'positive' or 'negative' symptoms of the depth of processing they had used. The positive signs (that is, signs of 'deep-level processing') were: 'having *what is signified* (what the discourse is about) as the object of focal attention'; and 'active processing, the subject being *the agent of learning*'. The corresponding negative signs (that is, signs of 'surface-level processing') were: 'having *the sign* (the discourse itself or the recall of it) as the object of focal attention'; and 'passive processing, the subject not being *the agent of learning*' (Marton 1975: 276; italics in original). Based on these criteria, nine of the 30 participants were classified as having exhibited deep-level processing, 14 of the participants were classified as having exhibited surface-level processing, and the seven remaining participants could not be unambiguously classified either way.

Marton and Säljö (1976a) subsequently paraphrased their findings in the following manner:

> We have found basically two different *levels of processing* to be clearly distinguishable. These two different levels of processing, which we shall

call *deep-level* and *surface-level processing*, correspond to the different aspects of the learning material on which the learner focuses. In the case of *surface-level processing* the student directs his attention towards learning the text itself (*the sign*), i.e., he has a 'reproductive' conception of learning which means that he is more or less forced to keep to a rote-learning strategy. In the case of *deep-level processing*, on the other hand, the student is directed towards the intentional content of the learning material (*what is signified*), i.e., he is directed towards comprehending what the author wants to say about, for instance, a certain scientific problem or principle.

(Marton and Säljö 1976a: 7–8; italics in original)

As Gibbs *et al.* (1982b) pointed out, these two levels of processing reflect qualitative variation within the semantic domain, and so both would count as 'deep' processing in the sense defined by Craik and Lockhart (1972). Indeed, Marton and Säljö (1984: 42) noted that there was merely a 'metaphorical resemblance' between their account and Craik and Lockhart's idea of levels of processing. It may be more accurate to say that surface-level and deep-level processing amount to local and global forms of semantic analysis (Richardson 1983). The expressions 'the sign' and 'what is signified' appear to constitute a very oblique reference to the distinction between *signifié* and *signifiant* in the writings of Saussure ([1916] 1955: 99, [1916] 1959: 67), although for Saussure the former was spoken rather than written. Elsewhere, Marton (1976b) discussed the various ramifications of his distinction between 'the sign' and 'what is signified', but he never explored nor even acknowledged the Saussurian connotation in any of his subsequent writings.

Marton (1975) found, as expected, that there was a clear relationship between his participants' levels of processing when reading the academic text and the levels of outcome apparent in their recall of the same text. All of the participants who showed deep-level processing had produced the two highest levels of outcome, but all but one of the participants who showed surface-level processing had produced the two lowest levels of outcome. Svensson (1976, 1977) elaborated the distinction between surface-level and deep-level processing in terms of a contrast between 'atomistic' and 'holistic' approaches:

The *atomistic* approach was indicated when students described their activities as involving: focusing on specific comparisons, focusing on the parts of the text in sequence (rather than on the more important parts), memorising details and direct information indicating a lack of orientation towards the message as a whole. In contrast the *holistic* approach was characterised by students' attempts: to understand the overall meaning of the passage, to search for the author's intention, to relate the message to a wider context and/or to identify the main parts of the author's argument and supporting facts.

These two types of activity were also apparent in students' reports on how they tried to remember the texts. 'Atomists' relied on remembering the introductory sentences, visualising the tables, parts of the text or the outline structure of the text, and/or a general orientation to details. 'Holists' mentioned their attempts to remember the main message, what the author had been trying to say, the basis steps in the argument, and the message in a wider context.

(Svensson 1977: 238)

This distinction was closely related to that between surface-level and deep-level processing, with 25 out of the 30 students being allocated to the corresponding categories. There was also a clear relationship between the atomist/holist distinction and the quality of the learning outcome. However, Svensson proposed that his terminology should subsume differences in both outcome and process, on the theoretical ground that knowledge and skill should be seen as unified, and on the conceptual ground that the categories of process and outcome were 'internally' (in other words, intrinsically) related to one another (see Marton and Svensson 1979).

Inducing different levels of processing

Of course, the research strategy developed by Craik and Lockhart (1972) would suggest that one could modify students' levels of processing (and consequently their levels of outcome) by manipulating the conditions of learning. Marton and his colleagues carried out four studies to address this question. First, Marton (1976a) asked social-science students at a campus-based university to read a text (in this case, the first chapter of an introductory textbook on politics) and attempted to induce a deep level of processing by asking them a series of content-neutral questions after they had read each section in the text (for instance, 'What subsections do you think there are in this section?' and 'Can you summarize the content of the whole section in one or two sentences?'). In comparison with students who read the text uninterrupted, this actually led to *poorer* retention of the text both immediately after reading it and at a follow-up session 2 months later. From the participants' accounts at interview, Marton attributed this finding to 'a kind of technification of the learning process' (Marton 1976a: 45): the participants' attention had been focused on the interpolated questions rather than the text itself, so that they interpreted the learning task in a much narrower manner than had been intended.

I mentioned earlier a study by Dahlgren (1975) in which 38 students had been asked to read two chapters from an introductory textbook on economics (see also Marton and Dahlgren 1976). In fact, for the first of the two chapters, half of the participants had been given explicit instructions to aim for depth, comprehension and an active approach in reading the text. Content-orientated questions (for instance, 'Why is that?' and 'What does this mean?') had been added to the page margins with the aim of reinforcing these instructions. The remainder of the participants were given general instructions and an unannotated text. For the second chapter, all the participants received an unannotated text and were just told to read the chapter in the same way as the first. The first group demonstrated better retention of the second chapter but not of the first. Dahlgren suggested that the instructions to aim for depth and comprehension had indeed induced a deeper level of processing, but that this had once again been counteracted in reading the first chapter by the participants' attention becoming fixated on the marginal annotations rather than the text.

Säljö (1975; see also Marton and Säljö 1976b) attempted to induce deep-level or surface-level processing by the use of appropriate test questions after participants had read abridged versions of two successive chapters from a textbook on comparative education. The participants were 40 female first-year students at a campus-based university. Half of the participants were tested on bare facts and other surface properties after each of the chapters; the other half were tested on the underlying content of the texts. All of the participants were then asked to read an abridged version of a third chapter, which was followed by questions on both surface and deep aspects of its content. Feedback and correction were provided on all of the questions and the participants were recalled for a follow-up test 45 days later. The participants' comments at interview and a qualitative analysis of their recall of the chapters confirmed that they had tended to adapt to the intended level of processing. Those participants who had been led to expect factual questions uniformly reported that they had attended to the surface properties of the third chapter and were able to recall such details accurately immediately afterwards, though not at the follow-up test. The participants who had been led to expect deeper questions demonstrated two quite different strategies. Some did appear to have attended to the intentional content of the chapter. However, others attempted to master by rote one or two sentences that summarized the main idea, which Marton and Säljö (1976b) regarded as a further example of 'technification'.

These studies confirm that it is possible to manipulate students' levels of processing and hence their levels of outcome or understanding. For instance, leading students to expect to be assessed on the surface properties of the learning material seems to induce surface processing. Academic staff should therefore beware that they do not encourage undesirable approaches to learning by the use of inappropriate forms of assessment. In particular, with the increasing use of so-called 'objective' examinations that involve multiple-choice questions, teachers should ensure that the selected test items are tapping students' understanding of the subject-matter as opposed to their memory for surface facts. Nevertheless, if they attempt to induce more desirable approaches to learning, the effects might be rather different from what was intended. Providing instructions to engage with the material in an active way, embedding prompts within the text itself or attaching reflective questions at the end of the material may turn out to be counterproductive if students concentrate on fulfilling these extra demands at the expense of normal reading comprehension. As Gibbs *et al.* (1982a) remarked, this casts considerable doubt on the value of self-assessment questions and other in-text teaching devices, which at the time were widely used in all kinds of self-instructional texts, including the course materials written for distance-learning students.

A fourth attempt to manipulate levels of processing was carried out by Fransson (1977), who examined the effects of test anxiety, intrinsic motivation and extrinsic motivation. In this study, the participants were asked to read a description of the examination system at the Institute of Education at the University of Göteborg. Roughly half of the participants were students from the Institute itself and were presumed to have a high intrinsic motivation to read this text; the remaining participants were sociology students, who were presumed to have a low intrinsic motivation. Within each of these two groups of students, roughly half of the participants were given instructions intended to make the task more demanding, and thus to produce a high level of extrinsic motivation; the remaining participants were given instructions intended to make the task undemanding, and thus to produce a low level of extrinsic motivation. All the participants had been classified in advance as being of high or low test anxiety on a simple questionnaire.

Unfortunately, it turned out that not all of the manipulations operated in the intended manner: some of participants assigned to the 'low extrinsic motivation' conditions perceived the task as demanding, and some of the sociology students found the text to be very interesting. However, when the participants were reclassified in terms of whether they had adapted to the expected demands of the experiment, the results were fairly clear:

> Lack of interest in the text, efforts to adapt to expected test demands, and high test anxiety, were all found to increase the tendency towards surface-processing and ineffective, reproductive attempts at recall. However, an adaptive approach allied to strong interest and low anxiety produced a high proportion of deep-level approaches with good factual recall.
>
> (Fransson 1977: 244)

Fransson concluded that the type of motivation for reading a particular text was an important factor influencing the level of processing and consequently also the level of outcome:

> A subject motivated by test demands to read a text for which he has very limited interest is very probable to adopt a surface-learning strategy, while deep-level learning seems to be the normal strategy chosen by a student motivated only by the relevance of the content of the text to his personal needs and interests.
>
> (Fransson 1977: 256).

In a subsequent study, van Rossum and Schenk (1984) asked 69 campus-based students to read a text under a standard set of instructions. They were give a short questionnaire about the kind of assessment that they were expecting, followed by a longer, open-ended questionnaire about how they had approached the task of reading the text and what they could remember of its contents. On the basis of their accounts, 34 students were classified as showing deep-level processing and 35 students were classified as showing surface-level processing. Although all the participants had been treated in the same way, the former students were more likely to have expected to be tested on their insight or understanding of the text, whereas the latter students were more likely to have expected to be tested on their basic knowledge of the text. Moreover, male students were more likely to exhibit deep-level processing than female students, which may conceivably have had to do with the content of the text (an article about criminal gangs in eighteenth-century Holland). These results tend to confirm that levels of processing depend on the students' intrinsic motivation in the learning material and the expected form of assessment.

Approaches to studying in campus-based education

All of the research discussed so far in this chapter was concerned with how students go about reading isolated academic texts in relatively artificial experimental situations, but is there any guarantee that similar conclusions apply to how they go about their normal academic studying? Marton (1975) had, of course, asked the 30 campus-based students in his original investigation about their general studies. He provided no details and only a few illustrative quotations, but he commented that the categories of description that were used to characterize levels of processing in the text-reading experiment could be also be used to classify the students' learning activities. He also claimed that there was an analogous relationship between process and outcome, in that the level of processing in academic learning was related to subsequent examination results.

Further evidence from this study was provided by Svensson (1976, 1977), who classified the 30 students as having an atomistic or holistic approach in their normal studies on the basis of their comments during the interviews:

> Students adopting a holistic approach to their normal studies related new material to their own knowledge and experience, stressing the importance of reorganising new information in terms of existing knowledge structures . . . The atomists were more likely to stress the importance of over-learning and memorising in preparation for examinations.
> (Svensson 1977: 240)

Svensson found that 23 out of the 30 students were assigned to the same category (atomists or holists) in terms of their level of processing when reading an academic text and in terms of their accounts of how they approached their academic studies. Moreover, there was a strong relation between the latter accounts and academic performance. Of the 19 students who were classified as atomists in their academic studies, only seven passed all their first-year examinations; but of the 11 students who were classified as holists, ten passed all their examinations. Svensson was able to arrive at an even better differentiation of the students who passed or failed one particular examination by taking into account an individual's approach to studying, the number of hours they had spent each day on private study, the amount of revision they had carried out for the examination and whether they had adopted an 'elaborated' study technique (making synopses, underlining important passages and making use of lecture notes) or a 'restricted' technique.

Clearly, then, the levels of processing identified in artificial experimental situations have their counterparts in the students' everyday academic work. To describe these counterparts, Marton (1976c) talked of a 'deep approach' and a 'surface approach', and he concluded:

> It would appear that a decisive factor in non-verbatim learning, both in experimental settings and in everyday academic work, is the learner's approach to learning. Those who succeed best (both qualitatively and quantitatively) seem to have an approach that aims beyond the written or spoken discourse itself towards the message the discourse is intended to communicate. These students feel themselves to be the agents of learning; they utilize their capacity for logical thinking in order to construct knowledge.
>
> (Marton 1976c: 37)

Although Marton's account suggested that the distinction between deep and surface approaches marked a qualitative difference between different kinds of student, the findings of his research on reading academic texts suggested that they were instead strategies adopted in response to the content, the context and the perceived demands of particular learning tasks. Indeed, despite his demonstration of consistency in levels of processing between experimental tasks and academic study, Svensson (1977: 242) suggested that there might well be 'intra-individual differences in cognitive approach, depending on how the student conceptualises what is required of him'. In the same way, Dahlgren and Marton (1978) suggested that many economics students failed to acquire a sophisticated understanding of concepts such as 'price' because they had been forced to engage in rote memorization in order to cope with the demands of an overburdened syllabus.

These ideas were investigated by Laurillard (1978, 1979, 1984), who interviewed 31 students of science and engineering at a campus-based university about how they were tackling coursework problems they had encountered on different courses. She found that 19 of these students demonstrated both deep and surface approaches, depending upon the context, whereas the other students only showed a deep approach. Laurillard illustrated the first pattern by two quotations from the same student talking about his approaches in dealing with two different learning tasks:

Deep level processing:
'This has to be handed in – it's an operation research exercise, a program to find a minimum point on a curve. First I had to decide on the criteria of how to approach it, then drew a flow diagram, and checked through each stage. You have to think about it and understand it first. I used my knowledge of O.R. [operational research] design of starting with one point, testing it and judging the next move. I try to work through logically. Putting in diagrams helps you think clearly and follow through step by step. I chose this problem because it was more applied, more realistic. You can learn how to go about O.R. You get an idea of the different types of problem that exist from reading.'

Surface level processing:
'This problem is not to be handed in, but it will be discussed in the lecture because the rest of the course depends on this kind of thing. I knew how I'd do it from looking at it; it practically tells you what equation to use. You just have to bash the numbers out. I knew how to do it before I started so I didn't get anything out of it. There's not really any thinking. You just need to know what you need to solve the problem. I read through the relevant notes, but not much, because you don't need to look at the system. It's really just a case of knowing what's in the notes and choosing which block of notes to use. You don't have to interpret it in terms of the system. It's only when things go wrong, you have to think about it then. In this sort of situation you've got to get through to the answer.'

(Laurillard 1979: 400)

Laurillard argued that different approaches to studying were characteristics not of individual students but of students in relation to particular learning contexts. She concluded that in their academic work students 'are responsive to the environment and their approach to learning is determined by their interpretation of that environment' (Laurillard 1979: 408).

Ramsden (1979, 1981) carried out a similar study in which he interviewed 57 students from six academic departments at a single campus-based university (see also Entwistle and Ramsden 1983: chapter 8; Ramsden 1984). The participants were asked about how they had tackled recent academic tasks set as part of their normal studies, about the context in which they had carried out those tasks, and about the main department in which they were based. Marton's distinction between deep and surface approaches to studying was very apparent in the students' accounts. Moreover, there was a statistically significant trend for those students who had shown a deep approach subsequently to obtain better degrees than those who had shown a surface approach. However, in explaining their approaches, the participants often referred to contextual factors, such as their relationships with members of teaching staff or the demands of assessment tasks. Indeed, many individual students indicated that they adopted different approaches to studying in different courses or even in carrying out different assessment tasks on the same course.

Nevertheless, Ramsden claimed to have identified a third approach by reference to a particular group of students who had been described by Miller and Parlett (1974) in a study of final year physics students at a campus-based university as 'cue seekers'. These students

> button-holed staff about the exam questions; sought them out over coffee; made a point of discovering who their oral examiner was, what his interests were and, most of all, deliberately attempted to make a good impression on staff. This for them seemed to constitute a very large part of what the exams were all about.
>
> (Miller and Parlett 1974: 52)

Ramsden found evidence of 'cue seeking' among some of his particip-ants who were studying in departments where the relationships between academic staff and students were informal and personalized. However, in departments in which staff–student relationships were more formal, stu-dents used other techniques to maximize assessment outcomes. Ramsden therefore devised the more general concept of a 'strategic' approach to assessment in higher education. As in the case of a surface approach and a deep approach, Ramsden found that those students who used a strategic approach did so in response to the specific demands made by the context of learning. Box 2.1 summarizes the defining characteristics of the three putative approaches to studying.

Unfortunately, subsequent research has failed to confirm the existence of a separate 'strategic' approach to studying. One possibility is that it reflects a sophisticated response in students with an extrinsic motivation to adopt a deep approach or a surface approach, depending upon which is the more likely to maximize their grades or marks in any particular context (see Newble and Entwistle 1986; Ramsden 1988). (The role of motivational fac-tors in determining approaches to studying will be discussed in Chapter 4.) In contrast, there does seem to be good evidence for a third approach to studying among students in China and Hong Kong. Kember and Gow (1990) interviewed 20 students from a campus-based institution in Hong Kong: many showed a deep or a surface approach to studying, but others demon-strated a 'narrow' approach characterized by a systematic step-by-step process-ing of information. Subsequent studies have indicated that this intermediate approach, which combines memorizing with understanding, is fairly com-mon among students in Hong Kong and China (see Tan 1994; Kember 1996; Watkins 1996).

Nevertheless, the basic distinction between deep and surface approaches has been confirmed in research carried out in campus-based institutions of higher education, not only in Europe but in other parts of the world as well. Indeed, nowadays, this kind of distinction is commonplace and per-haps even a cliché in discussions about teaching and learning in higher education. Of course, the use of the words 'deep' and 'surface' embodies a

---

Box 2.1   **Defining features of three approaches to learning**

Deep approach
Intention to understand
Vigorous interaction with content
Relate new ideas to previous knowledge
Relate concepts to everyday experience
Relate evidence to conclusions
Examine the logic of the argument

Surface approach
Intention to complete task requirements
Memorise information needed for assessments
Failure to distinguish principles from examples
Treat task as an external imposition
Focus on discrete elements without integration
Unreflectiveness about purpose or strategies

Strategic approach
Intention to obtain highest possible grades
Organise time and distribute effort to greatest effect
Ensure conditions and materials for studying appropriate
Use previous exam papers to predict questions
Be alert to cues about marking schemes

Source: Entwistle 1987: 16

---

judgement about the relative desirability of the two approaches (Webb 1996: 89, 1997). It is true that certain academic disciplines may require students to acquire a large knowledge base of bare facts (as in biology or medicine) or specific procedural skills (as in accountancy), and in these cases rote memorization may be an effective strategy. In general, however, the strategy of encouraging a deep approach to studying and discouraging a surface approach to studying can be readily justified by reference to the avowed goals and missions of institutions of higher education (for example, Entwistle 1997b).

Indeed, the latter strategy was explicitly adopted in a national programme which was carried out in the UK between 1989 and 1991 and which was aimed at improving the quality of student learning at institutions whose academic programmes were validated by a national body, the Council for National Academic Awards. In introducing a report on this programme, Gibbs (1992: chapter 1) provided two quotations from interviews with students at one campus-based institution of higher education. Box 2.2

Box 2.2 **Interview extract illustrating a deep approach to studying**

Interviewer: 'When you are going through and underlining, what sort of things are going through your mind?'

Student: 'Well, I read it, I read it very slowly, trying to concentrate on what it means, what the actual passage means. Obviously I've read the quotations a few times and I've got it in my mind, what they mean. I really try to read it slowly. There is a lot of meaning behind it. You have to really kind of get into it and take every passage, every sentence, and try to really think "Well what does this mean?" You mustn't regurgitate what David is saying because that's not the idea of the exercise, so I suppose it's really original ideas in this one, kind of getting it all together.'

Source: Gibbs 1992: 8

Box 2.3 **Interview extract illustrating a surface approach to studying**

Interviewer: 'When you use the word learning in relation to this course, what do you mean?'

Student: 'Getting enough facts so that you can write something relevant in the exam. You've got enough information so you can write an essay on it. What I normally do is learn certain headings. I'll write a question down, about four, five different headings, which in an exam I can go: "Introduction" and I'll look at the next heading and I know what I've got to write without really thinking about it really. I know the facts about it. I go to the next heading and regurgitate.'

Source: Gibbs 1992: 8

---

contains an extract from a student interviewed about a geography course that clearly illustrates the use of a deep approach; Box 2.3 contains an extract from a student interviewed about a computing course that clearly illustrates the use of a surface approach.

Gibbs used the second quote to support his assertion that a surface approach was very common in higher education within the UK. He went on to point out that the student in the second extract managed to obtain a good honours degree, which confirmed the students' own claim that the assessment system on the course in question served to reward rote memorization. Further, however, Gibbs pointed out that the extracts had been obtained, not from two different students, but from the *same* student on two different courses. Clearly, he inferred, this was not a lazy, stupid, incompetent or unaware student, but a competent student who had only responded strategically to the perceived demands of the two different courses.

Gibbs argued that negative characteristics of their courses induced students to adopt a surface approach in their learning. He identified the following characteristics as especially important:

- A heavy workload
- Relatively high class contact hours
- An excessive amount of course material
- A lack of opportunity to pursue subjects in depth
- A lack of choice over subjects and a lack of choice over the method of study
- A threatening and anxiety provoking assessment system.

(Gibbs 1992: 9)

In contrast, Gibbs argued that a deep approach could be fostered by relatively low class contact hours, intrinsic interest in the subject and freedom in learning, and that these could be achieved through the use of appropriate course design, teaching methods and assessment. In his book, he described ten case studies that were specifically intended to foster a deep approach to studying.

Approaches to studying in distance education

At the Open University in the UK, the Study Methods Group (consisting of Gibbs, Morgan and Taylor) carried out a longitudinal study to explore approaches to studying among distance-learning students. They focused upon 29 students who were taking the Social Science Foundation Course in their first year of study with the Open University. They were interviewed three times during the year about their general notions of learning and about their understanding of certain key concepts covered in two blocks roughly half-way through the course on 'Production and allocation' and 'Work'. The interviews took place just before the beginning of the course, whilst the students were engaged in studying the block on 'Work', and at the end of the course. Some students dropped out of the course or transferred to other institutions, and others moved house too far away to be visited by the researchers; as a result, only 24 students were interviewed on the second occasion, and only 18 students were interviewed on the third.

Taylor *et al.* (1981a) reported the detailed findings from this longitudinal study with regard to the students' understanding of the concepts of price control, political power and oligopoly (that is, a state of limited competition in a particular market among a small number of producers). In each case, the students' responses reflected four different levels of outcome or understanding. However, there was only mixed evidence for any changes in outcome that could be attributed to the students' having taken the foundation course. There was an overall shift in the direction of more sophisticated conceptions of oligopoly, and so the course did appear to have enhanced the students' understanding of competition and its effects on the price, quality or choice of relevant products. In contrast, positive and negative changes were equally likely in their conceptions of price control and political power; in both cases, all four levels of outcome were exhibited, even in students who had successfully completed the foundation course. Taylor *et al.* concluded that the changes in levels of outcome did not show any consistent effect of having taken this course. Taylor *et al.* (1981b) obtained similar findings when they examined the students' understanding of another key concept covered in the course, that of social class. Even so, the results replicated those obtained by Dahlgren (1975; Dahlgren and Marton 1978), and hence it would appear that Marton's (1975) analysis of levels of outcome applies to student learning in both campus-based education and distance education.

At the second interview, the participants in this study were interviewed in depth about how they had been studying the materials in the blocks on 'Production and allocation' and 'Work' and in particular how they had gone about producing the essay assignments for the course which they had recently submitted. Morgan *et al.* (1982) analysed transcripts of these interviews to try and uncover significant aspects of how Open University students study. They were able to confirm a basic distinction between deep and surface approaches to studying, analogous to Marton and Säljö's (1976a) distinction between deep-level and surface-level processing. Nevertheless, these approaches appeared to be manifested in ways that reflected an individual student's motivation. On the one hand, students seemed to adopt a deep approach either in an intrinsic manner (that is, related to their interests) or in an extrinsic manner (that is, related to the demands of their assessment). On the other hand, students seemed to adopt a surface approach either as a passive response to an overwhelming situation or as an active strategy to achieve verbatim retention of the course material. Morgan *et al.* concluded that approaches to studying in distance-learning students were constrained by the conceptions of learning that they held. This idea had already been anticipated by Marton and his colleagues and is the main focus of the following chapter.

Concluding summary

- In experiments where students are asked to read and recall short academic texts, they show a limited number of different levels of outcome. These define a hierarchy or 'outcome space' in terms of their proximity to the author's original conception of the relevant phenomenon.
- In these experiments, different participants also show two levels of processing, a deep level and a surface level, which are highly associated with the

quality of the subsequent outcome. The level of processing depends on the participants' level of interest in the material and the expected form of assessment and can be manipulated by appropriate instructions or prompts.

• When students are interviewed about their studies, they exhibit analogous levels of outcome in their understanding of key concepts and an analogous distinction between two approaches to studying, a deep approach and a surface approach. The use of a deep or surface approach seems to depend on the content, the context and the perceived demands of the learning task.

• The original findings concerning approaches to studying in higher education were obtained in experimental investigations carried out with campus-based students. However, they have been replicated in more naturalistic research with both campus-based and distance-learning students. Consequently, they do not appear to depend critically on the actual mode of course delivery.

3

Conceptions of Learning

In the experiments that were discussed in the previous chapter, Marton and his colleagues found evidence for two different levels of processing, a deep level and a surface level. A participant's adoption of one level of processing rather than the other could apparently be influenced to some extent, at least, by manipulating the conditions of learning, and this appears to be true in normal academic studying, too. Nevertheless, Marton's (1975) original point was that different students show different levels of processing even under constant conditions of learning, and that here the participants' adoption of one level of processing rather than the other seemed to depend on their conception of learning and their conception of themselves as learners. Participants who adopted deep-level processing generally took an active role and saw learning as something they did; those who adopted surface-level processing generally took a passive role and saw learning as something that just happened to them. Marton (1976c) argued that, in the same way, students' adoption of deep or surface approaches in the course of their normal academic studying would be constrained or facilitated by their conceptions of learning.

How could these conceptions of learning be investigated? Dahlgren's (1975) study had shown that Marton's (1975) analysis of levels of outcome could be applied to the acquisition of basic concepts in economic theory. Dahlgren and Marton (1978) extended this approach to explore the different kinds of understanding that resulted from academic studying. In their subsequent research, Marton and his colleagues were less interested in the study of 'on-line' processing in artificial experiments and more interested in the study of people's underlying conceptions of a particular domain or phenomenon. Marton (1978) argued that conventional research on learning had adopted a 'first-order' or 'from-the-outside' perspective that tried to describe both the learner and the learner's world in broadly the same terms. He characterized his own work as adopting a 'second-order' or 'from-the-inside' approach that sought to describe the world as the learner experienced it, an approach that Marton (1981) labelled 'phenomenography'. As he subsequently explained,

Phenomenography is a research method for mapping the qualitatively different ways in which people experience, conceptualize, perceive, and understand various aspects of, and phenomena in, the world around them.

(Marton 1986: 31; see also Marton 1988: 178–9)

This shift in the focus of interest of Marton and his colleagues was accompanied by a shift in the kind of research methods that they used. In their initial studies, students had been asked to recall the content of academic texts and different levels of outcome had been identified in the transcripts of the students' oral accounts. This process apparently involved a straightforward application of the techniques of content analysis (see, for instance, Krippendorff 1980) in which the participants' understanding of the texts was compared with the meanings that their original authors had intended to convey. (Nowadays, postmodernist critics would suggest that this was not quite so straightforward, in so far as it privileged one authorized conception, frequently the researchers' own understanding of the subject matter, as the ultimate point of comparison for the students' accounts: see, for example, Webb 1996: 87–9; 1997; Ashworth and Lucas 1998.)

In the initial studies that were described in Chapter 2, the students had also been asked about how they had tackled the task of reading the academic texts and about how they tackled their normal academic studies. Inspection of the transcripts of their oral accounts had given rise to the distinction between deep-level and surface-level processing in the former case and to the distinction between deep and surface approaches to studying in the latter case. Marton (1979) characterized this as an application of the 'introspective' method in psychology, where people were asked to describe their mental processes whilst carrying out an experimental task. As he noted, after the domination of behaviourism during the first half of the twentieth century, this approach was enjoying something of a revival in education and psychology and it subsequently came to be described as 'protocol analysis' (see, for example, Ericsson and Simon 1980, 1984).

Of course, the introspective accounts that were obtained by Marton and his colleagues took the form of *retrospective* reports rather than *concurrent* reports. This could be justified on the basis that giving concurrent reports tends to disrupt interpretative processing when participants are called upon to explain their thought processes (Ericsson and Simon 1984: 78–107, 1993: xvii–xxxii) or when the task demands creative insight (Hoc and Leplat 1983; Schooler *et al.* 1993). The validity of introspective reports depends on the fact that the mental episodes in question persist as objects of focal attention in short-term memory, from which it follows that accounts obtained soon after the completion of the task in question will usually be an accurate reflection of on-line cognitive processing (Erisson and Simon 1980, 1984: 19, 25–30). This is a plausible account of people's reports of how they have just set about the task of reading an academic text. Unless they can retain an accurate permanent record of the relevant mental activities, however, their accounts of normal academic studying are likely to depend, at least in part, on inferences and reconstructions derived from their own subjective and implicit theories of the processes involved (see Nisbett and Wilson 1977; Ericsson and Simon 1980, 1984: 19–20; White 1989). If this is case, there will be an intrinsic connection rather than an adventitious one between students' reported approaches to studying and their underlying conceptions of learning.

Marton and his colleagues were more circumspect in describing the analytic methods by which they had identified different conceptions of a particular domain or phenomenon. They appear to have subjected the transcripts of students' oral accounts to an iterative and interactive process in order to identify fundamental categories or themes, each illustrated by relevant quotations from the transcripts. According to Marton and Säljö (1984), the categories were expected to emerge from comparisons conducted within the data, whereas in traditional content analysis they would be defined in advance and imposed on the data. Precisely the same approach to the analysis of qualitative data can be found in 'grounded theory', which is a methodology devised by Glaser and Strauss (1967) according to which theoretical concepts and hypotheses are to be discovered in and refined against participants' accounts. The central idea is that theoretical development results from an iterative process based upon the constant sampling, comparison and analysis of excerpts from interviews or other discursive material (see Strauss and Corbin 1990, 1994).

Several authors have noted a broad similarity between phenomenography and grounded theory (for instance, Entwistle and Ramsden 1983: 14; Francis 1993; Baxter Magolda 1998). Marton himself only occasionally acknowledged such parallels (Marton 1978; Marton and Booth 1997: 134). Nevertheless, in the absence of published guidance on the analytic procedures involved in 'doing phenomenography', many researchers simply adopted the techniques of grounded theory in order to analyse transcripts of interviews with students about their experiences of studying in higher education (Laurillard 1978: 65–7; Morgan *et al.* 1982; Taylor 1983). In addition, Säljö (1982: 17, 1984) referred to Glaser and Strauss's (1967) book in explaining his own application of phenomenography, and he went on explicitly to identify the process of deriving categories of description within phenomenographic research with the analytic techniques of grounded theory (Säljö 1988). This identification is supported implicitly by several other accounts of the analytical methods involved in phenomenographic research (for example, Marton and Säljö 1984; Marton 1988, 1994; Entwistle and Marton 1994; Marton and Booth 1997: 129–35; Entwistle 1997a).

Since the 1970s, the phenomenographic approach has been widely used to investigate conceptions held by both children and adults about key concepts, principles and phenomena in a wide variety of domains, although much of the work has been focused upon the development of students' understanding in science and mathematics (for a convenient summary, see Marton 1994). Although it is widely held to be an important and influential approach to educational research, the phenomenographic approach is vulnerable to criticisms on both conceptual and methodological grounds (see, for instance, Ashworth and Lucas 1998; Richardson 1999). It is also generally concerned with the product of learning rather than the process of learning, and the majority of phenomenographic research is therefore of incidental interest in the present context. The most important exception is research on people's conceptions of learning itself, and this is the topic of the present chapter.

Conceptions of learning in campus-based education

Säljö (1979a,b; see also Säljö 1982: chapter 6) investigated conceptions of learning through interviews with 90 people between the ages of 15 and 73 years who had been recruited from a number of institutions of further and higher education in Sweden. (These institutions were not identified but, so far as one can tell, none of the students was studying by distance learning.) An initial analysis of their accounts indicated that for many people the nature of learning was taken for granted: it was described as an essentially reproductive activity that was tantamount to rote memorization. This conception of learning appeared to be self-evident and unproblematic and was linked to the consistent adoption of a surface approach in academic studies.

For other students, however, learning had become 'thematic', in the sense that they had become 'aware of the influence of the context of learning on what you should learn and how you should set about it' (Säljö 1979a: 448). For these participants,

> learning is something which can be explicitly talked about and discussed and can be the object of conscious planning and analysis. In learning, these people realize that there are, for instance, alternative strategies or approaches which may be useful or suitable in various situations depending on, for example, time available, interest, demands of teachers and anticipated tests.
>
> (Säljö 1979a: 446)

This was an interpretative conception of learning that involved the extraction of meaning from the materials to be learned, a process that was described as 'real learning' or 'learning for life', as opposed to the artificial kind of learning required in primary and secondary education. Some of the participants described a process of development from the former conception of learning to the latter, a process that in many cases had been occasioned by the transition from secondary school to university and the realization of the demands of learning in higher education. Säljö's account implies that the latter conception of learning would be linked to the use of either a deep approach or a surface approach in academic studies, depending on the perceived demands of the specific learning context. This is, of course, precisely what was described by Laurillard (1978, 1979, 1984), Ramsden (1979, 1981) and Gibbs (1992: chapter 1), as discussed in Chapter 2.

During the course of their interviews, the participants in this study had been asked specifically: 'Well, what do you actually mean by learning?'. On the basis of a more thorough analysis of their responses to this question, Säljö broadened his initial distinction between a reproductive conception and an interpretative conception into five more specific conceptions of learning:

1. Learning as the increase of knowledge.
2. Learning as memorising.
3. Learning as the acquisition of facts, procedures, etc., which can be retained and/or utilised in practice.
4. Learning as the abstraction of meaning.
5. Learning as an interpretative process aimed at the understanding of reality.

(Säljö 1979b: 19)

Säljö pointed out that the first two conceptions of learning represented a cognitive orientation towards learning tasks that was 'reproductive', whereas the last two conceptions of learning represented a cognitive orientation that was 'reconstructive'.

These five conceptions of learning had been found in different participants and so Säljö had no direct information concerning either the logical or the chronological relationships among them. Nevertheless, he claimed that they constituted a developmental sequence or hierarchy (see also Säljö 1982: chapters 12–13; Marton and Säljö 1984). Säljö justified this claim in two ways. First, as mentioned above, some of the participants had made comments during their interviews to do with a process of transition that they had gone through between school and university. Second, Säljö maintained that there were parallels between his own results and an account of intellectual development that had been presented by Perry (1970) on the basis of a longitudinal study that he had conducted in the 1950s and 1960s of students at Harvard University in the US.

According to Perry's model, students proceed through a series of nine possible developmental stages, moving from a simplistic or absolute stance on the fundamental nature of knowledge towards a complex, pluralistic one. These are described in detail in Box 3.1, but Perry (1970: 57) summarized the nine stages in the form of three broad 'divisions'. During the initial period of dualism (positions 1, 2 and 3), the student develops an attitude of multiplicity, an awareness that there might be an indefinite number of legitimate points of view in some specific area. Then, during the period of relativism (positions 4, 5 and 6), the student perceives the general legitimacy of uncertainty, but at the same time he or she appreciates the need to achieve some kind of personal commitment as a means of resolving this uncertainty. Finally, during the period of commitment in relativism

Box 3.1 **Perry's (1970) scheme of intellectual and ethical development in higher education**

Position 1: The student sees the world in polar terms of we–right–good vs. other–wrong–bad. Right Answers for everything exist in the Absolute, known to Authority, whose role is to mediate (teach) them. Knowledge and goodness are perceived as quantitative accretions of discrete rightnesses to be collected by hard work and obedience (paradigm: a spelling test).

Position 2: The student perceives diversity of opinion, and uncertainty, and accounts for them as unwarranted confusion in poorly qualified authorities or as mere exercises set by Authority 'so we can learn to find The Answer for ourselves'.

Position 3: The student accepts diversity and uncertainty as legitimate but still *temporary* in areas where Authority 'hasn't found The Answer yet'. He supposes Authority grades him in these areas on 'good expression' but remains puzzled as to standards.

Position 4: (*a*) The student perceives legitimate uncertainty (and therefore diversity of opinion) to be extensive and raises it to the status of an unstructured epistemological realm of its own in which 'anyone has a right to his own opinion', a realm which he sets over against Authority's realm where right–wrong still prevails, or (*b*) the student discovers qualitative contextual reasoning as a special case of 'what They want' within Authority's realm.

Position 5: The student perceives all knowledge and values (including Authority's) as contextual and relativistic and subordinates dualistic right–wrong functions to the status of a special case, in context.

Position 6: The student apprehends the necessity of orienting himself in a relativistic world through some form of personal Commitment (as distinct from unquestioned or unconsidered commitment to simple belief in certainty).

Position 7: The student makes an initial Commitment in some area.

Position 8: The student experiences the implications of Commitment, and explores the subjective and stylistic issues of responsibility.

Position 9: The student experiences the affirmation of identity among multiple responsibilities and realizes Commitment as an ongoing, unfolding activity through which he expresses his life style.

Source: Perry 1970: 9–10

(positions 7, 8 and 9), the student goes on to work out the implications of achieving that personal commitment through his or her own experience.

How general is Säljö's (1979b) scheme of conceptions of learning? In Chapter 2, I mentioned a study by van Rossum and Schenk (1984) that was carried out at a campus-based university in the Netherlands. In this study, 69 first-year psychology students were asked to read and recall a short text; they then completed a questionnaire about how they had approached the task of reading the text and about how they approached their academic studies in general. Van Rossum and Schenk were able to use Säljö's scheme to classify the students according to their responses to the specific question: 'What do you mean by learning?'. In addition, there was a relationship between their conceptions of learning and the levels of processing they had displayed when studying the text. Three-quarters of the students who exhibited Säljö's conceptions 1, 2 or 3 had used surface-level processing when reading the text; conversely, nearly all the students who exhibited Säljö's conceptions 4 or 5 had used deep-level processing when reading the text. Van Rossum *et al.* (1985) conducted a further study in which they interviewed 42 first- and second-year arts students at a campus-based university. Their accounts implied a similar set of learning conceptions that van Rossum *et al.* linked to the longitudinal model devised by Perry (1970).

Hounsell (1984a, 1984b, 1987) interviewed 17 history students and 16 psychology students at a campus-based university in the UK about how they had approached the task of writing a recent essay. He identified several different conceptions of what an essay was:

> Some history students conceived of essay-writing as a question of *argument*, coherently presented and well-substantiated; others saw it as concerned with the *arrangement* of facts and ideas. And amongst the psychology students, essay writing was seen by some as a matter of *cogency*, where substantive discussion was rooted in a solid and coherent core of empirical findings, and by others as *relevance*, in the sense of an ordered presentation of material pertaining to a topic or problem.
>
> (Hounsell 1987: 110; italics in original)

Hounsell claimed that these categories represented a general distinction between 'interpretative' and 'non-interpretative' conceptions of essay writing which essentially paralleled Perry's (1970) notion of contextual relativistic reasoning and Säljö's (1979a) thematic conception of learning. He suggested that the quality of tutorial feedback on essays was critical in enabling students to proceed from a non-interpretative conception of essay writing to an interpretative one.

Martin and Ramsden (1987) used Säljö's (1979b) scheme of conceptions of learning to classify 60 first-year history students at two campus-based universities in the UK. All of the students were interviewed twice, both before and after they had attended courses designed to improve their learning skills. In fact, the courses themselves seemed to have very little effect upon the students' underlying conceptions of learning. These were distributed between Säljö's conceptions 2 and 5 but were concentrated in conceptions 3 and 4 both before and afterwards. (No student exhibited conception 1 in this study.) Nevertheless, there was a direct relationship between the students' conceptions of learning and their academic performance at the end of the year. The students who achieved the lowest grades all exhibited Säljö's conceptions 2 or 3, whereas those students who achieved the best grades all exhibited Säljö's conceptions 4 or 5.

In the classifications of conceptions of learning that I have discussed thus far, 'memorization' and 'understanding' are essentially seen as being mutually exclusive. In Chapter 2, however, I mentioned that investigations carried out with students in Hong Kong and China had identified a distinctive approach to studying that appeared to combine memorization and understanding. This suggests that Chinese learners might possess somewhat different conceptions of learning. Marton *et al.* (1996) interviewed 18 teacher educators from China about their understanding of the phenomenon of learning and they indeed identified some fundamental differences from the conceptions of learning found in Western learners. First, most of the participants distinguished between purely mechanical memorization and memorization with understanding. Second, some participants regarded memorization with understanding as a way of retaining what had already been understood, but others regarded memorization with understanding as a way of attaining a deeper understanding. Third, some participants regarded understanding as a relation between a learner and an object, but others regarded understanding as a process of personal development. Marton *et al.* concluded that the conceptions of learning that had been identified in Western students were not adequate to describe learning practices within the Chinese culture.

Even in Western cultures, students on courses with a less academic focus might exhibit rather different conceptions of learning. Eklund-Myrskog (1997), working in Finland, interviewed 27 student nurses at the start of their training and 33 student nurses at the end of their training. She found evidence for five different conceptions of learning, which she defined as follows:

• learning in terms of remembering and keeping something in mind
• learning in terms of understanding
• learning in terms of applying knowledge, based on understanding
• learning in terms of getting a new perspective
• learning in terms of forming a conception of one's own.

Eklund-Myrskog suggested that the first was a quantitative or reproductive conception, whereas the others were qualitative conceptions concerned with understanding. There was a trend for the student nurses to be more likely to show qualitative conceptions of learning after their training than before, but this was not statistically significant. Thus, the training programme appeared to have only a weak effect upon the development of student nurses' conceptions of learning. They had also been asked to read a school text about the essence of caring, and there was a similar non-significant trend for them to be more likely to show deep-level processing in this task after their training than before. Nevertheless, all of the participants with a quantitative conception of learning displayed surface-level processing when asked about how they had read the text, and all of the participants with a qualitative conception of learning displayed deep-level processing.

Eklund-Myrskog (1998) then repeated this study with a class of male students who were taking a course in car mechanics at a vocational school. She interviewed 24 students at the start of the course and 30 students at the end of the course. She identified just four conceptions of learning:

• learning in terms of remembering
• learning in terms of applying knowledge, based on knowing how to do
• learning in terms of understanding
• learning in terms of forming a conception of one's own.

Eklund-Myrskog suggested that the first two were quantitative conceptions, whereas the other two were qualitative conceptions. On this basis, 79 per cent of the students had a quantitative conception at the start of the course, but only 50 per cent had a quantitative conception by the end. Here, the trend towards more sophisticated conceptions was statistically significant. Thus, even a course in car mechanics can bring about genuine intellectual development. Nevertheless, Eklund-Myrskog claimed that the differences among the conceptions of learning *within* each of the programmes was smaller than the differences in the conceptions of learning *between* the two different programmes. She concluded that conceptions of learning were contextually dependent.

Conceptions of learning in distance education

In Chapter 2, I mentioned the longitudinal study carried out by the Study Methods Group at the Open University in the UK to explore approaches to studying in distance-learning students. The first interview in this study was carried out with 29 students as they were about to embark on their first year of study with the Open University and included questions about their general notions of learning. On inspecting the transcripts, Morgan *et al.* (1981) found that Säljö's (1979b) scheme of five conceptions of learning could also be applied to these students. Indeed, some of the students appeared to be undergoing a transition in their conceptions, in so far as they could differentiate between their current understanding of learning and the learning demands they expected that Open University studies would be making of them.

In a similar investigation, Vermunt and van Rijswijk (1988) conducted interviews with students who had recently embarked on courses with the

Dutch Open University, which delivers courses primarily through specially prepared correspondence materials with tutorial support available at regional study centres. In analysing their transcripts, Vermunt and van Rijswijk compared their participants' accounts with the descriptions of conceptions of learning that had been provided by Säljö (1979b) and by van Rossum *et al.* (1985) in the case of campus-based students. They concluded that the same descriptions 'could easily be recognized' within the population of new students at the Dutch Open University (Vermunt and van Rijswijk 1988: 653). It would appear, then, that the scheme of learning conceptions devised by Säljö (1979b) applies both to campus-based students and to distance-learning students.

The Study Methods Group maintained contact with 12 students from their original sample into their second and third years of study with the Open University in the UK. At this point, the students were interviewed once again about their general understanding of learning, but they were also asked to compare their current understanding with that in their first year of study with the Open University. Morgan *et al.* (1983: 17) commented that there were 'many parallels' between their own students' accounts and the conceptions of learning that had been described by Perry (1970) and Säljö (1979b). Moreover, comparing the students' concurrent accounts of their present conceptions with their retrospective accounts of their own previous conceptions seemed to suggest the existence of a developmental process leading to increasingly sophisticated conceptions of learning over the course of time (see also Morgan 1991).

Unfortunately, retrospective accounts of this sort may not be valid. Social psychologists have shown that people sometimes denigrate their past capabilities in order to fit their own implicit theories about personal change, and this can certainly occur when students are asked to assess the value of recent educational experiences (see Conway and Ross 1984; Ross 1989). It would, instead, be more convincing to have evidence of progression through different conceptions of learning from concurrent accounts obtained from the same students at different stages of their academic careers. Case studies of just this sort were provided by Gibbs *et al.* (1984), showing development during the first year of study with the Open University, and by Beaty and Morgan (1992), showing development in subsequent years (see also Morgan and Beaty 1997).

In fact, out of the 29 students in the original cohort studied by the Study Methods Group, ten were interviewed over a period of 6 years at the end of every year in which they had taken a course with the Open University, and six of these students were interviewed on either five or six occasions. Marton *et al.* (1993) presented a detailed analysis of their conceptions of learning and of the changes in their conceptions of learning across the period of 6 years. Their accounts revealed five conceptions of learning that were broadly similar to those that Säljö (1979b) had originally described, but there was a sixth conception. Marton *et al.* characterized the resulting sequence of six conceptions of learning as follows:

(A) Increasing one's knowledge
(B) Memorizing and reproducing
(C) Applying
(D) Understanding
(E) Seeing something in a different way
(F) Changing as a person.

(Marton *et al.* 1993: 283–4)

The sixth conception was seen only during the later years of a student's academic career with the Open University and only in students who had previously exhibited the fifth conception, so it is reasonable to infer that it represents an even more sophisticated conception of learning. In fact, it appears to reflect the kind of personal commitment that is involved in the later stages of Perry's (1970) model of intellectual development. Out of the six students who were interviewed on five or six occasions, three had attained this conception by the conclusion of the study. Two of the remainder did not show any appreciable change in their conceptions of learning, but these students had exhibited the fourth and fifth conceptions, respectively, even at the outset of their studies with the Open University. The results obtained in the study mentioned earlier by Martin and Ramsden (1987) implied that academic progress in campus-based education depends on the attainment of more sophisticated conceptions of learning, and the findings obtained in the study by Marton *et al.* suggest that the same is true of distance education (Beaty and Morgan, 1992).

Coincidentally, all six of the students who had been repeatedly interviewed over 6 years by the Study Methods Group were women. In this regard, Perry's (1970) original study was of limited value because it had been based on a predominantly male sample. (At the time when it had been carried out, women studied for Harvard degrees at the separate institution of Radcliffe College.) In the 1970s and 1980s, researchers in the US sought to remedy this by investigating intellectual development in female students (see, for example, Clinchy and Zimmerman 1982; Gilligan 1982; Baxter Magolda 1988; Gilligan *et al.* 1988). In particular, Belenky *et al.* (1986) carried out interviews with 135 women who were students, graduates or clients at health clinics about their conceptions of learning and knowledge. From a content analysis of the transcripts, they produced an alternative account of intellectual development to that put forward by Perry (1970). This account is based on five 'ways of knowing' which are summarized in Box 3.2.

Belenky *et al.* acknowledged that these epistemological categories were not sufficiently well defined to be interpreted as stages of intellectual development. Nevertheless, they do appear to represent increasing levels of intellectual complexity organized around the metaphor of silence and voice. Beaty *et al.* (1997) reconsidered the earlier findings of the Study Methods Group at the Open University in the light of these developments. They felt that the extended scheme of conceptions of learning (that is, conceptions

---

Box 3.2 'Women's ways of knowing'

Silence, a position in which women experience themselves as mindless and voiceless and subject to the whims of external authority.

Received knowledge, a perspective from which women conceive of themselves as capable of receiving, even reproducing, knowledge from the all-knowing external authorities but not capable of creating knowledge on their own.

Subjective knowledge, a perspective from which truth and knowledge are conceived of as personal, private and subjectively known or intuited.

Procedural knowledge, a position in which women are invested in learning and applying objective procedures for obtaining and communicating knowledge.

Constructed knowledge, a position in which women view all knowledge as contextual, experience themselves as creators of knowledge and value both subjective and objective strategies for knowing.

Source: Belenky *et al.* 1986: 15

A–F above) was broadly compatible with Perry's (1970) original interpretation. However, a more detailed inspection of the students' interview responses suggested that, in their emphasis on personal perspectives and personal change, they were more consistent with the account that had been put forward by Belenky *et al.* (1986).

In a subsequent study, Hipp (1997) interviewed 16 women who were taking courses at Master's level by external study with an Australian university. They participated in groups of four in an interview and discussion session using teleconferencing about a number of issues that had been identified through an earlier postal survey. Hipp independently linked the women's conceptions of learning and their conceptions of themselves as learners with the different 'ways of knowing' that had been described by Belenky *et al.* (1986). She argued that positive, personal feedback from teachers was important in bringing about personal development and increased confidence in female students working by distance learning, although she suggested that specially designed workshops, teleconferences or self-help materials could also help to enhance their self-esteem.

Changing as a person

On the basis of their results, Beaty *et al.* concluded 'Although we expect the architecture of the variations and commonalities in the experience of learning to be generalisable, the individually characteristic themes may be gendered' (Beaty *et al.* 1997: 164). In particular, they argued that this was true of the conception of learning as changing as a person. However, Crawford (1989) had criticized the study carried out by Belenky *et al.* (1986) because they had not included any comparison group of male participants and yet had readily speculated about gender differences in ways of knowing. In the same way, the results obtained by Beaty *et al.* are quite unclear as to whether the conception of learning as changing as a person was distinctive of female students because no men were included in their final sample of participants. At the same time, it should also be noted that later writers have rejected the idea of *female* ways of knowing in favour of distinctively *feminist* epistemologies (see Alcoff and Potter 1993; Lennon and Whitford 1994).

To try to reconcile Perry's (1970) original model of intellectual development with subsequent theories, Baxter Magolda and Porterfield (1985) developed a structured instrument called the Measure of Epistemological Reflection. This contained a series of open-ended questions about different domains: decision making, the role of the learner, the role of the instructor, the role of peers, evaluation of learning, and the nature of knowledge, truth or reality. An analysis of the responses given by campus-based students identified four different developmental stages, which are summarized in Box 3.3. This classification of students demonstrated a high level of reliability and, in subsequent studies, it was found to be highly correlated with findings obtained from semi-structured interviews (Baxter Magolda, 1987, 1988). Baxter Magolda (1992) carried out interviews with 101 students at a campus-based university in the US over 5 years, and she found clear evidence for development through the scheme shown in Box 3.3.

This developmental scheme appeared to fit the accounts produced by both women and men, although they tended to use different patterns of reasoning at each of the first three developmental stages, at least; that is, there are 'qualitative differences in how students justify epistemic assumptions within the same way of knowing and, thus, different but equally valid approaches to knowing' (Baxter Magolda 1992: 37). At the absolute knowing stage, women tended to use a 'receiving' pattern based on a private approach to acquiring knowledge, whereas men tended to use a 'mastery' pattern based on a public approach. At the transitional knowing stage, women tended to use an 'interpersonal' approach based on sharing the views of others, whereas men tended to use an 'impersonal' approach based on challenging the views of others. At the independent knowing stage, women tended to use an 'interindividual' approach based on sharing one's views with others, whereas men tended to use an 'individual' approach based on independent thinking. Different patterns of reasoning were not identified at the contextual knowing stage because of the small numbers of students who were classified as being at this stage.

In short, Baxter Magolda identified the same four 'ways of knowing' in both male and female students, and to that extent there do not appear to

Box 3.3 **Baxter Magolda's Epistemological Reflection Model**

Domains	Absolute knowing	Transitional knowing	Independent knowing	Contextual knowing
Role of learner	Obtains knowledge from instructor	Understands knowledge	Thinks for self Shares views with others Creates own perspective	Exchanges and compares perspectives Thinks through problems Integrates and applies knowledge
Role of peers	Share materials Explain what they have learned to each other	Provide active exchanges	Share views Serve as a source of knowledge	Enhance learning via quality contributions
Role of instructor	Communicates knowledge appropriately Ensures that students understand knowledge	Uses methods aimed at understanding Employs methods that help apply knowledge	Promotes independent thinking Promotes exchange of opinions	Promotes application of knowledge in context Promotes evaluative discussion of perspectives Student and teacher critique each other
Evaluation	Provides vehicle to show instructor what was learned	Measures students' understanding of the material	Rewards independent thinking	Accurately measures competence Student and teacher work towards goal and measure progress
Nature of knowledge	Is certain or absolute	Is partially certain and partially uncertain	Is uncertain – everyone has own beliefs	Is contextual; judge on basis of evidence in context

Source: Baxter Magolda 1992: 30

be qualitative differences in the conceptions of learning and knowledge that are held by men and women in higher education. She did find qualitative differences in students' patterns of reasoning at three of these development stages, but she argued that these patterns were 'related to, but not dictated by, gender', and that they had been socially constructed on the basis of the students' differential experiences of learning (Baxter Magolda 1992: 20–2). Severiens and ten Dam (1998) confirmed Baxter Magolda's scheme through open-ended interviews with 53 students of 'adult secondary education' in the Netherlands, except that none was assessed as exhibiting a stage beyond independent knowing. (This is probably not surprising, given that these students had yet to achieve the qualifications required for admission to higher education.)

A different point is that students who pursue courses by distance learning are often much older than campus-based students. For instance, the mean age of students registered for courses with the Open University in the UK is typically around 40 years. This observation suggests the possibility that the conception of learning as changing as a person is distinctive of older students, possibly as a result of their greater lifetime experience. Once again, the results obtained by Beaty *et al.* (1997) do not allow one to address this issue because they had not interviewed any comparison group of younger people taking courses with the Open University. It will be noted in a moment that conceptions of learning seem to vary directly with students' ages, even within the same year of study.

Most crucially, the results obtained by Beaty *et al.* are unclear as to whether the conception of learning as changing as a person was distinctive of students taking courses by distance learning because they had not interviewed a comparison group of campus-based students. Nevertheless, Marton *et al.* (1993) commented that an 'identical' conception of learning had previously been found in an investigation of students at a campus-based university in the Netherlands conducted by van Rossum and Taylor (1987). These researchers had interviewed 91 first-year arts students (22 men and 69 women aged between 17 and 41 years) and broadly confirmed the classification of conceptions of learning presented by Säljö (1979b). However, in five students they found a sixth conception that they characterized as 'a conscious process, fuelled by personal interests and directed at obtaining harmony and happiness or changing society' (van Rossum and Taylor 1987: 19). Unfortunately, they provided no demographic information about these five students. There was no significant gender difference in the distribution of the 91 students across the six learning conceptions, but conceptions of learning varied with age, such that younger students were disproportionately represented within Säljö's conceptions 1–3.

In a subsequent investigation, Figueroa (1992) interviewed two groups of 20 students who were taking second-, third- or fourth-year courses in modern languages and literature with a Mexican university. One of the groups (consisting of students aged between 19 and 32 years) was taking courses by distance learning, while the other group (consisting of students aged between 18 and 26 years) was campus-based. In general, the former students appeared to be more interested and involved in their own learning than the latter students. Nevertheless, in response to the question, 'What does learning mean to you?', eight students in both of these groups gave accounts that implied that learning was a personally meaningful experience and, in response to the question, 'How would you explain quantity and quality in learning?', five distance-learning students and four campus-based students gave accounts that identified 'quality in learning' with personal and meaningful experiences.

Watkins and Regmi (1992) asked 333 students who were taking courses at one of the campuses of Tribhuvan University in Nepal to write down answers to the question: 'What do you mean by learning?'. They carried out a content analysis of the students' responses and identified the learning conceptions described by Marton *et al.* (1993) with just two exceptions. First, Watkins and Regmi found no evidence to support Marton *et al.*'s second conception: that is, learning as 'memorizing and reproducing'. Watkins and Regmi concluded that reproductive conceptions of learning were not common in Nepal. However, this conclusion subsequently had to be amended in the light of the results of a study by Dahlin and Regmi (1997), who found that campus-based students in Nepal repudiated rote learning as trivial and essentially useless but that they valued memorization as a way of keeping in mind material that one is in the process of understanding. Dahlin and Regmi suggested that this was very much akin to the 'narrow' approach to studying that Kember and Gow (1990) had identified among students in Hong Kong (see Chapter 2). It is also very close to the conception of 'memorization with understanding' identified by Marton *et al.* (1996) among Chinese learners in a study that was mentioned earlier in the present chapter.

The second discrepancy in the learning conceptions identified by Watkins and Regmi (1992) had to do with the conception of learning as 'changing as a person', which was found in 13.6 per cent of their respondents. In some students, this could be regarded as a more sophisticated conception that built upon the view of learning as 'seeing something in a different way':

'Learning means to broaden our mind, to be able to face any situations in life . . . I get full satisfaction out of learning.'

'Learning means to acquire knowledge, to be able to communicate with appropriate ideas, with good understanding. After having learned one is able to face the world boldly.'

However, in other students, the personal change in question did not appear to be dependent on a more sophisticated conception of learning:

'Learning is a process by which one can have knowledge of unknown things leading towards self-satisfaction.'

'The process which changes our behaviour is learning. Changes should come in our knowledge, attitude, and behaviour.'

(Watkins and Regmi 1992: 107)

In these students, Watkins and Regmi concluded that the conception of learning as changing as a person did not represent the most sophisticated level in a developmental hierarchy but instead had been induced by exposure to the religious and philosophical traditions prevalent in Nepal. As Dahlin and Regmi (1997) commented, 'changing as a person' seems to reflect the impact of an individual existentialism in the West but the prevalence of a collective moralism in Nepal.

Landbeck and Mugler (1994) carried out interviews with 16 second- and third-year students who were taking a course in linguistics on campus at the University of the South Pacific. Two of these students described learning in a way that appeared to the researchers to correspond to the sixth conception of learning postulated by Marton *et al.* (1993):

> 'My opinion is, when one learns, one is being enlightened. Learning is for improvement, change for the better . . . One learns in order to accommodate the change in the demands of life . . . In fact to be able to adjust to society one has no option, no other alternative but to learn . . . But learning, unfortunately, we also learn bad things.'

> 'Learning is when changes occur, happen to you, either changes your life to be more negative or positive, or changes how you think, look at people and things around you.'

> (Landbeck and Mugler 1994: 46)

Elsewhere in their report, Landbeck and Mugler identified the first of the students as male and the second as female, which clearly implies that this sixth conception of learning can be found both in men and in women. However, for present purposes, the more important implication of all these studies is that the conception of learning as changing as a person can be found among students taking campus-based courses as well as among those studying by distance learning.

Concluding summary

- Students at campus-based institutions of higher education in Sweden, the Netherlands and the UK display a limited number of conceptions of learning that are described by the scheme that was originally presented by Säljö (1979b). However, the same scheme may well not apply to learners from Chinese cultures or to students in Western cultures who are taking courses with less of an academic focus.
- These conceptions of learning are directly associated with the students' levels of processing when they engage in reading academic texts under neutral learning conditions, and also with their subsequent performance in academic assessments.
- Similar conceptions of learning have been identified in students taking courses by distance learning in both the Netherlands and the UK and there is fairly good evidence that they constitute a developmental

sequence or hierarchy through which students proceed during the course of a degree programme.

- The same studies of distance-learning students suggested the existence of a sixth conception of learning as 'changing as a person'. Although, initially, this appeared to be distinctive of students in distance education, it has subsequently been identified in students taking courses at campus-based institutions in Nepal, the Netherlands, Mexico and the South Pacific. This does appear in some cases to represent a developmentally more sophisticated conception of learning. However, it has been argued that this conception of learning can also be induced by exposure to local cultural traditions in the absence of any genuine intellectual development.

- In short, there is no evidence that delivering courses by means of distance education leads to any qualitative differences in the general pattern of students' intellectual development; any quantitative differences between conceptions of learning in campus-based students and distance-learning students are likely to be due to differences in their ages.

4

Orientations to Studying

Chapters 2 and 3 were concerned with approaches to studying and conceptions of learning, respectively. These constructs are mainly concerned with the cognitive or intellectual aspects of studying in higher education. However, academic progress and attainment may depend at least as much upon the motivational aspects of learning. The concept of a study orientation was introduced to cover both the cognitive and the motivational aspects of how students approach the business of learning in higher education: this chapter traces the development of this concept in research into both campus-based and distance education.

In Chapter 1, I pointed out that students in distance education were physically and socially separated both from their teachers and from their institutions. In fact, they are often isolated not only from their teachers but from other students as well (Kahl and Cropley 1986). It has been suggested that this isolation might have negative consequences for the development of generic skills such as critical thinking (Anderson and Garrison 1995). Pugliese (1996) referred to 'the loneliness of the long distance learner', but the evidence he presented indicates that loneliness *per se* is not related either to the likelihood of course completion or to academic performance in those students who do complete their courses (see also Pugliese 1994).

Even so, it is clear that students taking courses in distance education may often lack immediate social support in their learning from both their teachers and their fellow students. Consequently, motivational aspects of learning may be more important than the intellectual aspects of learning in the context of distance education, and it is certainly true that student motivation has been a particular concern for researchers into distance education. As in previous chapters, however, I will discuss the development of research on orientations to studying in campus-based education before turning to the findings of research into orientations to studying in distance education.

Orientations to studying in campus-based education

In Chapter 2, I described an investigation by Laurillard (1978, 1979, 1984), who interviewed 31 students of science and engineering at a campus-based university about how they were tackling the coursework problems that they had encountered on different courses. Laurillard noted that her participants often referred to their interests and their aims in their courses of study, but she considered that 'motivation' and 'attitude' were not appropriate terms to describe these aspects of their studying. Instead, their comments seemed to reveal the nature of the factors that the students took into account in deciding upon the use of different methods of studying, and these Laurillard characterized as their 'orientation'. She concluded:

> A student's overall orientation to his course influences the nature of his response to the requirements of the task which, together with his perception of what these are, determines his approach to the learning task. This in turn, together with the teaching and nature of the learning task, influences the student's learning style.
>
> (Laurillard 1978: 170)

Laurillard identified three different types of orientation to studying according to the transcripts of the interviews: ' "academic" (interested in the subject), "vocational" (interested in career opportunity), and "social" (interested in general self-education)'. Nevertheless, she emphasized that the students whom she had interviewed

> seldom ascribed to themselves a single overall orientation, although usually one would appear to have greater priority than the others. The different types of orientation should not therefore be seen as dividing students into groups. Each student seemed to be aware of having all three types, but to varying degrees.
>
> (Laurillard 1978: 172)

Laurillard suggested that these orientations were linked to methods of studying through motivational factors. She suggested that students with an academic orientation had an 'intrinsic' motivation based upon an interest in the subject for its own sake, but that students with a vocational orientation had an 'extrinsic' motivation based upon an interest in obtaining qualifications. A social orientation had little bearing upon the study method adopted, except in so far as students with this orientation did less work overall than the students who were academically or vocationally orientated to their studies (Laurillard 1978: 174).

Taylor (1983) carried out a more detailed investigation of students' orientations towards their courses at the same campus-based institution of higher education (see also Taylor *et al.* 1980, 1981c). She defined an

---

Box 4.1 **Students' orientations, interests, aims and concerns**

Orientation	Interest	Aim	Concerns
Vocational	Intrinsic	Training	Relevance of course to career
	Extrinsic	Qualification	Recognition of worth of qualification
Academic	Intrinsic	Follow intellectual interest	Room to choose work, stimulating lectures
	Extrinsic	Educational advance	Grades, academic progress
Personal	Intrinsic	Self improvement	Challenge, interesting material
	Extrinsic	Proof of capability	Feedback, passing course
Social	Extrinsic	Have a good time	Facilities for sport and social activities

Source: Adapted from Taylor *et al.* 1981b: 4

'orientation' as 'all those attitudes and aims that express the student's individual relationship with a course and the university' (Taylor *et al.* 1981c: 3; Taylor 1983: 130). On the basis of structured interviews with 39 students on two different degree courses, Taylor identified four principal types of study orientation: vocational, academic, personal and social. However, these could be expressed in terms of either an intrinsic or an extrinsic interest in their degree course itself. Box 4.1 illustrates how these different orientations were linked to the different concerns expressed by the students while they were studying their courses.

Taylor argued that students' orientations constituted their personal context for studying, and that the latter was a primary determinant of how they subsequently approached their academic studies. She initially interviewed her students towards the end of either their first or second year of study and then annually for 2 years thereafter. She found that some students tackled their studies in a way that accommodated both their orientations and the demands of their courses. However, some students had to adapt their orientations to suit the demands of their courses, while other students failed to achieve such a compromise and left the university altogether. Taylor concluded that students' study patterns resulted from a complex negotiation between their orientations to studying and their perceptions of the situational context.

Orientations to studying in distance education

Goodyear (1976) carried out a group interview to explore the motives of a sample of students who were about to embark on courses by distance learning with the Open University in the UK. She identified two basic motives:

- obtaining a specific qualification to achieve some promotion in one's job
- searching for something to compensate for perceived inadequacies or dissatisfaction in one's current life.

The latter motive might amount to making up for missed opportunity in one's past experience, escaping from everyday routine in one's current situation or investing in one's future. Goodyear also interviewed some students who were currently taking courses at the Open University and other students who had failed to complete their courses. Many claimed that their motivation had changed during their studies, but Goodyear did not analyse their comments in any depth.

In Chapters 2 and 3, I mentioned the longitudinal study conducted by the Study Methods Group at the Open University in the UK. The first set of interviews in this investigation was carried out with 29 students who were about to embark on their first year of study with the Open University by taking the Social Science Foundation Course. On examining the interview transcripts, Taylor *et al.* (1980) found evidence for all of the different study orientations that Taylor had identified at the campus-based university (see Box 4.1), except that none of the distance-learning students appeared to exhibit a social orientation to studying (see also Taylor *et al.* 1981c). Presumably, aspiring students with a strong social orientation simply choose not to study by means of distance learning. Even so, Gibbs *et al.* (1984) pointed out that some students taking courses with the Open University placed a high priority upon their tutorials because these did provide a limited opportunity to meet other people.

As I mentioned in Chapter 2, 18 of these students were interviewed at the end of the year, when they were asked, among other things, what they felt they had gained from studying the course in question. Taylor *et al.* (1983) found evidence of an association between their study orientations at the start of the course and their perceptions of what they had gained at the end of the course (see also Morgan *et al.* 1983):

> Where there had been a wish for personal development at the start of the course, in the interview at the end of the course there appeared to be a corresponding emphasis on personal gains. Similarly, where initially students had expressed a wish to follow up an interest in particular subjects, either for academic or vocational reasons, they tended to emphasize their increased understanding of those subjects in the later interview.
>
> (Taylor *et al.* 1983: 143)

However, this association was more apparent where the original orientation had been intrinsic in nature; where the orientation had been extrinsic, the outcome of the course was presumably seen merely as a means to a further end and was therefore not mentioned as an actual gain.

In Chapter 3, I also mentioned an investigation by Vermunt and van Rijswijk (1988) in which interviews were carried out with students who had recently embarked on courses with the Dutch Open University. In analysing their interview transcripts, Vermunt and van Rijswijk compared their own participants' accounts with the descriptions of orientations to studying that had been provided in the publications of the Study Methods Group (see, for example, Gibbs *et al.* 1984). They remarked in passing that their interviews with distance-learning students had resulted in descriptions of orientations to studying that were 'comparable to those of Gibbs *et al.*', and this would indicate that the scheme shown in Box 4.1 has a fairly high degree of generality.

Marland *et al.* (1984) carried out a small-scale study in which four people who were registered as external students at an Australian university were video recorded while they were studying genuine course materials. The participants then watched a replay of themselves carrying out the task and attempted to recall their thought processes during the task. Their accounts suggested that just two basic types of study orientation encompassed their motivations, study strategies, role perceptions and levels of processing while carrying out the task. One of these involved intrinsic motivation, optimizing strategies, a divergent role and deep processing. The other orientation involved extrinsic motivation, satisficing strategies (that is, fulfilling the minimum requirements to achieve a particular goal), a compliant role and surface processing.

Clearly, the value of this study is limited by the very small number of participants. However, in a subsequent investigation using the same methodology, Marland *et al.* (1990, 1992) classified 17 students who were taking courses by distance learning as having either a 'surface' approach or a 'deep' approach with regard to their motivations, their strategies and their conceptions of learning. Thirteen of the students were classified consistently across all three domains, and only four combined indicators of both a surface approach and a deep approach. However, even those students who had espoused a deep approach towards studying seemed to engage with the course materials in a rapid and superficial manner. Marland *et al.* argued that the latter finding was a matter for some concern. Nevertheless, it might simply have reflected the participants' response to the perceived demands of what seems to have been a singularly unrealistic experimental task.

Olgren (1993, 1996) interviewed 20 distance-learning students at an institution in the US about how they had actually been studying one module on marketing. She found that their accounts could be categorized as representing three different 'approaches' – reproducing, comprehension and application – that varied in terms of:

- the learner's goal orientation;
- the learner's perceptions of the value of the task, the demands of the examination and the outcome of learning; and
- the learner's knowledge about effective learning strategies.

Although Olgren's students typically had multiple goals that were vocational, academic and personal in nature, these goals tended to be consistently orientated towards either intrinsic or extrinsic concerns in the manner that was described by Taylor *et al.* (1981c). Olgren concluded that the outcome of distance learning depended not only on the learners' cognitive strategies but also on their perceptions, their goals and other possible factors that affected their mental involvement and their self-direction in learning.

Campus-based versus distance education

As in Laurillard's (1978) earlier study, the orientations shown in Box 4.1 were not intended to be seen as mutually exclusive. Instead, they represented idealized extremes that might well be combined in any particular student's orientation (see Taylor *et al.* 1980, 1981c). An academic orientation or a vocational orientation was the major component for most of the campus-based students interviewed by Taylor (1983), whereas signs of a personal orientation were shown by all the students who were embarking on distance-learning courses at the Open University. An analogous pattern was obtained by Saga (1992) in a postal survey of distance-learning students in Pakistan. However, von Prümmer (1990) found that distance-learning students in the former West Germany endorsed vocational and personal motives to roughly the same extent.

Presumably, extrinsic vocational motives are more important than intrinsic academic motives when the course is being taken as a prerequisite for a degree that leads to a particular career. Yellen (1998) obtained replies to a postal survey from 36 students who were taking courses in information systems with four different distance-learning institutions in the US. He also obtained responses from 123 students who completed the same questionnaire in class time while taking comparable courses in a campus-based institution. Yellen found no difference in the extent to which these two groups rated their motivation for taking their course 'to learn the material' rather than 'to get a degree'. In this context, the motivation for both distance-learning and campus-based students was primarily extrinsic rather than intrinsic in nature.

In addition, Taylor (1983) had found a personal orientation in some of the students whom she had interviewed at the campus-based university. Taylor *et al.* (1981c) observed that nearly all the students in question were 'mature' students: that is, they had been over the age of 26 years at the time of their admission to the university. (These students are often referred to as 'adult' students in the US and as 'mature-age' students in Australia, although the age limit used to define such students varies from one institution to another and has changed over time.) In both respects, they were more like distance-learning students than the majority of campus-based students. (As I mentioned in Chapter 3, the average age of Open University students is about 40 years.) As Taylor *et al.* themselves suggested: 'It may be that personal orientation is a feature of mature students rather than just Open University students' (Taylor *et al.* 1981c: 10).

Indeed, a survey of students in the final year of a psychology degree at another campus-based university in the UK indicated that older students may well have personal goals that are not shared by younger students (Marshall and Nicolson 1991). When asked why they had chosen to study psychology, ten out of 15 'mature' students (in this case, those who had been over the age of 25 years at the time of their admission to the course) indicated that they had chosen to study psychology to make more of their own lives by opening up professional and intellectual opportunities and also by enhancing their self-confidence. As one stated:

'I came through school without any qualifications at all. I wasn't particularly encouraged to believe in myself . . . Then through events in my own life I realised that I had more potential than I'd ever given myself credit for and I didn't know what it was – but I was going to find out!'
(Marshall and Nicolson 1991: 27)

However, not one of the 24 younger students who were included in this survey gave answers of this sort. This implies that there are no inherent differences in the orientations of campus-based students and distance-learning students once the difference in their ages is taken into account.

Earlier in this chapter, I referred to an investigation by Vermunt and van Rijswijk (1988) that had involved 34 first-year students who had recently embarked on four different courses with the Dutch Open University. Although Vermunt and van Rijswijk indicated the broad rationale for their research, they did not present any detailed analysis of their qualitative data. The latter was provided in a subsequent paper by Vermunt (1996), which also presented comparable data from 11 first-year students who were studying psychology at a campus-based university in the Netherlands. The account that follows is, therefore, based on information contained in both of these publications.

Vermunt and van Rijswijk began by arguing that one important dimension underlying student learning was the extent to which educational tasks and activities were regulated by students themselves rather than by their teachers. It would therefore be important to determine not only the different ways in which their students went about learning specific materials, but also the different ways in which they or their teachers tried to coordinate the learning of those materials. In looking for common themes in the transcripts of their interviews, Vermunt and van Rijswijk identified two different kinds of activities – *processing* and *regulation*:

Processing activities are directed at elements of the learning content, such as facts, concepts, definitions, arguments, conclusions, theories,

Box 4.2   Learning styles and their components

Components	Learning styles			
	Undirected	Reproduction directed	Meaning directed	Application directed
Cognitive processing	Hardly any processing	Stepwise processing	Deep processing	Concrete processing
Regulation of learning	Lack of regulation	Mostly external regulation	Mostly self-regulation	Both external and self-regulation
Affective processes	Low self-esteem Failure expectations	Fear of forgetting	Intrinsic interest	Practical interest
Mental model of learning	Cooperation and being stimulated	Intake of knowledge	Construction of knowledge	Use of knowledge
Learning orientation	Ambivalent	Certificate and self-test oriented	Person oriented	Vocation oriented

Source: Vermunt 1996: 47

perspectives, etc. Regulation activities are directed at the processing activities; students employ them to orchestrate, coordinate, regulate and check their own processing activities and so to exert control over their own learning.

(Vermunt and van Rijswijk 1988: 649)

In addition, whether and how students are able to regulate their own learning activities clearly depends upon their conceptions of learning and their motivation or orientation to their studies. Consequently, Vermunt and van Rijswijk looked for major themes under these headings, too. Although they identified variation among different students at each of these levels, this seemed to be subsumed under four overarching learning 'styles', which they described as 'undirected', 'reproduction directed', 'meaning directed' and 'application directed'. These differed in how the students processed the materials to be learned, in how they regulated their learning, in the affective processes that arose during their studying, in their conceptions – or, as Vermunt (1996) characterized them, their 'mental models' – of learning and in their learning orientations. The characteristics of the four learning styles are summarized in Box 4.2.

These were prototypical styles or idealized extremes that once again could be combined in any particular student. However, in fact every respondent showed a single dominant style. Vermunt did not report how frequently the four different styles were identified within each of the groups of students (that is, campus-based versus distance-learning). This would not in itself have been very informative for two reasons:

1. The relative frequency of each learning style probably varies from one discipline to another, and yet the two groups were studying different academic disciplines.
2. The relative frequency of each learning style probably varies with age, and yet the two groups differed in their mean ages (distance-learning students, 33.0 years; campus-based students, 22.4 years).

Nevertheless, the illustrative extracts from the interviews that Vermunt included in his article implied that all four learning styles had been exhibited by both distance-learning students and campus-based students. This implies that the two groups were essentially comparable in their learning activities, in their conceptions or mental models of learning, and in their basic orientations towards studying in higher education.

Concluding summary

- Students at campus-based institutions of higher education in the Netherlands and the UK display a limited number of orientations to studying that are characterized by the scheme originally presented by Taylor (1983). These reflect their motivation for engaging in higher education and are a primary determinant of how they approach their academic studies.
- Similar orientations to studying have been identified in students taking courses by distance education at 'open universities' in Germany, the Netherlands, Pakistan and the UK and and in students taking courses as 'external' students at universities in Australia and the US.
- Distance-learning and campus-based students seem to be comparable in their orientations to studying. The chief exception is that students taking courses by distance learning tend not to show a social orientation to studying. This is hardly surprising, given the physical separation from teachers and other students that is inherent in distance education.
- Students taking courses by distance learning are instead likely to show a personal orientation to studying. In this respect, they resemble older campus-based students and differ from younger campus-based students. To the extent that a personal orientation is more common in distance-learning students than campus-based students, this is probably due to differences in their ages rather than to differences in the mode of course delivery.

5

The Study Process Questionnaire

The research described in Chapters 2–4 consists mainly of qualitative investigations based on structured or semi-structured interviews with campus-
based and distance-learning students. These investigations have identified
certain approaches, conceptions, orientations and learning styles in both
campus-based and distance education. Nevertheless, the number of such
studies that have been carried out with distance-learning students is actually quite small, partly because of the sheer practical difficulty involved in
arranging face-to-face interviews with students who are located at a geographical distance from the institutions where they are registered. In other
words, the physical separation between students and teachers in distance
education affects not only the students' experience but also how research
is carried out into the students' experience.

Instead of face-to-face interviews, it is possible to carry out postal surveys that use open-ended questionnaires. This was the approach that was
employed by van Rossum and Schenk (1984), for example, even with campus-
based students. However, this still leaves the burden of analysing a substantial
body of qualitative data, even with only a relatively modest sample of participants. If a much larger sample is required then the process of data analysis
becomes quite intractable unless there are a limited number of response
alternatives to each question that can be encoded in a fairly straightforward
manner. In research on distance education, therefore, the adoption of
inventories and questionnaires (typically ones yielding quantitative data)
has been dictated by the problem of geographical distance and organizational constraints (see Morgan 1984, 1991).

Four main instruments have been used to collect quantitative data from
students in distance education, and these will constitute the focus for the
present chapter and the four that follow:

- the Study Process Questionnaire (Chapter 5)
- the Approaches to Studying Inventory (Chapters 6 and 7)
- the Distance Education Student Progress inventory (Chapter 8)
- the Inventory of Learning Styles (Chapter 9).

In addition, a number of other instruments will be discussed in Chapter 10. In most cases, the main function of these instruments has been to operationalize the various constructs that have emerged from qualitative investigations in order to generate quantitative scores on particular dimensions or scales that reflect different aspects of learning and studying in higher education. Most of these instruments were devised for use with students taking courses at campus-based institutions of higher education but, in principle, there is no reason why they should not adapted for use with students who are taking courses by distance learning. This in turn means that they could then be used to make direct statistical comparisons between campus-based students and distance-learning students in their distributions of scores on the relevant dimensions or scales.

The Study Behaviour Questionnaire

This chapter is mainly concerned with the Study Process Questionnaire, but I need to begin by discussing its precursor, the Study Behaviour Questionnaire (SBQ). This was devised by Biggs (1970a, b), who, in common with other researchers at the time, characterized differences in how students went about their academic studying as the product of 'certain enduring personality characteristics' (Biggs 1970a: 163). Although Biggs used the expression 'study behaviour', the SBQ actually contains items that relate to students' beliefs, attitudes and mental processes, as well as examples of observable behaviour such as note-taking or engaging in group discussion. In each case, respondents indicate how often a statement is true of them on a five-point scale from 1 ('This is always or nearly always true of me') to 5 ('This is never or very rarely true of me'), so that a high score on a given item means that the item has been rejected. The initial version of the SBQ contained 72 items, and Biggs (1970a) administered this to 314 campus-based students who were beginning teacher training courses at an Australian university. At the end of the first year of study, 260 of these students completed the SBQ for a second time. Their responses were encoded numerically and then submitted to a factor analysis.

The latter is a technique for identifying the constructs (usually called 'factors' or 'components') that seem to underlie a set of quantitative data. If several variables are all very highly correlated with one another then it is reasonable to assume that they are all tapping the same underlying construct. For example, if a lot of people are asked which hand they prefer to use for writing, for throwing, for cutting with a pair of scissors, and so on, their responses prove to be highly associated with one another (that is, most people – although not all – will report using the same hand for most of these activities). This then makes it sensible to talk about a single underlying dimension that might be called 'handedness' (see Richardson 1978). In other cases, however, the pattern of correlations will imply the existence of two or more underlying constructs, and there exist different methods for identifying these. It may then be necessary to transform (or 'rotate') these factors to achieve the most meaningful interpretation and, depending upon the analytic techniques that are used, this can result in rotated factors that are either orthogonal (that is, independent of one another) or oblique (that is, correlated with one another).

In Biggs's (1970a) study, the factor analysis generated six orthogonal factors that he interpreted as follows:

- study organization
- tolerance of ambiguity
- cognitive simplicity
- capacity for intrinsic motivation
- dogmatism
- independence of study behaviour.

The test–retest reliability of the students' scores on these factors was only moderate (less than 0.50 in all cases) and typically lower in science students than in arts students. However, this could be attributed to the fairly long test–retest interval, during which many students might have modified their approaches to studying in the light of their learning experiences. Scores on four of these factors showed statistically significant correlations with performance in the end-of-year examinations in the case of students taking arts subjects, but the relationships in question were very weak and none was statistically significant in the case of students taking science subjects. The fact that individual differences in studying consisted of a number of distinct components and could not be reduced to a single dimension of 'good' versus 'bad' in terms of subsequent attainment led Biggs to reject the view that studying could be identified with a specific set of teachable skills. It follows that the value of 'study skills programmes' is highly questionable.

In a subsequent paper, Biggs (1970b) examined the relationships between the students' scores on the six factors that he had identified and various measures of personality and attainment. Some of the correlations were statistically significant, and the pattern of correlations generally tended to reinforce his previous interpretation of the factors. However, the relationships were typically very weak, and most of these correlation coefficients were not statistically significant. In some cases, the relationships were statistically significant for arts students but not for science students, which led Biggs to conclude that the SBQ was tapping strategies that were important in arts subjects but not in science subjects. However, the discrepancies can also be attributed to the fact that he had included nearly four times as many arts students as science students in his study, so that weak relationships would be less likely to be significant in the latter group.

Biggs commented that gender differences in the correlation coefficients were 'minimal' (Biggs 1970b: 290). However, scores on the 'dogmatism' factor were found to be negatively related to performance in the end-of-year examinations in male arts students, but not in science students or in female arts students. Biggs suggested that this factor was concerned with the insulation or 'encapsulation' of personal values from the university experience to protect them from change. He argued that insulating one's value system would be irrelevant in studying science as the course content would be only marginally related to personal values, but it would be maladaptive in arts students as the course content would often confront their personal values. He went on:

> The fact that this relationship between encapsulation of values and performance does not appear in Arts females is possibly due to the selectivity of the present sample. Many prospective female teachers possibly regard their academic careers in fairly superficial terms. Their ultimate career would be marriage; in the meantime, they could regard their departmental bond as a means of obtaining a degree with minimal effort and with less self-involvement than would males.
>
> (Biggs 1970b: 294)

The views expressed in this quotation would not, of course, be acceptable nowadays.

In two later papers, Biggs (1973, 1976) developed the SBQ into an instrument that measured ten scales by means of 80 items concerned with motivational and strategic aspects of studying:

- Academic aspiration: 'Pragmatic, grade-oriented, university as means'
- Academic interest: 'Intrinsically motivated, study as end'
- Academic neuroticism: 'Confused, overwhelmed by demands of course work'
- Internality: 'Sees "truth" coming from within not external authority'
- Study skills and organization: 'Works consistently, reviews regularly, schedules work'
- Fact-rote strategy: 'Centres on facts, details, rote learns'
- Dependence: 'Rarely questions instructors, tests; needs support'
- Meaning assimilation: 'Reads widely, relates to known, meaning oriented'
- Test anxiety: 'Very concerned about tests, exams, fear of failure'
- Openness: 'University place where values are questioned'

(Biggs 1976: 72)

Although Biggs made no explicit comment about the scoring of the items in this version of the SBQ, it would seem that he had reversed the response scale so that a high score on a given item meant that the participant had accepted the item as true of them. Their responses to the relevant items were then summed to yield a total score on each of the ten scales.

Biggs (1976) obtained responses from 464 campus-based students who were starting courses in arts and science subjects at a Canadian university. Several of the scales were correlated with the students' grade-point averages at the end of the academic year. However, academic attainment proved to be associated with different patterns of studying in men and women, especially in the science students. For men, optimal performance was apparently achieved 'by seeing "truth" as emerging from external sources and authorities, and not worrying too much about inter-relating past knowledge with what one is in the process of acquiring'. However, for women, it tended to be achieved 'by making up one's own mind about "truth", by avoiding rote learning of detail, and by actively using transformational strategies' (Biggs 1976: 77). This does rather contradict Biggs's (1970b) earlier suggestion that many female students were interested only in marriage.

The 80-item version of the SPQ

Subsequently, however, Biggs (1978a) adopted a revised position in which academic attainment was a result of both 'personological' factors (such as personality, intelligence and background) and 'institutional' factors (such as academic subject, teaching method and mode of assessment). (Strictly speaking, 'personological' means 'pertaining to the study of personality', but it is also sometimes used to refer to individual differences of all kinds: that is, to variables relating to the *person* as opposed to their situation or context.) Biggs argued that the effects of personological and institutional factors on students' academic performance were mediated by 'study processes', which encompassed students' values, motives and strategies. In this scheme, the personological and institutional factors constitute independent variables; study processes constitute intervening variables; and measures of academic attainment constitute dependent variables (Biggs 1984).

Biggs's (1978a) account drew upon the 'presage–process–product' model of classroom teaching that had been put forward by Dunkin and Biddle (1974: 36–48). The latter researchers described the characteristics of teachers as 'presage variables' and differentiated them from the contextual variables (including characteristics of their students) that influenced the nature of their teaching. Biggs simply reversed this distinction, stressing the role of the students rather than that of their teachers and regarding characteristics of the teachers simply as part of the institutional context in which learning occurred. Biggs also subsumed both personological and institutional factors under the heading of 'presage variables' (see Figure 5.1).

Originally, Biggs characterized the causal connections as running in one direction, from presage to processes to product (that is, to academic performance) (see also Biggs 1984, 1985, 1987: 9, 96). However, in a subsequent account, Biggs (1991) incorporated feedback loops whereby observations of learning outcomes could lead students to modify their beliefs about their own capabilities and could also induce teachers and institutions to modify their teaching practices. Eventually, Biggs (1993a) allowed for the possibility of interactions among all of the different components of this system. Although this introduces a much greater degree of flexibility into the model, there is a danger that it also deprives it of any explanatory power, in so far as it can now accommodate virtually any pattern of empirical results that might be obtained.

To operationalize the domain of study processes, Biggs (1978a) developed a revised instrument in which certain of the 80 items in the SBQ had been

Figure 5.1 Biggs's (1978, 1985) general model of study processes

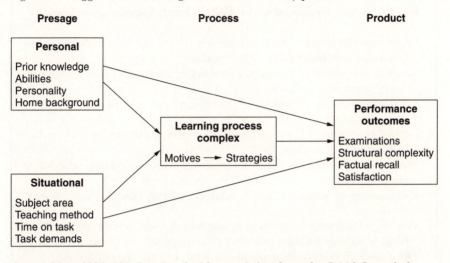

Source: Biggs 1985: 185. Reprinted with permission from the *British Journal of Educational Psychology*, © The British Psychological Society 1985

reclassified and the ten scales relabelled. He called this new instrument the 'Study Process Questionnaire' (SPQ) (Box 5.1). Biggs carried out separate factor analyses on the scores obtained by 420 campus-based students at a Canadian university and by two samples consisting of 150 and 148 campus-based students at an Australian university. In each case, he found that the ten scales could be subsumed under three second-order factors, which he interpreted as representing the 'reproducing', the 'internalizing' and the 'organizing' dimensions of study processes. These encompassed the values, motives and cognitive strategies that were associated with different aspects of learning (Box 5.2).

At a cognitive level, these corresponded closely to the distinction between surface approach, deep approach and strategic approach that was discussed in Chapter 2. At a motivational level, Biggs (1979) implied that they corresponded to the distinction between extrinsic motivation, intrinsic motivation and achievement motivation. The first two kinds of motivation were discussed in Chapter 4. The third had been widely discussed by researchers in the US as a personality dimension that reflected the need to succeed in contrast to a need to avoid failure (for example, see McClelland 1961; Atkinson 1964). In Biggs's subsequent writings, he referred to the reproducing dimension as an 'instrumental' or 'utilizing' dimension, and he also referred to the organizing dimension as an 'achieving' dimension (Biggs 1978b, 1979, 1982).

Biggs (1978b) administered this version of the SPQ to a class of 60 students at a campus-based university in Australia and then asked them to read two short texts that summarized educational experiments. Half of the

***Box 5.1*   Scales contained in the 80-item Study Process Questionnaire**

Pragmatism (10 items): Grade oriented; student sees university qualifications as a means to some other end.

Academic motivation (10 items): Intrinsically motivated; sees university study as an end in itself.

Academic neuroticism (7 items): Overwhelmed and confused by demands of course work.

Internality (8 items): Uses internal, self-determined standards of truth, not external authority.

Study skills (8 items): Works consistently, reviews regularly, schedules work.

Rote learning (8 items): Centres on facts and details and rote learns them.

Meaningful learning (8 items): Reads widely and relates material to what is already known; oriented to understand all input material.

Test anxiety (6 items): Worries about tests, exams, fear of failure.

Openness (8 items): Student sees university as a place where values are questioned.

Class dependence (7 items): Needs class structure; rarely questions lecturers or texts.

Source: Biggs 1978: 268

students were instructed to read the first text for meaning (relating the purpose of the experiment to the evidence, procedures and conclusions) but the second text for fact (concentrating on facts and experimental details). The remaining students received the two sets of instructions in the reverse order. All the participants then received a list of highly factual questions about both texts, and these were repeated at a follow-up test 1 week later. When the students were split into subgroups on the basis of their scores on the three main dimensions of the SPQ, there were no significant differences between the students who had obtained high and low scores on the internalizing and achieving dimensions. Those who had obtained high scores on the instrumental (reproducing) dimension gave significantly more correct answers than those who obtained low scores, but only on the text read for fact, not on the text read for meaning.

Biggs noted that the best performance in this study had been obtained by students who tended to adopt an instrumental or surface approach to learning under conditions in which they had been explicitly instructed to focus upon the facts and details contained in the learning materials. This remained the case even in the follow-up test 1 week later. This is perhaps unsurprising, given that the retention test in question had itself demanded the retrieval of factual information. However, Biggs pointed out that this pattern of

Box 5.2 **Value–motive–study dimensions in the 80-item Study Process Questionnaire**

Dimension	Value	Motive	Strategy
Reproducing	Pragmatism: instrumental values, university is a means to another end	Test anxiety, neuroticism: motive to study is fear of failing	Class dependence, fact-rote, minimax: goals are those defined in the course, no more; rote learned to a reproductive criterion
Internalizing	Openness, internality: self-growth or actualization seen as overall goal, university permits this	Academic motivation: intrinsic, what contributes to growth is interesting, self-motivated	Meaning: work unsatisfying unless understood and incorporated with existing knowledge. Class only *basis* for stimulation
Organizing	Winning through competition: university a game to show excellence	Achievement motivation: need for success, low anxiety	Structuring, organizing work, meets deadlines, plays the game

Source: Biggs 1978: 276

results was inconsistent with the assumption made by Craik and Lockhart (1972) that the use of deeper or more abstract processing would inevitably lead to better retention than the use of shallow or surface processing (see Chapter 2). As Biggs noted, there was some evidence from psychological experiments on human memory that shallow processing could in some circumstances lead to good retention, partly depending upon the aspects of the material that were being tested (see Baddeley 1978; Eysenck 1978).

Watkins and Hattie (1980) distributed this version of the SPQ in a postal survey of full-time campus-based undergraduate students at an Australian university. Responses were obtained from 562 students, representing a 60 per cent response rate, and these were used to explore the psychometric properties of the instrument. First, they obtained measures of the internal consistency of each scale (that is, the extent to which the scores that are obtained on the individual items correlate with one another). Each of the eight scales showed a moderate but not outstanding level of internal consistency. However, there was also evidence that each of the eight scales was measuring more than one underlying dimension. Next, Watkins and Hattie carried out a factor analysis on the scores obtained by the 562 students on the eight scales. This produced clear evidence for a reproducing factor (measured by rote learning, class dependence, academic neuroticism, pragmatism and test anxiety) as well as an internalizing factor (measured by academic motivation, meaningful learning, internality and openness). Unfortunately, Biggs's (1978a) 'organizing' dimension appeared to be split into two separate factors, one measured by test anxiety and neuroticism, the other by study skills and academic motivation. Biggs himself had acknowledged difficulty in interpreting this dimension, and Watkins and Hattie suggested that this was because he had extracted too few factors from his data sets. On balance, they felt that they had obtained some support for Biggs's account of study processes, but that there was considerable scope for improving the 80-item version of the SPQ.

Watkins and Hattie (1981b) conducted further analyses of the same students' scale scores to investigate possible differences related to gender, faculty and year of study. Complete data on the latter variables were provided by 282 men and 236 women in the Faculties of Arts, Science, Rural Science and Economics. The main results were as follows:

• Men tended to achieve higher scores than women on pragmatism, academic neuroticism and class dependence, whereas women tended to achieve higher scores than men on academic motivation, study skills and openness. This suggested that men were more likely to exhibit a reproducing approach, but that women were more likely to exhibit an internalizing approach.
• Science students tended to achieve higher scores than arts students on pragmatism, academic neuroticism, study skills and rote learning. This suggested that science students were more likely to exhibit a reproducing approach than arts students.
• Finally, students in the later years of their degree courses tended to achieve higher scores on internality and openness but lower scores on study skills. This suggested that students in the later years of their degree courses were more likely to exhibit an internalizing approach than students in the earlier years of their courses. Nevertheless, Watkins and Hattie acknowledged that the interpretation of this result was ambiguous because the effects of academic level had been confounded with the possible effects of age.

The 42-item version of the SPQ

Biggs (1982) reduced the SPQ to just seven items in each of six sub-scales that were intended to reflect the respondents' motives and strategies on each of the three dimensions. For each item, respondents produced a response to a statement along a five-point scale between 1 ('this item is never or only rarely true of me') and 5 ('this item is always or almost always true of me'). The responses to the relevant items were summed to obtain a score on each scale and each subscale. Biggs then employed this 42-item version of the SPQ in a survey of campus-based students at five universities and nine colleges of advanced education in Australia. At the time, the latter institutions were seen as having a more vocationally oriented and less research oriented role than universities. The university students obtained higher scores than the college students on internalizing motive and strategy and on achieving strategy, but the college students obtained higher scores than the university students on utilizing motive. These differences seem to have been due, in part, to the different subject 'mix' in the two kinds of institutions. However, these data were included in a more extensive report to be discussed in a moment (Biggs 1985, 1987).

Watkins and Hattie (1981b) used the 42-item version of the SPQ in a postal survey of first-year campus-based students at an Australian university and obtained 249 responses. The main results were as follows:

- Men obtained higher scores than women on utilizing strategy, whereas women obtained higher scores than men on internalizing motive and strategy.
- Science students obtained higher scores than arts students on utilizing strategy, whereas arts students obtained higher scores than science students on internalizing motive and strategy.
- Students aged 21 years or older obtained higher scores on internalizing motive and strategy and lower scores on utilizing motive than students aged between 18 and 20 years.

These results were broadly consistent with those of Watkins and Hattie's (1981b) initial study using the 80-item version of the SPQ. They concluded that younger students, male students and science students would benefit from counselling in the use of appropriate study methods.

To simplify the terminology, and also to recognize the similarity between his own account and the ideas of other researchers into student learning in higher education, Biggs (1985, 1987: 10) relabelled his three dimensions of study processes as a 'surface approach', a 'deep approach' and an 'achieving approach', each of which had a motive component and a strategy component (Box 5.3). The 42 items making up this version of the SPQ were published as an appendix to Biggs's (1987: 132–3) book. He also produced a similar instrument, the 36-item Learning Process Questionnaire, which was intended for use with children in secondary education (see Biggs 1985, 1987: 130–2). Biggs (1987: chapter 5) conducted an analysis of the responses

---

Box 5.3   Scales and subscales contained in the 42-item Study Process Questionnaire

Approach	Motive	Strategy
SA: Surface	Surface motive (SM) is instrumental: main purpose is to gain a qualification with pass-only aspirations, and a corresponding fear of failure	Surface strategy (SM) is reproductive: limit target to bare essentials and reproduce through rote learning
DA: Deep	Deep motive (DM) is intrinsic: study to actualise interest and competence in particular academic subjects	Deep strategy (DS) is meaningful: read widely, inter-relate with previous relevant knowledge
AA: Achieving	Achieving motive (AM) is based on competition and ego-enhancement: obtain highest grades, whether or not material is interesting	Achieving strategy (AS) is based on organising: follow up all suggested readings, schedule time, behave as 'model student'

Source: Biggs 1985: 186

---

given to the 42-item version of the SPQ by 2365 campus-based students in five universities and ten colleges of advanced education in Australia. He put forward a number of conclusions:

• University students produced higher scores on deep approach and lower scores on surface approach than students in colleges of advanced education. This was not simply due to a different subject mix, because the recruitment of participants was restricted to students who were taking subjects taught in both universities and colleges, and because Biggs's analysis controlled for the effect of subject under three broad headings (arts, education and science).
• Men tended to produce higher scores than women on surface approach, but women tended to produce higher scores than men on achieving strategy. Although there was no overall gender difference on deep approach, men tended to produce higher scores than women on this scale in university courses (and especially in education courses), while

women tended to produce higher scores than men on this scale in colleges of advanced education.

- Science students tended to produce higher scores than arts or education students on surface strategy. Science students also tended to produce higher scores on achieving strategy, with arts students being intermediate and education students lowest on this scale. Arts students tended to produce higher scores than science students on deep motive; education students tended to produce scores as high as arts students in university courses but scores as low as science students in colleges of advanced education.
- Scores on both deep approach and achieving approach tended to decline with year of study. As Biggs noted, this finding is contrary to the idea that educational experience encourages a deep approach to studying. He suggested that the trend might be due to increasing workload and concern over unemployment as students enter the later stages of a degree programme.
- Scores on deep approach tended to increase whereas scores on surface approach tended to decrease with the students' age. Scores on achieving approach showed a U-shaped function, being fairly high in the youngest students (aged 18–19 years), lowest at the age of 22 years, and highest after the age of 40 years.

Subsequent research in campus-based institutions

Although originally intended for use with students in Australia, some researchers have used the 42-item version of the SPQ in other countries. Miller *et al.* (1990) administered this instrument to students taking a general psychology undergraduate course at a campus-based university in the US. These researchers obtained usable questionnaires from 1119 students, which they examined for the existence of gender differences. They found no difference between men and women in their scores on deep and surface motives and strategies. Men tended to produce higher scores than women on achieving motive but women produced higher scores than men on achieving strategy. However, Miller *et al.* observed that even these statistically significant differences were fairly modest in their magnitude, and none of the subscale scores proved to be significantly correlated with academic performance in terms of cumulative grade-point average.

Kember and Gow (1990, 1991; Gow and Kember 1990) administered this version of the SPQ to students in different years of study at one campus-based institution of higher education in Hong Kong. For the purpose of this study, each of the 42 items was presented both in English and in a Chinese translation. In the initial stage of their research (Gow and Kember 1990), they obtained data from 1043 students and conducted a multiple regression analysis to predict their scores on the six subscales from a number of demographic characteristics. They found, in particular, that students' scores on deep and achieving motives and strategies declined with their year of study. Gow and Kember noted that Biggs (1987) had obtained a similar trend in the case of Australian students. They inferred that students tended to become less likely to employ a deep approach as they progressed through a programme of study, and they concluded that it was most questionable whether higher education was succeeding in meeting the goals espoused by both governments and academic staff, particularly with regard to the promotion of independent learning.

Nevertheless, Kember and Gow's main aim was to test the anecdotal stereotype that students in Hong Kong relied on rote learning and memorization in their academic studies. They eventually obtained responses from 2143 students, and they compared their scores on the three main scales of the SPQ with those obtained by the students at Australian colleges of advanced education in the study by Biggs (1987). Kember and Gow found that the students in Hong Kong tended, if anything, to obtain higher scores on deep approach and lower scores on surface approach than Australian students. They concluded that any tendency for students in Hong Kong to engage in rote learning was due to the nature of the curriculum and the teaching environment rather than to any inherent characteristic of the students. Biggs (1991) presented results from several other studies using either the SPQ with tertiary students or the Learning Process Questionnaire with secondary students, and these all confirmed that students in Hong Kong tended to produce high scores on deep approach and achieving approach but low scores on surface approach.

Tooth *et al.* (1989) devised a shortened version of the SPQ in which just three items were used to measure each of the six subscales. They used this instrument in a postal survey of candidates who had applied for admission to medical school, and they then administered it to the students who had actually been admitted towards the beginning and the end of their first year of study. The students' scores on deep approach and achieving approach tended to decline over the three occasions of testing, whereas their scores on surface approach tended to increase over the same period. Tooth *et al.* also found that the students' performance in their end-of-year examinations varied directly with their scores on achieving approach and inversely with their scores on surface approach, but that it was not related at all to their scores on deep approach. They argued that the adoption of apparently maladaptive strategies was caused partly by poor performance in the mid-year examinations and partly by the students' perceptions that their assessments would place excessive emphasis on the recall of factual knowledge at the expense of understanding.

Subsequently, Wilding and Valentine (1992) administered this 18-item version of the SPQ to 263 campus-based students who had just started courses in medicine and dentistry in the UK. They found that the students' marks in their end-of-year examinations were predicted by their scores on achieving strategy and, in the case of the medical students, with their scores on deep strategy. Finally, Wilding and Hayes (1992) found that this version of the SPQ could predict how first-year psychology students at a campus-based university in the UK took notes during a lecture: those who obtained high scores on surface motive or achieving strategy produced longer notes that recorded more of the key points in the lecture.

Volet *et al.* (1994) devised another short version of the SPQ to assess cross-cultural differences in approaches to studying. This contained a total of 21 items: four items drawn from each of the three motive subscales and three items drawn from each of the three strategy subscales. Volet *et al.* criticized earlier investigations comparing students in Hong Kong with students in Australia because these had confounded effects of individual characteristics (in other words, Hong Kong students versus Australian students) with those of contextual variables (in other words, students taking courses in Hong Kong versus students taking courses in Australia). Instead, they focused on students who were taking the same first-year unit in economics at a campus-based university in Australia. These consisted of 434 students who were described as 'local Australian' and 120 students who were described as 'south-east Asian'. All of these students completed the 21-item version of the SPQ at the start of the academic year and 359 students completed it for a second time during the last week of the 13-week course. For the purpose of comparing the two groups, Volet *et al.* identified 63 pairs of Australian and south-east Asian students who had completed the SPQ twice and were matched in terms of their age, gender and prior study of economics.

The south-east Asian students obtained significantly higher scores than the Australian students on surface approach and achieving approach. The two subgroups did not differ in their scores on deep approach, although the Australian students obtained significantly higher scores than the south-east Asian students on deep strategy. Volet *et al.* claimed that these differences were due not to cultural differences but to the south-east Asian students' successful use of survival skills in an unfamiliar educational environment. The general pattern of results was similar on the two occasions and there were no significant differences between the two subgroups in the changes in their scores over the course of time. These took the form of a significant decline in the scores on both deep approach and achieving approach, a pattern similar to that obtained by both Biggs (1987) and Gow and Kember (1990) in cross-sectional research (that is, testing different groups of students at different points in the same programme). There is, unfortunately, a basic problem in that Volet *et al.* did not report the cultural origins of any of the participants. Both 'south-east Asian' and 'Australian' students are culturally and ethnically extremely diverse and so this was not an ideal situation in which to evaluate cross-cultural differences in approaches to studying.

Murray-Harvey (1994) evaluated the stability of students' scores on the 42-item version of the SPQ by measuring its test–retest reliability over 8 weeks and over 12 months and by comparing it with the Productivity Environmental

Preference Survey (Price *et al.* 1991). This instrument is widely used in the US as a measure of physical, environmental, social and emotional learning preferences or 'learning styles' (for a fairly comprehensive summary, see Jonassen and Grabowski 1993: chapter 21). Murray-Harvey obtained responses to both of these questionnaires from 406 campus-based students at an Australian university and carried out a factor analysis on their subscale scores. There was very little overlap between the factors associated with the two instruments, which implied that they represented different conceptualizations of how students learn and study. A subgroup of 280 students completed the SPQ for a second time roughly a year later and the correlations between their subscale scores on the two occasions varied from 0.42 to 0.64. A separate group of 72 students completed the SPQ on two occasions with an 8-week interval, and in their case the correlations varied from 0.48 to 0.83. These results suggested that scores on the SPQ's subscales are not wholly reliable but are nevertheless relatively stable over the course of time in the absence of any intervention.

Wilson *et al.* (1996) argued that previous research using the SPQ to investigate the possibility of gender differences in approaches to studying had suffered from methodological limitations. They administered the 42-item version of the SPQ to two cohorts of students who were in the first year of a psychology programme at a campus-based university in Australia. They found no sign of any difference in the scores obtained by the men and women in either of the two cohorts. Of course, by focusing on first-year psychology students, these researchers had achieved a high level of homogeneity in their participants, but there is no guarantee that similar findings would be obtained with students in other years, other programmes or other countries.

Processes or predispositions?

As mentioned earlier, the SPQ was originally an attempt to operationalize the domain of study processes (Biggs 1978a, 1985, 1987: 8–10, 95–6). However, Kember and Gow (1989) remarked that the terms 'deep' and 'surface' were used to refer both to students' general predispositions to learn in different ways and to different strategies that they adopted in specific learning tasks. They suggested that Marton and Säljö (1976a) had used the expression 'approaches to learning' when classifying the ways in which students had gone about reading specific academic articles. However, Kember and Gow noted that, when items in questionnaires mentioned 'approaches to studying', this was characteristically in a predispositional sense. From a practical point of view, they noted that it might be possible to induce students to shift from a surface strategy to a deep strategy when carrying out a particular learning task but that the more important issue was whether it was possible to induce them to shift from a surface predisposition to a deep predisposition.

In a similar manner, though without acknowledging Kember and Gow's article, Biggs (1993b) observed that the expression 'approaches to learning' had come to have two different meanings:

- 'the *processes* adopted prior to, and which directly determine, the outcome of learning'
- '*predispositions* to adopt particular processes'

(Biggs 1993b: 6)

Like Kember and Gow, Biggs claimed that Marton and Säljö (1976a) had used 'approaches to learning' in the former sense. Nevertheless, this is quite incorrect. As I explained in Chapter 2, Marton and Säljö consistently used the different expression 'levels of processing' in referring to students' strategies when reading isolated passages of text. In contrast, they used the expression 'approaches to studying' when referring to the different ways in which students typically went about their academic studies. It follows that Marton and Säljö (1976a) had used the expression 'approach to studying' in a predispositional sense rather than in a strategic sense. Nevertheless, like Kember and Gow, Biggs went on to point out – correctly – that questionnaires such as the SPQ were actually concerned with students' predispositions to set about learning in particular ways. He inferred that the theoretical dimensions that the SPQ was seeking to measure should more properly be located at the presage level than at the process level (see also Biggs 1988, 1991).

Biggs pointed out that questionnaires such as the SPQ could be reworded to refer to students' approaches to learning in particular contexts, although, even here, the latter expression would still seem to have a predispositional connotation. One example of this was an investigation by Eley (1992), who looked for pairs of second-year course units at a campus-based Australian university 'in which one course unit was of a reflective nature, allowing for possible student variation in elective emphasis and interpretation of content, and in which the other was of a more defined nature, with a fixed body of content to be studied' (Eley 1992: 234). Eley asked students who had completed such pairs of course units to fill out the 42-item version of the SPQ in relation to each unit separately. He found that the first kind of course unit tended to elicit higher scores on deep approach, but lower scores on surface approach, than the second kind.

The magnitude of the differences between the scores obtained on the pairs of courses was not very great. In addition, statistically significant differences were obtained only when comparing combinations of units in some academic disciplines (for instance, accounting versus law and biochemistry versus microbiology), and not when comparing combinations of units in other disciplines (for instance, chemistry versus mathematics and statistics, and English literature versus politics and philosophy). Eley ascribed this to the apparently considerable variation in how different students tended to perceive the same course units. However, this does not affect the main conclusion from this study: that students' approaches to learning according to the SPQ depend upon the nature and the demands of each specific course.

Scouller (1998) obtained analogous results when asking students how they prepared for two different kinds of assessment: an assignment essay and an examination with multiple-choice questions. She devised a 28-item questionnaire based upon the SPQ to measure deep approach and surface approach and supplemented it with items about the intellectual skills and abilities being tapped by a particular assessment method. She then asked 206 education students at a campus-based university in Australia to respond to all the items with regard to both kinds of assessment. She found that students perceived assignment essays as assessing higher levels of intellectual processing based on their understanding of the curriculum, and were likely to adopt deep approaches when preparing their essays. In contrast, they perceived multiple-choice examinations as assessing lower, knowledge-based levels of intellectual processing and were likely to adopt surface approaches in preparing for such examinations. These findings confirm the importance of the perceived demands of assessment in determining approaches to studying.

Of course, the decision to deliver and assess a course in a particular way is not an arbitrary one. It may be constrained by institutional factors and by the demands of external accrediting bodies, but it is partly influenced by the teacher's predisposition to teach in a specific manner, which in turn depends upon the teacher's understanding of the nature of teaching and learning. Dall'Alba (1991) interviewed 20 teachers of four different disciplines at an Australian university about the teaching of their subject, and she identified seven different conceptions of teaching:

- teaching as presenting information
- teaching as transmitting information (from teacher to student)
- teaching as illustrating the application of theory to practice
- teaching as developing concepts/principles and their interrelations
- teaching as developing the capacity to be expert
- teaching as exploring ways of understanding from particular perspectives
- teaching as bringing about conceptual change.

Similar findings were obtained by other investigators (for reviews, see Kember 1997; Prosser and Trigwell 1999: 142–7). Moreover, Trigwell *et al.* (1994) identified five different approaches to teaching first-year science courses, expressed in terms of teachers' intentions and strategies:

- Approach A: A teacher-focused strategy with the intention of transmitting information to students
- Approach B: A teacher-focused strategy with the intention that students acquire the concepts of the discipline
- Approach C: A teacher/student interaction strategy with the intention that students acquire the concepts of the discipline

- Approach D: A student-focused strategy aimed at students developing their conceptions
- Approach E: A student-focused strategy aimed at students changing their conceptions

(Trigwell *et al.* 1994: 78)

Trigwell and Prosser (1996a) went on to show that the teachers' use of particular approaches to teaching was strongly associated with their holding corresponding conceptions of teaching and also with their attributing corresponding conceptions of learning to their own students.

Gow and Kember (1993) interviewed teachers at a campus-based institution in Hong Kong and identified different analytic categories in their beliefs about teaching and learning. They used these to construct sub-scales in a questionnaire on conceptions of teaching. On the basis of the responses given in a pilot study involving teachers in five departments, this was revised into a final instrument containing 46 items that measured nine subscales under two orientations:

Learning facilitation	**Knowledge transmission**
Problem solving	Training for specific jobs
More interactive teaching	Greater use of media
Facilitative teaching	Imparting information
Pastoral interest	Knowledge of subject
Motivator of students	

They then administered this questionnaire to teachers from 15 departments whose students had participated in longitudinal research in which they had completed the SPQ soon after starting their course and again just before their final examination. There were a number of statistically significant relationships between the mean subscale scores obtained by the students on the SPQ and the mean subscale scores obtained by the staff on the teaching questionnaire. In particular, in departments where the predominant teaching orientation was towards knowledge transmission, the students' use of a deep approach tended to decline over their course of study. In contrast, in departments with an orientation towards learning facilitation, the students were less likely to report the use of a surface approach (see also Kember and Gow 1994).

Trigwell and Prosser (1996b) developed a similar questionnaire, the Approaches to Teaching Inventory, which contains 16 items measuring teachers' intentions and strategies with regard to two approaches to teaching: a conceptual change/student-focused approach and an information transmission/teacher-focused approach (see also Prosser and Trigwell 1999: 176–9). Trigwell *et al.* (1999) administered this instrument to members of staff teaching 48 first-year courses in chemistry and physics, and they gave a modified version of the SPQ to the students who were taking those courses. Both the teachers and the students were asked to complete the appropriate questionnaire in relation to the particular topic being taught. Trigwell *et al.* found a relationship between the teachers' approach to teaching and the students' approach to learning: an information-transmission/ teacher-focused approach to teaching was linked with higher scores on surface approach and with lower scores on deep approach on the part of their students; in contrast, a conceptual-change student-focused approach to teaching was associated with lower scores on surface approach and (to a lesser extent) with higher scores on deep approach.

These findings are, of course, purely correlational in nature, and Trigwell *et al.* were careful not to make assumptions about the underlying causal relationships. Although a teacher's approach to teaching may constitute part of the institutional context that influences a student's approach to learning, it is equally possible that teachers modify their approaches to teaching to respond to the preferences or predispositions of their students. Trigwell *et al.* cited an example, which they themselves had observed, of tutors adapting their approach to teaching in response to requests from students to go through problems in an information transmission/teacher-focused manner. However, the implication of their findings, as well as those obtained by Eley (1992), by Gow and Kember (1993) and by Scouller (1998), is that students could be induced to adopt desirable approaches to studying by the use of appropriate forms of course design and assessment.

McKay and Kember (1997) had an opportunity to test this idea at a campus-based institution in Hong Kong where there was a widespread assumption that students relied on rote learning and expected to be spoon fed by their teachers. Students who were taking an established three-year diploma course had been given the 42-item version of the SPQ at the beginning and the end of their course. Consistent with the findings obtained by Biggs (1987), there was a non-significant decline in their scores on deep approach between the two occasions. In the light of a decision to develop a new degree course to replace the diploma, the opportunity was taken to introduce an alternative student-centred curriculum that stressed independent learning. Quite contrary to the prevailing stereotype, the students taking this course appeared to prefer the new curriculum and there was a significant increase in their scores on deep approach over the 3-year degree.

All of these findings are entirely consistent with the conclusion drawn from the interview-based research discussed in Chapter 2 that students' approaches to studying depend upon the content, the context and the demands of the relevant learning task. As McKay and Kember (1997) pointed out, although students may have a predisposition towards one particular learning approach, the latter can be influenced by extrinsic factors such as the choice of curriculum and mode of assessment. Nevertheless, this poses a fundamental problem for the presage–process–product model:

• On the one hand, if, following Biggs (1978a, 1985, 1987), the SPQ is assumed to measure study processes, it implies that 'process' variables are inherently predispositional in nature.

- On the other hand, if, following Biggs (1988, 1991, 1993b), the SPQ is assumed to measure predispositions, it implies that 'presage' variables can be influenced by extrinsic factors.

The solution to this dilemma is presumably to decompose or 'fractionate' the process level into two components. One component represents the student's general predisposition towards a particular approach; this is determined partly by 'personological' factors and partly by the persisting quality of the institutional context including the nature of the curriculum and the conceptions of teaching that are prevalent in their department. The other component reflects the actual processes or strategies employed in a specific learning situation; this is determined partly by the student's general predisposition towards a particular approach but also partly by the contingent properties of that situation. In other words, Biggs's original theoretical account needs to be elaborated into a series of four different stages: presage, predisposition, process and product. Indeed, a model with precisely this structure had been put forward by Newble and Entwistle (1986).

Research in distance education

Biggs (1987: 102–23, 1988, 1989) proposed that the SPQ could be used both to inform teachers about how students respond to their teaching and to inform counsellors when helping individual students. Indeed, some researchers have employed the SPQ as a diagnostic instrument in order to identify approaches to learning in individual students taking courses by distance learning in Australia (Parer 1988; Parer and Benson 1989; Relf and Geddes 1992).

The SPQ was also employed by Ekins (1992a,b) in an investigation of distance-learning students in the Hong Kong/Macau region who were being taught in English. This investigation yielded a number of interesting findings:

- The students' scores on deep motive increased and their scores on surface motive decreased with the number of years for which they said they had been studying.
- The students' scores on deep and achieving motives and strategies increased with their self-ratings of their command of English, but their scores on surface motive and strategy were largely unrelated to their self-rated language competence.
- The students' scores on both deep motive and achieving strategy increased with the number of credits they said they had obtained.
- The students' scores on both deep and achieving motives and strategies increased and scores on surface motive and strategy decreased with the grades they said they usually obtained.

Ekins checked the reports of credits and grades produced by a small sample of students against official institutional records and found that they were accurate. Nevertheless, as I mentioned in Chapter 3, it remains the case that students' retrospective accounts of their past capabilities and perform-ance are vulnerable to reconstructive biases based on their implicit theories of personal change, and it is conceivable that these theories are in turn related to their habitual approaches to studying (as might be suggested by the account given by Conway and Ross 1984).

A more serious problem is that Ekins did not appear to have adapted the SPQ for use in distance education. She employed the bilingual (English and Chinese) format that had been used previously with campus-based students in Hong Kong, but she apparently made only minimal and incid-ental changes to the items that explicitly referred to face-to-face teaching in classes, lectures or laboratories. It is simply not clear, for example, what students taking courses by distance learning were supposed to make of the following (slightly adapted) items in the SPQ:

> I learn best from teachers/lecturers who work from carefully prepared notes and outline major points neatly on the blackboard.

> After a class/lecture or lab I reread my notes to make sure they are legible and that I understand them.

(Ekins 1992a: 342–3)

In fact, both of these items were significantly correlated with the students' reported grades. This suggests that the students might have produced hypo-thetical responses based upon their academic performance rather than veridi-cal accounts of their actual approaches to studying.

Unfortunately, none of the research studies carried out with distance-learning students using the SPQ has included a comparison group of tradi-tional, campus-based students, and none has directly addressed the issue of whether the SPQ possesses reliability, validity and a coherent structure when it is employed in either campus-based education or distance education. In fact, researchers have tended to assume that the SPQ can be taken from campus-based education and applied in the context of distance learning in a wholly unproblematic manner.

Problems with the SPQ

Hattie and Watkins (1981) administered the 42-item version of the SPQ to 255 campus-based students in their first year of study at an Australian university and 173 campus-based students in their first year of study at a university in the central Philippines. The internal consistency of each of the three main scales and the six subscales was satisfactory for the Australian students and adequate for the Filipino students. A factor analysis of the Australian students' responses to the individual items yielded a six-factor solution in which the subscales outlined by Biggs were said to have been 'clearly evident' (Hattie and Watkins 1981: 243). A factor analysis on the students' scores on the six subscales generated three factors that could be identified with the three major approaches to learning. In the case of the Filipino students, however, both kinds of factor analysis yielded only a two-factor solution differentiating between motives and strategies. This suggested, at the very least, that the 42-item SPQ was not suitable for use with Filipino students.

However, subsequent attempts to reproduce the constituent structure of the 42-item SPQ proved less successful. In his own analyses of the subscale scores obtained by campus-based Australian students, Biggs (1987: 16; Biggs and Rihn 1984) consistently failed to retrieve three factors and instead found only two factors, which Biggs and Rihn described as a generalized deep approach to learning and a generalized surface approach to learning. A very similar pattern was obtained by Murray-Harvey (1994) in her factor analysis of the subscale scores obtained by campus-based Australian students on the 42-item SPQ and the Productivity Environment Preference Survey (Price *et al.* 1991). Kember and Leung (1998) analysed the subscale scores on the 42-item version of the SPQ obtained by 3254 students at a campus-based university in Hong Kong. They used confirmatory factor analysis to test whether Biggs's model involving three major scales and six subscales gave a satisfactory fit to their data in comparison with six other theoretical models. In fact, Biggs's model showed the worst fit, whereas the best fit was achieved by a model based upon a generalized deep approach and a generalized surface approach, both of which were partially tapped by the achieving motive and strategy subscales.

In fact, Biggs and Rihn (1984) made use of this factor structure with students who had opted to take a learning skills intervention programme at Stanford University in the US. This programme had the explicit goal of encouraging a deep approach to learning and discouraging a surface approach. In a pilot study, Biggs and Rihn found that students taking this programme tended to produce relatively high scores on all three motive subscales of the SPQ but that (in comparison with other Stanford students) they produced higher scores on the surface strategy subscale and lower scores on the deep and achieving strategy subscales. In the main study, 58 students completed the SPQ both before and after they had taken the intervention programme and were assigned scores on deep approach and surface approach on both occasions as follows:

- deep approach = deep motive + deep strategy + achieving motive + achieving strategy
- surface approach = surface motive + surface strategy + achieving motive.

Biggs and Rihn showed that there was a clear and highly significant increase in the students' scores on deep approach as a result of taking this course, accompanied by a less pronounced but nevertheless statistically significant decrease in their scores on surface approach. (This is, it should be said, one of the few instances in which a 'learning skills' programme has been shown to generate desirable and significant changes in students' approaches to learning.)

In any particular learning task it would seem that a surface approach and a deep approach are mutually exclusive, in which case one might expect that the two dimensions identified in these factor analyses should be negatively correlated with one another. In fact, in Biggs's (1987: 16; Biggs and Rihn 1984) analyses, the two factors were independent of one another, but this was simply because he had used orthogonal rather than oblique rotation. Similarly, in the 'best fit' model identified by Kember and Leung (1998), the two factors in question had been stipulated to be independent of one another. In both cases, then, the apparent independence of the factors stemmed from an artefact which the researchers imposed upon their data and which prejudged the question of whether the factors were actually correlated in any way.

Watkins and Regmi (1990) and Watkins and Akande (1992) administered the 42-item SPQ to campus-based students in Nepal and Nigeria, respectively, and carried out factor analyses with oblique rather than orthogonal rotation. They obtained two-factor solutions that were similar to those obtained by Biggs with Australian students, but they did not indicate the magnitude of the correlation between the two factors in question. O'Neil and Child (1984) administered the 42-item SPQ to 277 campus-based students in the UK and reported the full set of correlation coefficients among their participants' scores on the six subscales. These data indicate the existence of two factors and Table 5.1 shows the results of factor analyses carried out using both orthogonal rotation and oblique rotation. The data shown are the factor loadings, which are (very roughly) analogous to correlation coefficients between the subscale scores and the underlying factors. Both solutions are once again similar to those obtained by Biggs with Australian students and confirm the existence of a generalized deep approach and a generalized surface approach to studying. The correlation coefficient between the two factors obtained in the oblique solution is +0.08, which implies that they are effectively independent of each other.

The latter finding means that individual students might score high or low on both factors. This has the practical implication that interventions aimed at improving student learning should be concerned specifically with encouraging a deep approach and not necessarily with discouraging a surface approach, because achieving the latter need itself have no implications for the former (see Trigwell and Prosser 1991a). Nevertheless, the remarkable consistency between the results of factor analyses of the 42-item SPQ carried out in Australia, Hong Kong, Nepal, Nigeria and the UK casts doubt upon the existence of a separate 'achieving' approach. Indeed, Biggs had himself expressed reservations about the nature of the achieving approach:

It should be noted that deep and surface approaches are different in kind from the achieving approach. The strategies involved in the first two describe ways in which students engage the actual content of the task, while the achieving strategy describes the ways in which students organise the temporal and spatial contexts in which the task is carried

Table 5.1 Results of factor analyses of the data reported by O'Neil and Child (1984)

SPQ subscale	Orthogonal solution		Oblique solution	
	Factor 1	Factor 2	Factor 1	Factor 2
Achieving motive	0.38	0.60	0.36	0.59
Achieving strategy	0.58	0.28	0.57	0.25
Deep motive	0.64	−0.07	0.64	−0.10
Deep strategy	0.76	−0.11	0.76	−0.14
Surface motive	−0.03	0.67	−0.06	0.67
Surface strategy	−0.13	0.71	−0.15	0.72

Technical note: Both the eigenvalues-one rule and the scree test indicated the existence of two factors that explained 65.1 per cent of the variance among the six variables. A common factor analysis was carried out using squared multiple correlations as initial estimates of commonality. The orthogonal solution used a varimax rotation; the oblique solution used an oblimin rotation.

out. There is, then, no inconsistency in rote learning in a highly organised way ('surface-achieving') or reading for meaning in an organised way ('deep-achieving').

(Biggs 1985: 187)

This concurs with the implication of the interview-based research discussed in Chapter 2 that what seems to be a 'strategic' or 'achieving' approach actually reflects a sophisticated response in students with an extrinsic motivation to adopt either a deep approach or a surface approach, depending on which appears likely to maximize their grades or marks in any particular course. This is how Biggs (1978b) had originally conceived of this 'approach'. Moreover, in his most recent accounts, Biggs (1999a: 13–19, 1999b) made no mention of an achieving approach at all.

Other problems have been raised in reports that have described factor analyses carried out on the responses produced by campus-based students to the 42 individual items in the SPQ. O'Neil and Child (1984) carried out separate factor analyses on data that had been obtained by Biggs from 827 university students and 1638 students at colleges of advanced education in Australia. In both cases, there were six interpretable factors, four of which could be readily identified with the scales relating to deep and achieving motives and strategies. However, the scales relating to the surface approach were much less clearly supported. O'Neil and Child then carried out factor analyses on the data that they themselves had obtained from 277 students at an institution of higher education in the UK and these produced very similar results. They argued that the robustness of the scales relating to a surface approach was highly questionable.

As mentioned above, Kember and Gow (1990, 1991) employed the 42-item version of the SPQ with campus-based students at an institution of higher education in Hong Kong. In spite of the different cultural context, a factor analysis of the students' responses to the individual items of the SPQ produced clear support for the scales relating to achieving motive, achieving strategy and deep strategy. However, the items relating to deep motive were split across two different factors, and it was very difficult to associate any factors with surface motive and strategy. The consistency between these results and those reported by O'Neil and Child (1984) suggests that the SPQ is 'portable' between Western cultures and Hong Kong but is unsatisfactory in either setting. Finally, Christensen *et al.* (1991) administered the SPQ to 328 students at an Australian college of advanced education and carried out a factor analysis on the responses to the 42 items. They did identify six orthogonal factors but, once again, found only weak support for the scales relating to a surface approach.

Biggs (1993b) responded to the latter article with a spirited defence of the SPQ. In particular, he argued that seeking an orthogonal factor structure was inappropriate as the six subscale scores were meant to constitute the motive and strategy components of the three approaches to learning. He also claimed that previous independent evaluations of the original SPQ supported its basic theory and construction in this regard. These comments are rather disingenuous as, according to O'Neil and Child (1984), Biggs himself had initially evaluated the SPQ by using analytic techniques that imposed an orthogonal structure on the factor solution. Indeed, it was precisely in order to replicate Biggs's methods that Kember and Gow (1990, 1991) had used the same techniques and generated orthogonal solutions from their data.

In addition, O'Neil and Child (1984) had explicitly allowed for the possibility that the factors underlying responses to the 42 items of the SPQ might not be independent. They carried out a separate factor analysis on their data, which led to an oblique (that is, non-orthogonal) solution. The pattern of factor loadings was very similar to that obtained in an orthogonal solution and the intercorrelations among the factors in the oblique solution were described as 'low'. This implies that, even to the extent that the six subscales of the SPQ were confirmed in the factor solution, these subscales were 'virtually independent' of each other (see also Volet *et al.* 1994). Finally, O'Neil and Child conducted a second-order factor analysis to investigate whether there was a coherent structure underlying the factors identified in their oblique solution. However, they found that this 'gave no discernible pattern' (O'Neil and Child 1984: 232).

In short, even using analytic techniques that accommodate the theoretical assumptions in the presage–process–product model, there appear to be problems in the composition of the subscales that were intended to measure surface motive and surface strategy, and there is no evidence that the factors that do result constitute associated components of three underlying approaches to learning. They cannot, therefore, be said to provide distinctive, homogeneous and appropriate measures of the theoretical constructs on which the SPQ was supposed to be based. Moreover, as mentioned earlier, even when the integrity of the subscales is taken for granted by carrying out factor analyses on the total scores obtained on the subscales themselves, there is support only for a generalized surface approach and a generalized deep approach to learning. On both theoretical and practical grounds, then, the SPQ cannot be recommended as a useful research instrument.

Concluding summary

- The SPQ has been used in a number of studies concerned with campus-based education, and it has been shown to be sensitive to differences between individual students related to their age, year of study and academic discipline. In contrast, gender differences in students' scores on the SPQ are inconsistent in direction, small in magnitude and sometimes not statistically significant at all. However, the SPQ has also been used to refute an anecdotal stereotype that students in Hong Kong rely upon rote learning and memorization.
- Students' scores on the scales of the SPQ are most naturally interpreted as measuring their predispositions to adopt different approaches to learning. However, the SPQ also appears to be sensitive to contextual factors, such as the demands of the specific courses that students are taking and in particular the conceptions of teaching that are held by their teachers. This seems to demand modification or elaboration of the original presage–process–product model of student learning that was put forward by Biggs (1978a, 1985).
- Only a few studies have been carried out using the SPQ in the context of distance education. The researchers in question have tended to assume that the constructs underlying the SPQ can be applied to the context of distance learning in an unproblematic manner, and they do not even appear to have adapted the constituent items of the SPQ to ensure that they were meaningful and appropriate for students taking courses by distance learning.
- The findings of research studies carried out with campus-based students in Australia, Hong Kong, Nepal, Nigeria and the UK indicate that the SPQ simply measures a generalized surface approach and a generalized deep approach to learning. The findings of research studies carried out with campus-based students in Australia, Hong Kong and the UK have also cast doubt upon the integrity of the subscales concerned with a surface approach. As a result, the SPQ cannot be recommended as a research instrument.

6
The Approaches to Studying Inventory

Probably the most widely used questionnaire on student learning in higher education has been the Approaches to Studying Inventory (ASI). This was devised by Entwistle and his colleagues at the University of Lancaster, which is a campus-based institution in the UK. As in the case of the SPQ, the ASI evolved from other instruments over a number of years and, in due course, it gave rise to a number of different variants that have been used by other researchers around the world. Although Entwistle himself has now abandoned the original ASI in favour of a new instrument, a substantial body of research evidence has been obtained with different versions of the original ASI. In this chapter, I will describe the development of the original version of the ASI and summarize the main findings of research carried out with this instrument, before considering the more specific results of investigations in which it has been administered to students taking courses by distance learning. In Chapter 7, I will discuss the results of investigations carried out with other versions of the ASI.

Development of the ASI

In the 1960s, there was a good deal of interest in both the UK and North America over whether academic attainment in higher education could be predicted by personality characteristics such as introversion–extroversion and neuroticism. Entwistle and Wilson (1970) suggested that any effects of such variables might depend upon students' working habits or study methods. They devised a questionnaire containing items relating to both study methods and motivation that their colleagues and graduate students had identified as relevant to academic attainment. To try to disguise the purpose of the questionnaire, these were interspersed with other items measuring extroversion and neuroticism, and the resulting inventory was then administered to 72 graduate students at a campus-based university in Scotland, together with a conventional personality test, the Eysenck

Personality Inventory (EPI: Eysenck and Eysenck 1964). It was found that students classified as introverts according to their scores on the EPI reported higher academic motivation and better study methods than those classified as extroverts, and that the former students also tended to have obtained better results in their first degrees, which they had completed the previous year.

On the basis of these results, Entwistle and Entwistle (1970) produced a revised instrument, the Student Attitudes Questionnaire (SAQ), which contained 91 items relating to motivation, study methods, extroversion and neuroticism. This was administered to 257 first year students at two different campus-based institutions of higher education, along with the EPI. Students who were classified as introverts according to their scores on the EPI and those who reported better study methods achieved better results in their end-of-year assessments than those who were classified as extroverts or who reported poorer study methods. Entwistle *et al.* (1971) extended the SAQ by including two additional scales relating to 'examination technique' and 'lack of distractions', and the revised instrument was used in a survey of 1650 first-year students at 12 campus-based institutions of higher education. On this occasion, academic attainment was predicted by study methods and motivation, but the correlations were fairly modest and these variables were much less important in predicting academic attainment than the students' entrance qualifications.

In a follow-up survey that involved 1087 of these students in their third and final year of study, Entwistle and Wilson (1977: 38–43, 180–3) revised the SAQ once more by including two additional scales that were intended to measure 'syllabus-boundness' and 'syllabus-freedom'. These notions had been introduced by Hudson (1968: 11–14) and Parlett (1970) to describe the extent to which different students seem to prefer direction as opposed to autonomy in their learning. In the event, the students' final degree results were predicted by motivation and study methods but not by syllabus-boundness or syllabus-freedom. Once again, the correlations were fairly modest, and the best predictors of academic attainment were the students' qualifications on entry to their courses and especially their performance at the end of their first year of study (Entwistle and Wilson 1977: 211).

Each of these versions of the SAQ consisted of a series of statements with which respondents were asked either to agree or to disagree as descriptions of themselves. Entwistle and Wilson (1977: 41) reported that a simple choice of two responses had been adopted partly in order to simplify the scoring procedure and partly to follow the method of responding used in the EPI. However, they added that some students had indicated that they would have preferred to use a broader range of responses, such as a five-point scale, and this was subsequently adopted in the case of the ASI. Another feature of the SAQ is that responses were scored in terms of whether they were in accordance with the meaning of the relevant scale. However, the relevant response was 'agree' for some items and 'disagree' for others. This provided some protection against the possibility that respondents had a bias consistently to agree or to disagree with all of the items. (In fact, this feature was not retained in the case of the ASI: all of the items reflect the meaning of the corresponding scales and so the ASI is vulnerable to the operation of response biases.)

In these early investigations, 'motivation' was simply interpreted as a uni-dimensional construct that was tantamount to a drive for academic achievement. At the time, this merely represented current practice in educational research both in the UK and North America. However, students may have different motivations for participating in higher education, as was seen in Chapter 4. Entwistle *et al.* (1974) compared the scores obtained by 60 final-year students at a campus-based university on the revised version of the SAQ with the accounts that were given by the same students in semi-structured interviews designed to investigate motivational factors. They concluded, on the basis of their own findings and a review of the previous literature, that it was important to differentiate between intrinsic motivation (or an interest in the subject matter), extrinsic motivation (or an interest in the rewards or qualifications that could be gained) and achievement motivation (or an interest in the maintenance of self-esteem as opposed to the fear of failure). Accordingly, these constructs were incorporated into the ASI as separate subscales.

Equally, the study methods scale of the SAQ was also interpreted as a uni-dimensional construct concerned just with whether students were organized or disorganized in their studying and with whether their general attitudes towards studying were positive or negative. The research carried out by Marton and his colleagues (see Chapter 2) showed these considerations to be inadequate as a means of characterizing differences among students in higher education. Consequently, the ASI included new subscales that were devised to represent the deep and surface approaches described by Marton (1975) and the strategic approach that was described by Ramsden (1979). These were supplemented by two other subscales concerned with certain cognitive processes that were presumed to be associated with a deep approach to learning: a propensity for interrelating ideas and making use of evidence. More fundamentally, the distinction between deep, surface and strategic approaches to learning was subsumed within a broader framework that involved a 'meaning orientation', a 'reproducing orientation' and an 'achieving orientation'.

Finally, these three domains were supplemented by a fourth that represented particular styles and pathologies of learning described by Pask, who had used an interview-based approach to investigate the strategies adopted in artificial learning tasks that demanded understanding of a particular domain. Pask and Scott (1972) claimed that two general categories of strategy were employed in such tasks, a 'serialist' approach and a 'holist' approach:

Serialists learn, remember and recapitulate a body of information in terms of string-like cognitive structures where items are related by simple data links: formally, by 'low order relations' . . . Holists, on the other hand, learning, remember and recapitulate as a whole: formally, in terms of 'high order relations'.

(Pask and Scott 1972: 218)

In academic learning, however, Pask (1976) claimed that the requirement for understanding was relaxed. In this case,

some students are disposed to act 'like holists' (*comprehension* learners) and others 'like serialists' (*operation* learners), with more or less success. There are also students able to act in either way, depending upon the subject matter, and if they excel in both pursuits, we refer to those students as *versatile*. It is these distinctions which can, more appropriately be referred to as learning style.

(Pask 1976: 133)

Pask went on to suggest that comprehension learners were able to acquire an overall picture of the subject matter by using global 'description building operations', whereas operation learners acquired rules, methods and details by using specific 'procedure building operations'. However, comprehension learners were disposed to the learning pathology of 'globetrotting' in their use of inappropriate speculations or analogies, and operation learners were disposed to the converse pathology of 'improvidence' in their failure to exploit valid analogies and general principles. For Pask, truly effective learning resulted from a versatile approach that integrated description building and procedure building operations in an appropriate manner (see also Pask 1988). The ASI incorporated the 'learning styles' of comprehension learning and operation learning and the corresponding 'pathologies of learning' of globetrotting and improvidence.

The ASI

The ASI itself went through a process of development during the latter half of the 1970s (see Entwistle *et al.* 1979; Entwistle and Ramsden 1983: chapter 4) and was presented in its final form by Ramsden and Entwistle (1981). In this form, it contains 64 items in 16 subscales, the latter being grouped under four general headings (see Box 6.1). The 64 items themselves were published as an appendix to the book by Entwistle and Ramsden (1983: 228–33). In each case, respondents are asked to indicate the extent of their agreement or disagreement with a statement along a five-point scale between 'definitely agree', scoring 4, and 'definitely disagree', scoring 0. (The middle category on this scale, scoring 2, was 'only to be used if the item doesn't apply to you or if you really find it impossible to give a definite answer'.) The responses given to the relevant items are summed to obtain a score on each subscale and the scores on the relevant subscales are then summed again to obtain a score on each scale.

Box 6.1   **Subscales contained in the 64-item Approaches to Studying Inventory**

Subscale	Meaning
Meaning orientation	
Deep approach	Active questioning in learning
Interrelating ideas	Relating to other parts of the course
Use of evidence	Relating evidence to conclusions
Intrinsic motivation	Interest in learning for learning's sake
Reproducing orientation	
Surface approach	Preoccupation with memorisation
Syllabus-boundness	Relying on staff to define learning tasks
Fear of failure	Pessimism and anxiety about academic outcomes
Extrinsic motivation	Interest in courses for the qualifications they offer
Achieving orientation	
Strategic approach	Awareness of implications of academic demands made by staff
Disorganised study methods	Unable to work regularly and effectively*
Negative attitudes to studying	Lack of interest and application*
Achievement motivation	Competitive and confident
Styles and pathologies	
Comprehension learning	Readiness to map out subject area and think divergently
Globetrotting	Overready to jump to conclusions
Operation learning	Emphasis on facts and logical analysis
Improvidence	Overcautious reliance on details

Source: Ramsden and Entwistle 1981: 371
* These subscales are meant to be scored in reverse

Factor analyses conducted on the subscale scores obtained by campus-based students on earlier versions of the ASI identified three major constructs that seemed to integrate the cognitive and motivational aspects of learning rather in the way that Biggs (1979) had described (Entwistle *et al.* 1979; Entwistle and Ramsden 1983: 38–41):

- deep approach + comprehension learning + intrinsic motivation
- surface approach + operation learning + extrinsic motivation
- organized study methods + achievement motivation.

As mentioned above, Entwistle *et al.* (1979) described these three constructs as 'orientations to studying' and Ramsden and Entwistle (1981) specifically labelled them 'meaning orientation', 'reproducing orientation' and 'achieving orientation', respectively.

Ramsden and Entwistle (1981) arranged for the administration of the final version of the ASI to 2208 (predominantly second-year) campus-based students at 54 institutions of higher education in the UK. A factor analysis was carried out upon their scores on the 16 subscales, together with their own reports of their school examination results and their own ratings of their academic performance in higher education. This produced four factors. The first two could be identified with meaning orientation and reproducing orientation. However, the other two factors showed a less clear relationship with the dimensions of 'achieving orientation' and 'styles and pathologies', as these constructs had been defined. Instead, they appeared to be associated with an achieving orientation that was defined merely by a strategic approach to studying, combined with both extrinsic and achievement motivation, and a 'non-academic orientation' that reflected a disorganized and dilatory approach to studying (see also Entwistle and Ramsden 1983: 48–9).

In this research, the term 'orientation' was being used to encompass major aspects of studying that might be correlated with academic attainment (Entwistle and Ramsden 1983: 51–5) and to reflect a student's intention or focus in studying (Entwistle *et al.* 1979). In particular, Entwistle and Ramsden (1983: 195–6) pointed out that at the heart of the distinction between a meaning orientation and a reproducing orientation was a contrast between an 'internal' focus on the content of the learning materials and on the knowledge, experience and interests of the learner, and an 'external' focus on the learning task and on the demands of assessment. This is a rather different notion of a learning orientation from that put forward by Taylor (1983) and discussed in Chapter 4. In fact, Entwistle and Ramsden themselves noted that deep and surface approaches to learning could be regarded simply as a special case of the intrinsic and extrinsic aspects of the goals or orientations to studying that had been described by Taylor *et al.* (1981c).

Entwistle and Ramsden (1983: 44–7) examined the relationships between their students' scores on the 16 subscales of the ASI and their ratings of their own academic progress. The latter ratings were most highly (though negatively) correlated with their scores on disorganized study methods and negative attitudes to studying. Moreover, they were positively correlated with their scores on all the subscales grouped under meaning orientation and negatively correlated with their scores on all the subscales grouped under reproducing orientation. Ramsden and Entwistle (1981) went on to compare two specific groups of students who said that they were doing either 'very well' or 'badly' in their courses. The subscales that discriminated the most clearly between these two groups were disorganized study methods, negative attitudes to studying and strategic approach. However, in Chapter 5, I questioned the validity of self-reports because they might be biased by students' implicit theories of personal change. In Ramsden and Entwistle's investigation, those students who adopted a meaning orientation might simply have felt that they were doing well in their courses, regardless of their actual academic performance; alternatively, those students who really were doing well in their courses might have rated their approaches to studying in the ASI in accordance with their implicit theories of how a 'good student' would respond.

Watkins (1982) administered the ASI by means of a postal survey to campus-based students in their first year of study at an Australian university and obtained responses from 540 students. He found that the older students obtained lower scores than the younger students on extrinsic motivation and negative attitudes to studying; that women produced higher scores than men on fear of failure, comprehension learning and improvidence; and that there were differences on five of the subscales between arts, economics and science students. Watkins and Hattie (1985) repeated the survey with the same sample of students 2 years later and obtained responses from 244 of the original 540 students. In this study, women produced higher scores than men on fear of failure and interrelating ideas, there were again differences between arts, economics and science students on five of the subscales, but there was no significant effect of age.

Nevertheless, this last study is of interest mainly because Watkins and Hattie were able to look back at the scores obtained by these 244 students in their initial survey. They found that their scores on the ASI were systematically different from the scores obtained by those students who had subsequently withdrawn from their studies, and also from the scores obtained by those students who had not withdrawn but who simply did not respond to the follow-up survey. There is evidence that students who respond to surveys are different from non-respondents in terms of their academic attainment and many other variables (Astin 1970; Nielsen *et al.* 1978). Watkins and Hattie's results show that students who respond to surveys also differ from non-respondents in terms of their approaches to studying. Consequently, any survey of approaches to studying that fails to achieve a 100 per cent response rate will be vulnerable to sampling bias.

Newble and Clarke (1986, 1987) used the ASI to compare Australian campus-based students in two different medical schools: one had a traditional curriculum (that is, one in which preclinical training was followed by clinical training), and the other had an innovative curriculum that was based on the use of problem-based learning. In both cases, responses to the ASI were obtained from students in their first year, their third year or their final year (in other words, Year 6 in the traditional school and Year 5 in the innovative school). The students at the innovative school obtained higher scores on meaning orientation and lower scores on reproducing orientation than the students at the traditional school. These comparisons were statistically significant in every case, except that the final-year scores on meaning orientation were not significantly different. This demonstrates once again that approaches to studying depend on the context of learning.

In Chapter 5, I mentioned a study by Miller *et al.* (1990), which compared men and women who were taking a general psychology course at a campus-based university in the US. In this study, the researchers also compared the scores obtained by men and women on the ASI. There were statistically significant gender differences on 12 of the 16 subscales. Men produced higher scores than women on deep approach, use of evidence, extrinsic motivation, negative attitudes to studying, achievement motivation and comprehension learning. Women produced higher scores than men on interrelating ideas, intrinsic motivation, surface approach, fear of failure, strategic approach and improvidence. Miller *et al.* did not report any analysis on the scores across the four general study orientations but the pattern of results on the constituent subscales makes it unlikely that there would have been gender differences at this level. Miller *et al.* remarked that the significant differences they had found were small and had often achieved statistical significance just because of the very large size of their sample (over 1100 students).

Severiens and ten Dam (1994) reviewed a number of research studies that had compared the scores obtained by men and women on the ASI and used the statistical technique known as 'meta-analysis' to integrate quantitative estimates of the gender difference on each of the 16 subscales. There were only three subscales where the gender difference over all the studies was statistically significant (in other words, significantly different from zero): men produced higher scores than women on achievement motivation and on extrinsic motivation; in contrast, women produced higher scores than men on fear of failure. There was a tendency for women to produce higher scores than men on intrinsic motivation, but this gender difference was not statistically significant. The general implication of all these results is that any gender differences are on the motivational aspects of studying rather than the cognitive or intellectual aspects of studying.

Severiens and ten Dam also included tests of the homogeneity of gender differences across the different studies included in their meta-analysis. These examine whether the gender differences obtained in different studies are homogeneous (that is, they are estimates of the same effect) or whether they are heterogeneous (that is, they are estimates of different effects). They found that for 12 out of the 16 subscales the different estimates of the gender difference were significantly heterogeneous. In other words, the gender differences obtained on these subscales varied from one study to another, even though they had all used the same instrument. This suggests that any gender differences on the ASI depend upon exactly how, when and where it is administered. In fact, a general phenomenon in the study of human cognition is that the existence and magnitude of gender differences depend upon the exact testing and scoring procedures that are used. This suggests that they reflect contextualized interactions between researchers and participants rather than fundamental differences between men and women (see Crawford and Chaffin 1997).

However, a fundamental problem with the kind of analysis conducted by Severiens and ten Dam is that, in investigating whether men and women are different in their approaches to studying, it assumes that men and women are commensurable in their approaches to studying: that is, that it makes sense to compare them on the same dimensions. Two investigations with campus-based students in South Africa (Meyer *et al.* 1994) and the UK (Meyer 1995) have found evidence for subtle but statistically significant differences between the results of factor analyses carried out separately on the responses given by men and women to the ASI. It is of interest that the courses being taken by the students in both of these investigations were, broadly speaking, scientific in nature, as interview-based research has indicated that these are more likely to challenge the personal identity and confidence of female students than courses in the arts (Thomas 1988, 1990). Nevertheless, the main point is that, if 'meaning orientation' and 'reproducing orientation' have different meanings for male and female students, then it does not really make sense to compare them on these dimensions.

The ASI has indeed been used with campus-based students in countries around the world, and many investigators have carried out factor analyses on the students' scores on the 16 subscales. Factor solutions broadly similar to that obtained by Ramsden and Entwistle (1981) have been found in studies conducted in Australia (Watkins 1982, 1983; Watkins and Hattie 1985; Clarke 1986), the United States (Speth and Brown 1988), Venezuela (Entwistle 1988) and Hong Kong (Kember and Gow 1990). In contrast, studies carried out in South Africa (Meyer 1988, 1995; Meyer and Parsons 1989a; Meyer and Dunne 1991), Nepal (Watkins and Regmi 1996) and Spain (Cano-Garcia and Justicia-Justicia 1994) produced solutions with only two interpretable factors. Meyer and Parsons (1989a) compared the factor solutions obtained in some of these studies with the results obtained by Ramsden and Entwistle (1981), and they concluded that there was consistent evidence across different populations for two orientations to studying:

• a meaning orientation indexed by the subscales concerned with deep approach, interrelating ideas, the use of evidence, intrinsic motivation and comprehension learning; and
• a reproducing orientation indexed by the subscales concerned with surface approach, syllabus-boundness, fear of failure, disorganized study methods, negative attitudes to studying, globetrotting and improvidence.

Meyer and Parsons also concluded that there was no evidence at all to support the existence of additional constructs concerned with an achieving orientation or a non-academic orientation, as defined by Ramsden and Entwistle (1981). The failure to demonstrate any achieving orientation is, of course, consistent with the failure to identify a 'strategic' approach in the interview-based research that was discussed in Chapter 2 and with the failure to identify a separate 'achieving' approach in the research on the SPQ that was discussed in Chapter 5.

Moreover, several researchers have carried out factor analyses upon students' responses to the 64 individual items in the ASI, and their solutions have typically failed to reproduce certain of the subscales. Indeed, Entwistle and Ramsden (1983: 50–2) carried out such an analysis on the data produced by the 2208 students in their main study. They first extracted just five factors to examine broad domains. In this case, the dimensions of 'meaning orientation' and 'reproducing orientation' were apparent both in the total sample and in each of six different subject groups. However, there was only ambiguous evidence for a non-academic orientation, and none at all for an achieving orientation. Next, they extracted 17 factors in an attempt to reconstruct the 16 original subscales. Unfortunately, this analysis 'produced few identifiable groupings of items'.

Speth and Brown (1988) administered the ASI along with other questionnaires to 383 campus-based students who were taking a course in educational psychology at a large state university in the US. A factor analysis of their responses to the 64 individual items produced only eight factors. Two of these factors subsumed many of the items measuring meaning orientation (including comprehension learning) and reproducing orientation, respectively. There was little support for the subscales concerned with operation learning, improvidence and globetrotting. Schmeck (1988) carried out a similar study in which 269 students taking different courses at a campus-based university in the US completed the ASI and the Inventory of Learning Processes (ILP; see Chapter 10). A factor analysis of their responses to the 126 items identified only eight factors, and these were based on groups of items that corresponded to the scales in the ILP rather than to the subscales in the ASI (see also Schmeck and Geisler-Brenstein 1989).

On the one hand, the results of these two studies could mean that the ASI does not transfer well to the educational context of the US; there is some evidence for this suggestion from research using a shortened version of the ASI, and this will be discussed in Chapter 7. On the other hand, it could mean that there are inherent weaknesses in some of the ASI's subscales. Entwistle and Waterston (1988) created a new instrument by combining 30 items from the ASI with 30 items from the ILP and 15 further items intended to reflect additional constructs. They obtained responses from 218 first-year campus-based students in the UK and a factor analysis of their responses to the 75 items yielded ten factors. These appeared to be dominated by concepts and items drawn from the ILP rather than from the ASI, which raises doubts about the integrity of the constituent subscales of the ASI even when they are used in a British setting.

Finally, in an investigation to be discussed in more detail in a moment (see p. 97), Meyer and Parsons (1989a,b) obtained responses to the ASI from 1194 English-speaking students across 12 disciplinary areas at a campus-based institution of higher education in South Africa. A factor analysis produced just nine factors. Even though this meant that in some cases items defining two or more subscales loaded on the same factor, Meyer and Parsons considered that their factor solution confirmed the integrity of the majority of the subscales in the ASI. However, three sub-scales (globetrotting, intrinsic motivation and strategic approach) were barely apparent and were subsumed within other constructs and one subscale (syllabus-boundness) was not represented in the factor solution at all. Meyer and Parsons (1989b) obtained very similar data from 590 Afrikaans-speaking students at the same institution and from 290 students at another campus-based institution in South Africa. In short, the integrity of the ASI subscales associated with an achieving orientation and with the 'styles and pathologies' scale is open to question.

Approaches to studying and perceptions of the learning environment

One of the main purposes of Entwistle and Ramsden's research was to correlate approaches to studying with students' perceptions of their academic environment. For this purpose, Ramsden (1979, 1981) had developed a separate inventory, the Course Perceptions Questionnaire (CPQ), in which students assessed eight different aspects of their academic environment (Box 6.2). The CPQ had been distributed to the 2208 campus-based students who participated in Ramsden and Entwistle's (1981) main study. A factor analysis of their responses to the eight scales of the CPQ produced two (largely independent) factors. One factor measured good teaching, openness to students and freedom in learning; this appeared to represent a positive evaluation of teaching across all departments. The other measured vocational relevance, formal teaching methods and clear goals and standards; this appeared to distinguish between different departments (see also Entwistle and Ramsden 1983: 121–30). Ramsden and Entwistle then carried out a single factor analysis that combined the ASI subscales and the CPQ scales; this yielded six factors. They acknowledged that there was not a great deal of overlap between the two sets of measures but there were some relationships of interest (see also Entwistle and Ramsden 1983: 184–9):

- Perceptions of a heavy workload were associated with high scores on the subscales that defined a reproducing orientation (surface approach, syllabus-boundness, fear of failure and extrinsic motivation).
- Perceptions of clear goals and standards were associated with high scores on the subscales that defined an achieving orientation (strategic approach, disorganized study methods, negative attitudes to studying and achievement motivation, where the second and third are scored in reverse).
- High scores on intrinsic motivation and the use of evidence were associated with high scores on the scales that defined a positive evaluation of

---

Box 6.2 **Subscales contained in the Course Perceptions Questionnaire**

Scale	*Meaning*
Formal teaching methods	Lectures and classes more important than individual study
Clear goals and standards	Assessment standards and ends of studying clearly defined
Workload	Heavy pressures to fulfil task requirements
Vocational relevance	Perceived relevance of course to careers
Good teaching	Well-prepared, helpful, committed teachers
Freedom in learning	Discretion of students to choose and organize own work
Openness to students	Friendly staff attitudes and preparedness to adapt to students' needs
Good social climate	Quality of academic and social relationships between students

Source: Ramsden and Entwistle 1981: 371

---

teaching (that is, good teaching, openness to students and freedom in learning).

Parsons (1988; Meyer and Parsons 1989a) tried to replicate Ramsden and Entwistle's study by giving the ASI and the CPQ to 1194 English-speaking students at a campus-based institution in South Africa. Despite the different cultural context, Parsons found that perceptions of a heavy workload were associated with high scores on the subscales defining a reproducing orientation and that a positive evaluation of teaching was associated with positive attitudes to studying. He also administered the ASI and the CPQ to 590 Afrikaans-speaking students from the same institution. Once again, perceptions of a heavy workload were associated with high scores on reproducing orientation, and perceptions of formal teaching methods were associated with high scores on syllabus-boundness and with low scores on globetrotting and interrelating ideas.

Nevertheless, Parsons' results confirmed the general impression from Ramsden and Entwistle's study that there are few associations between the two major orientations to studying and scores on scales of the CPQ, and that even those associations that do attain statistical significance are relatively weak and unlikely to be of much practical importance. Ramsden and Entwistle (1981) obtained clearer results when they aggregated the students' scores in each of the 66 departments involved in their study. They found that the students' average score on meaning orientation was significantly correlated with high scores on good teaching and freedom in learning, whereas the average score on reproducing orientation was significantly correlated with a lack of freedom in learning and a heavy workload (see also Entwistle and Ramsden 1983: 187–8). However, the failure to find any stronger association between the two instruments might, of course, be due to inherent weaknesses in the CPQ, which measures only global aspects of the academic setting.

Meyer (1988) devised a far more detailed questionnaire, the Awareness of Context Inventory, which covered 91 more specific aspects of the academic environment. Respondents were asked to rate their level of awareness of each item in their learning experience and, to avoid confusing the participants, Meyer asked for similar ratings of the items in the ASI. He gave both questionnaires to two successive cohorts of accounting students at a campus-based university in South Africa and found a large number of associations between their overall scores on meaning orientation, reproducing orientation and achieving orientation and their ratings of specific items in the Awareness of Context Inventory. Indeed, he was able to classify the items as representing deep, surface or strategic perceptions of the context. However, while students with high scores on reproducing orientation appeared to respond mainly to items reflecting a surface perception, students with high scores on meaning orientation appeared to have 'a rich, holistic perception of learning context that embraces deep, strategic and surface perceptions' (Meyer 1988: 81).

On the basis of these findings, Meyer and Muller (1990a, b) devised six scales measuring 'deep' and 'surface' perceptions of the learning context and combined them with the workload scale from the CPQ to yield a new questionnaire, the Qualitative Context Inventory (QCI). All the items were to be rated using the five-point scale from the ASI and scores on the scales were obtained in the normal manner by summing the responses to the individual items. Data obtained using the QCI could be subjected to a factor analysis to explore the relationships among the subscales. Nevertheless, factor analysis is based on aggregate data generated by large groups of individuals, and it is possible that the features of a group do not adequately capture the range of features exhibited by its constituent members. Instead, Meyer and Muller advocated the use of multi-dimensional unfolding analysis because it allowed them to make comparisons between the patterns of scores obtained by different students. This procedure interprets a score on a scale as a measure of the proximity or affinity of the person to the relevant construct and is used to represent both subscales and students as specific locations within a multi-dimensional space.

Using the scores on the ASI obtained by students at a campus-based university in South Africa, Meyer and Muller (1990a) found that multi-dimensional unfolding analysis produced a coherent representation in which the subscales defining a meaning orientation were both tightly clustered and clearly differentiated from the remaining subscales. They then considered the scores that had been obtained on the ASI and the QCI by students at the University of Namibia, a campus-based institution that was at the time still under the jurisdiction of South Africa. In this case, the subscales defining a meaning orientation were closely associated with those relating to deep perceptions of the learning context, a phenomenon that Meyer and Muller (1990a: 148) called the 'contextual orchestration' of approaches to studying. Meyer and Muller (1990b) went on to find similar results in educationally disadvantaged (mainly Black) students taking a foundation course in engineering at a third campus-based university in South Africa. Meyer and Watson (1991) also obtained similar findings in students who were following a course in occupational therapy at the same institution, except that in this case their study orchestrations evolved over the 4 years of the degree and took subtly different forms in different areas of the curriculum.

As I have said, multi-dimensional unfolding analysis can be employed to represent both subscales and students as locations within the same multi-dimensional space. Meyer and Muller (1990a) found that most students were clustered together within the core of the representations they had derived, whereas other students were scattered around the periphery. They argued that the latter students might be regarded as being at risk of academic failure because they did not share their peers' perceptions of the learning context. Meyer *et al.* (1990a) then compared successful and unsuccessful students in their first year of a degree in electrical engineering at a campus-based university in South Africa. Those who went on to pass their end-of-year assessment replicated the pattern of results just described: a well-defined study orchestration of their subscale scores on the ASI and the QCI combining a meaning orientation with deep perceptions of the learning context. However, the students who went on to fail their end-of-year assessment failed to show any coherent pattern at all. Meyer *et al.* inferred that in the latter students there had been a total disintegration of the normal study orchestration based around a meaning orientation.

Meyer *et al.* (1990b) investigated this issue in the next cohort of students to take the foundation course in engineering studied by Meyer and Muller (1990b). In this study, the students had been asked to complete the ASI and the QCI on two separate occasions during the course. The cohort as a whole once again produced a study orchestration that combined a meaning orientation with deep perceptions of the learning context. Those students who showed a high degree of fit to the ideal theoretical model tended to be highly consistent in their study orchestrations and typically passed the foundation course. However, those students who showed a poor fit to the theoretical model were less consistent and, in some cases, showed deterioration in their study orchestrations. The latter students seemed to be particularly vulnerable to failing their end-of-year assessments. Meyer *et al.* (1992) obtained similar findings when educationally disadvantaged students taking foundation courses in engineering at three different universities in South Africa were instructed to complete the ASI and the QCI retrospectively with regard to their experiences at high school and then to complete the ASI and the QCI to describe their current experience on two occasions during the course itself. Once again, they identified a group whose initial subscale scores were coherently 'orchestrated' and who typically were academically successful, and a second group whose scores showed no coherent orchestration and who were vulnerable to academic failure.

A useful overview of all these studies and their practical implications was provided by Meyer (1991). The findings showed that, at least in the case of academically successful students, there is a consistent relationship between approaches to studying in higher education and perceptions of the academic environment. This conclusion is consistent with the inference that was drawn from interview-based research in Chapter 2, that approaches to studying depend on the content, context and perceived demands of the learning task. In this instance, however, the data are correlational in nature and so, strictly speaking, say nothing about the direction of any causal relationship between approaches to studying and perceptions of the academic environment. It is possible that students' perceptions of their learning context affect their approaches to studying. However, it is equally possible that students' approaches to studying influence their perceptions of their learning context, or else that other factors (such as students' conceptions of learning and teaching) affect both their approaches to studying and their perceptions of the learning context.

Entwistle and Tait (1990) constructed a shortened version of the ASI that simply measured four study orientations, a short version of the CPQ that contained merely ten items, a set of questions about study habits and 16 items concerning preferences for contrasting aspects of the academic environment. They gave these various instruments to 123 electrical engineering students and 148 psychology students at a campus-based university in the UK and carried out factor analyses on their scale scores and their responses to the other individual items. Within both groups, those students with high scores on meaning orientation preferred environments that were likely to promote understanding, whereas students with high scores on reproducing orientation preferred environments that were likely to promote rote learning. Entwistle and Tait argued that students with different orientations would tend to define effective teaching in ways that reflected those orientations and would evaluate their academic environments accordingly.

Entwistle *et al.* (1991) obtained end-of-year examination results for the electrical engineering students in this study and carried out separate factor analyses on the data from the 80 students who subsequently passed the examination and on the data from the 43 students who had failed. The analysis for the successful students showed the same, broadly coherent pattern of findings as the analysis for the entire sample of students: in particular, a meaning orientation was linked to features that would facilitate understanding, whereas a reproducing orientation was linked to features that would encourage memorization. However, the factor analysis for the unsuccessful students produced only 'bizarre and uninterpretable combinations of loadings' (Entwistle *et al.* 1991: 252). The application of multi-dimensional unfolding analysis to the two sets of data also led to the conclusion that poor academic performance was associated with a disinteg-ration or a fragmentation of the normal patterns of studying.

Research in distance education

In Chapters 2, 3 and 4, I described the research carried out by the Study Methods Group at the Open University in the UK. Morgan *et al.* (1980) had noted the development of the 64-item version of the ASI at the University of Lancaster and modified it for use with students who were taking courses by distance learning with the Open University. They obtained responses from a total of 357 students who were attending two residential schools as part of the Technology Foundation Course and the Social Science Foundation Course, respectively. They carried out a factor analysis of the students' scores on the 16 subscales and this produced four factors with a pattern of loadings relatively similar to that which had been obtained by Ramsden and Entwistle (1981) in the case of campus-based students. In particular, the two main factors could be readily interpreted as a meaning orientation and a reproducing orientation, and the only substantive difference was that extrinsic motivation did not seem to contribute to the latter construct in the case of Open University students. Morgan *et al.* inferred that the back-ground research on approaches to learning in campus-based students that had been used in developing the ASI was equally valid for describing stu-dent learning with the Open University.

Morgan *et al.* then compared their students' scores on the 16 subscales of the ASI with those that had been obtained in campus-based students by Ramsden and Entwistle (1981). There were statistically significant differ-ences on ten of the 16 subscales, and some of the differences were still significant even when the subscale scores of Open University students were compared with those of campus-based students who had been taking courses in similar academic subjects. In particular, the Open University students obtained much higher scores on intrinsic motivation than campus-based students taking psychology or engineering. Nevertheless, these differences were confounded with other differences between the two groups of stu-dents in terms of several characteristics that might (in principle, at least) have influenced their approaches to studying:

- First, most of the campus-based students included in Ramsden and Entwistle's study would have entered higher education immediately after the successful completion of their advanced secondary education. In con-trast, Open University students often lack any recent experience of formal education or intensive studying.
- Second, all of the campus-based students included in Ramsden and Entwistle's study were in either their second or third year of study in higher education. However, foundation courses at the Open University are intended for people who are returning to formal education. Many of

the students seen by Morgan *et al.* would accordingly have been in their first year of study.

- Third, and perhaps most notably, the vast majority of the campus-based students included in Ramsden and Entwistle's study would have been young adults around the ages of 18–22. In contrast, as was mentioned in Chapters 3 and 4, the majority of Open University students are older than this. In fact, similar differences have been obtained in comparisons between older and younger students on campus-based courses: in general, older students are both more likely to adopt a meaning orientation and less likely to adopt a reproducing orientation than younger students (see Richardson 1994b for a review).

Finally, Morgan *et al.* employed the 64 items in the ASI as the basis for an interview schedule with a small number of Open University students in an attempt to check the instrument's face validity. They found that their interviewees could readily make sense of these questions in the context of their own experience of distance learning. In particular, a meaning orientation and a reproducing orientation could be easily identified as global accounts of approaches to studying in the interview responses that had been given by different students. This confirmed that the distinction between a meaning orientation and a reproducing orientation was as valid for Open University students as it was for campus-based students. Morgan *et al.* seem to have found no evidence for a separate achieving orientation in either their factor analysis of subscale scores or their interview data. On the one hand, this is not surprising, as students who take courses by distance learning have little opportunity to indulge in the kind of 'cue seeking' behaviour that was described by Miller and Parlett (1974) and provided the basis for Ramsden's (1979) notion of a 'strategic' approach. On the other hand, it might also be recalled from Chapter 2 that there has been little subsequent support for such an approach, even in campus-based students.

The Open University is, of course, a 'single-mode' institution, as this was defined in Chapter 1. Consequently, Morgan *et al.* were not able to make any direct comparisons between the pattern of scale scores produced by distance-learning students and those from any comparison group of campus-based students who were taking exactly the same courses. This problem was addressed by Harper and Kember (1986) in a study involving 348 internal (that is, campus-based) students and 431 external (that is, distance-learning) students taking courses in four academic disciplines with two colleges of advanced education in Australia. They adapted the 64-item version of the ASI for use in this specific context and carried out separate factor analyses on the subscale scores obtained by the external students and by the total sample. Although Harper and Kember did not carry out any formal statistical comparison of the factor solutions, they were remarkably similar at a purely descriptive level. Harper and Kember inferred that the ASI was valid for use with distance-learning students as well as with campus-based students and that the approaches to studying that were shown by distance-learning students were not qualitatively different from those that were shown by campus-based students (see also Kember and Harper 1987a).

Harper and Kember (1989) went on to provide a comparative review of their own findings and those obtained by other researchers with regard to the factor structure of the 64-item version of the ASI. They concluded that there was consistent evidence in both campus-based and distance-learning students for two major factors underlying the ASI:

(a) a 'deep orientation' factor that was indexed by deep approach, interrelating ideas, the use of evidence, intrinsic motivation and comprehension learning
(b) a 'surface orientation' factor that was indexed by surface approach, syllabus-boundness, fear of failure, disorganized study methods, negative attitudes to studying, globetrotting and improvidence.

This concurs with the conclusions of Meyer and Parsons (1989a) that were mentioned earlier in this chapter. In addition, some studies (but not all) had produced evidence for two other factors:

(c) a 'narrow orientation' factor indexed by the subscales concerned with operation learning and strategic approach
(d) a 'goal orientation' factor indexed by the subscales concerned with extrinsic motivation and achievement motivation.

Harper and Kember acknowledged that the two latter factors were much less consistent than the first two factors across different investigations. In fact, they are not evident at all in some of the research with campus-based students in South Africa (Meyer 1988; Meyer and Dunne 1991).

Harper and Kember (1986) presented means and standard deviations for their internal students and their external students on each of the 16 subscales of the 64-item version of the ASI. They did not themselves report the results of any statistical tests carried out on these data. However, it is fairly straightforward to show that the external students obtained significantly higher scores than the internal students on the subscales concerned with deep approach, interrelating ideas, the use of evidence, intrinsic motivation and operation learning and significantly lower scores than the internal students on the subscales relating to surface approach, negative attitudes to studying and globetrotting. Even so, Harper and Kember did not themselves come to any such conclusions, apparently because they would have confounded effects of the mode of study with differences in the students' age, gender and academic disciplines.

Instead, Harper and Kember carried out analyses of covariance that statistically controlled for possible effects of the last three variables. They also identified a different problem that arises when one carries out large numbers of independent statistical tests: the increased probability of making Type I errors (or obtaining spuriously significant results in statistical decision making). To guard against this, they argued that it was more appropriate to use the stringent criterion of statistical significance of 0.5 per cent than the normal threshold criterion of 5 per cent. Using this more stringent criterion, Harper and Kember found no overall difference between the internal students and the external students on any of the subscales when possible differences in their age, discipline and gender had been taken into account. This indicates that there were no intrinsic differences between the approaches to studying of distance-learning and campus-based students when possible effects of these background variables had been statistically controlled.

Wong (1992) conducted a very similar study that involved 89 internal students and 112 external teleconferencing students at a Canadian university. Separate factor analyses of the scores on the 16 subscales of the ASI obtained by the external students and by the total sample yielded factor solutions that were relatively similar both to each other and to the modal structure described by Harper and Kember (1989). Simple comparisons between the two groups generated significant differences on seven of the 16 subscales: the external students obtained significantly higher scores than the internal students on the subscales concerned with deep approach, interrelating ideas, intrinsic motivation and comprehension learning and significantly lower scores than the internal students on surface approach, fear of failure and achievement motivation. Wong ascribed these differences to the fact that the external students were generally older than the internal students. However, in analyses of covariance that took into account any effects of age and gender and that used the more stringent criterion of statistical significance of 0.5 per cent, three of the differences between the two groups remained significant: the external students obtained higher scores than the internal students on deep approach, interrelating ideas and intrinsic motivation.

Unfortunately, even with these precautions, at least two confounded variables in this study might have given rise to spurious differences between the two groups of students. First, Wong had originally surveyed students taking selected courses in business studies, but the study was extended to include all teleconferencing students at the institution in question. Thus, internal students in the field of business studies were compared with external students from all academic disciplines. It has been shown that subscale scores on the 64-item version of the ASI vary systematically across different disciplines (see, for instance, Entwistle and Ramsden 1983: 181–4; Harper and Kember 1986), and so this is a potential source of bias in this study. Second, the overall response rate was much higher in the case of the internal students (74 per cent) than in the case of the external students (19 per cent). As I mentioned earlier in this chapter, students who respond to surveys differ in some respects from those who do not (Astin 1970; Nielsen *et al.* 1978) and in particular in their subscale scores on the ASI (Watkins and Hattie 1985). It follows that the differences in the subscale scores produced by the internal students and the external students in Wong's study might simply have been due to sampling bias.

Nevertheless, Kember and Harper (1987b) found some interesting differences between internal and external students with regard to the prognostic value of their subscale scores on the 64-item ASI in terms of which students would pass or fail their courses. For both internal and external students, passing was associated with low scores on surface approach and high scores on fear of failure. For the internal students, passing was also associated with high scores on globetrotting and low scores on disorganized study methods. However, for the external students it was linked with high scores on syllabus-boundness and low scores on negative attitudes to studying. Kember and Harper carried out a corresponding analysis to predict which of the students who passed their courses would receive a credit or better. For the internal students, better attainment was associated with low scores on globetrotting, fear of failure and syllabus-boundness, and with high scores on achievement orientation. For the external students, better attainment was linked with low scores on negative attitudes to studying, disorganized study methods and strategic approach, and with high scores on syllabus-boundness. The different patterns of results produced by internal and external students suggest that the implications of adopting particular approaches to studying are somewhat different in campus-based courses and in distance-learning courses.

Working with colleagues at the Open University in the UK, I was able to examine the responses to a postal survey of 'post-foundation' students, defined as those who had already achieved one-third of the credits needed for a bachelor's degree (Richardson *et al.* 1999). We carried out a factor analysis on the scores obtained by 2288 such students on the 16 subscales. This produced four factors that were similar to those obtained by Morgan *et al.* (1980) in the case of students taking foundation courses with the Open University and similar to the modal factor solution described by Harper and Kember (1989). We then compared the mean subscale scores with those obtained by Morgan *et al.* in students taking foundation courses. Even using the stringent criterion of statistical significance of 0.5 per cent, the post-foundation students were found to have significantly lower scores on the subscales concerned with surface approach, syllabus-boundness, fear of failure, disorganized study methods, negative attitudes to studying, globetrotting and improvidence. In Chapter 5, I mentioned research findings that implied that campus-based students were less likely to employ a deep approach as they proceeded through a programme of study in higher education (see Gow and Kember 1990). However, the results of this study indicate that Open University students, at least, do not show a progressive shift from a meaning orientation to a reproducing orientation over the course of their degrees.

We noted that our participants were working at broadly the same academic level as the students described by Ramsden and Entwistle (1981) and we therefore compared the subscale scores obtained in these two groups of students. Even using the same stringent criterion of statistical significance, the two groups were significantly different on all except one of the 16 subscales in the ASI. The distance-learning students produced significantly higher scores than the campus-based students on all four aspects of meaning orientation and also on strategic approach and operation learning. The campus-based students produced significantly higher scores than the distance-learning students on all four aspects of reproducing orientation, on the other three aspects of achieving orientation and on three of the four learning styles and pathologies. We concluded that distance-learning students were more likely than campus-based students to exhibit approaches to studying that were more desirable in the sense of being more appropriate to the avowed aims of higher education. However, in the light of the findings obtained by Harper and Kember (1986), we suggested that these apparent effects of mode of study on students' approaches to learning could be attributed to the confounded effects of age.

Finally, we examined the relationships between our participants' scores on the four factors that we had identified and their demographic characteristics and academic outcomes. There were few gender differences in approaches to learning, although women obtained higher scores on reproducing orientation than men. (Even so, they also obtained better grades on their courses than men.) Older students obtained significantly higher scores on meaning orientation but lower scores on extrinsic motivation than younger students, consistent with the findings from research carried out in campus-based institutions that older students adopt more desirable approaches to studying (Richardson 1994b). There were also significant differences among different academic disciplines and a significant effect of the students' level of prior education: those students with a higher level of prior education obtained lower scores on reproducing orientation.

When the effects of these variables were taken into account, the probability that students would complete their courses was unrelated to their approaches to studying. This is of interest in so far as completion rates are an issue of concern in distance education, and it has been assumed that approaches to studying are an important factor here (for instance, Kember 1995; see also Chapter 8). (It should, however, be recognized that the outcome being measured in this study was that of the students' completion or non-completion of a single course unit rather than their withdrawal from higher education altogether.) Nevertheless, even when the possible effects of gender, age, academic discipline and level of prior education had been taken into account, the probability that students would pass their courses (given that they had completed them) was negatively related to their scores on reproducing orientation and was positively related to their scores on operation learning; in addition, the final grades in those students who passed their courses were negatively related to their scores on reproducing orientation. We concluded that discouraging the latter orientation should have major benefits for students' academic performance.

Concluding summary

• The ASI has been used in a large number of studies concerned with campus-based education, and has been shown to be sensitive to differences between individual students in their age, year of study and academic discipline. Gender differences may be more likely to arise on the subscales concerned with motivational aspects of studying but, in practice, these differences are inconsistent in direction, small in magnitude and often not statistically significant.

- Students' scores on the ASI have also been shown to be sensitive to contextual factors, such as the nature of the curriculum (traditional versus innovative) and the students' perceptions of their courses or departments. This supports the idea that approaches to studying depend upon the content, context and perceived demands of the learning task.

- The findings of research studies carried out with campus-based students in Australia, Hong Kong, Nepal, South Africa, Spain, the UK and Venezuela all indicate that the ASI measures a meaning orientation and a reproducing orientation to studying, but other constructs are much less consistent across different studies. The findings of research carried out with campus-based students in South Africa, the UK and the US have also cast doubt upon the integrity of some of the subscales, especially those concerned with an achieving orientation and with styles and pathologies of learning. Finally, research studies in South Africa and the UK have shown that the constituent structure of the ASI is fragmented in students who fail or who are vulnerable to academic failure.

- The factor structure of the ASI has been reproduced in research involving distance-learning students in Australia, Canada and the UK. There is consistent evidence from these studies that distance-learning students tend to obtain higher scores than campus-based students on the subscales associated with a meaning orientation and to obtain lower scores than campus-based students on the subscales associated with a reproducing orientation. However, these effects can be ascribed to confounded differences in the students' ages. There may be genuine differences between campus-based and distance-learning students in the extent to which the subscales of the ASI predict their subsequent academic attainment.

7

Variants of the Approaches to Studying Inventory

In Chapter 6, I noted the rather doubtful status of certain of the subscales in the original version of the ASI, particularly those associated with an achieving orientation and the 'styles and pathologies' scale. It is also rather a long instrument to complete, which is an important practical consideration for at least two reasons. First, there might well be restrictions on the time and opportunities available for completing questionnaires, especially if they are to be given to campus-based students in a classroom setting before or after their normal academic activities. Second, if the task of completing the questionnaires proves too onerous, it might well lead to poor response rates, especially when they are administered by postal surveys to either campus-based or distance-learning students and when their completion and safe return depends upon the students' compliance and cooperation.

For these reasons, it was thought useful to develop a shortened form of the ASI that focused on the more reliable orientations to studying. One strategy for doing this was to choose fewer items to define the main constructs that the ASI was intended to measure; this led to the 30-item and 18-item versions of the ASI. Another strategy was to select the more robust scales and subscales, which led to the 32-item version of the ASI. Finally, a wholesale revision of the entire ASI was undertaken, resulting in the Revised Approaches to Studying Inventory (RASI). In this chapter, I shall describe the original derivation and subsequent application of each of these four instruments. In practice, they have proved more popular in research in campus-based education, probably because they tend to be used in formal teaching situations where there are competing pressures on staff and students in formally timetabled teaching activities. In contrast, distance-learning students are well used to dealing promptly with materials received from their institutions through the post, and as a result their response rates even to long questionnaire surveys can be very high indeed.

The 30-item version of the ASI

Entwistle (1981: 57–60, 100–3, 273–4) described a variant of the ASI in which 30 items drawn from the original instrument defined seven different subscales:

- achieving orientation (6 items)
- reproducing orientation (6 items)
- comprehension learning (3 items)
- meaning orientation (6 items)
- operation learning (3 items)
- improvidence (3 items)
- globetrotting (3 items).

As in the original ASI, respondents are asked to indicate their agreement or disagreement with each item on a five-point scale between 'definitely agree', scoring 4, and 'definitely disagree', scoring 0. The responses to the relevant items are simply summed to obtain a score on each subscale. 'Achieving orientation', 'reproducing orientation' and 'meaning orientation' are used as major scales in their own right. However, other measures can be determined as follows:

- comprehension learning + globetrotting = comprehension learning style
- operation learning + improvidence = operation learning style
- meaning orientation + comprehension learning + operation learning = versatile approach
- reproducing orientation + improvidence + globetrotting = pathological symptoms
- achieving orientation + versatile approach + (48 − pathological symptoms) = predictor of overall academic success.

Entwistle (1981: 274) presented some 'provisional norms' for this version of the ASI for arts, science and social science students. However, it would appear that these had been obtained by examining the mean responses to the relevant items in the main study reported by Ramsden and Entwistle (1981), which had of course involved the 64-item version of the ASI. In other words, the norms had been arrived at by calculating average scores as if the participants in that study had merely completed the 30 items in the shortened inventory. Their self-ratings of academic progress were found to be directly related to their scores on achieving orientation, meaning orientation and versatile approach and to be inversely related to their scores on reproducing orientation and learning pathologies. Finally, their self-ratings of academic progress were also shown to be moderately correlated with the predictor of overall academic success.

In Chapter 6, I questioned the validity of self-reports of academic progress and argued that it could not be inferred from findings such as these that academic success was the result of students adopting more desirable approaches to studying. There is, however, a more fundamental problem in Entwistle's (1981) uncritical assumption that data obtained with the 64-item version of the ASI could used to construct norms (albeit 'provisional' ones) for the 30-item version. In deciding how to interpret items in question-naires like the ASI, participants will make use of the immediate context: in other words, the content of neighbouring items. If the context is changed, then their responses may well be different (see Strack and Schwarz 1992). In this case, some of the context (namely, the other 34 items) has actu-ally been removed. It should not, therefore, be assumed that students would respond to the 30-item version of the ASI in the way they respond to the relevant items when they are embedded within the 64-item version of the ASI.

It seems that this version of the ASI was intended simply as an expository device in a textbook on educational psychology, rather than as a serious research instrument. Nevertheless, Entwistle and Ramsden (1983: 53–5) referred to a 'pilot study' in which it had been modified for use with sixth form (that is, upper secondary school) students. Data were presented from a small number of students and these suggested that high scores on repro-ducing orientation and improvidence were associated with good academic performance in science students but poor academic performance in arts students. In a much more extensive study, Watkins (1984; Watkins *et al.* 1986) gave the 30-item version of the ASI to 445 secondary school children in the Philippines; a second set of responses was obtained from 425 of these children at a follow-up session 6 months later. Even when variations in their IQs had been taken into account, the children's overall academic grades were positively correlated with their scores on meaning orientation and operation learning but negatively correlated with their scores on reprodu-cing orientation and globetrotting.

For each of the two sessions, Watkins *et al.* found that factor analyses carried out on the scores on the seven subscales identified two factors: one measured the subscales that Entwistle (1981) had associated with academic success (meaning orientation, comprehension learning, achieving orienta-tion and operation learning) and the other measured the subscales that Entwistle had associated with academic failure (globetrotting, reproducing orientation and improvidence). However, the internal consistency of the subscale scores was rather low, which Watkins (1984) ascribed to the brevity of the individual scales. Ford (1985) obtained responses to this version of the ASI from 25 postgraduate students at a campus-based university in the UK. He found no significant association between their relative bias towards comprehension learning or operation learning according to the ASI and their relative degree of competence in holist or serialist learning on arti-ficial learning tasks of the sort devised by Pask (1976). This casts doubt on whether the latter constructs are actually being measured by the 30-item version of the ASI.

Coles (1985) used the 30-item version of the ASI to compare students who were taking courses at medical schools with a traditional curriculum and a problem-based curriculum. The students in question had very similar scores on the ASI when they began their courses. During their first year, the students who were taking the traditional curriculum showed an increase in reproducing orientation but a decrease in meaning orientation and versatile approach. However, the students who were taking the problem-based curriculum showed a decrease in reproducing orientation, with no change in their scores on any of the other scales. As a result, by the end of the first year, the students taking the problem-based curriculum showed higher scores on meaning orientation and versatility and lower scores on reproducing orientation than the students who had taken the traditional curriculum. As in the study by Newble and Clarke (1986, 1987) mentioned in Chapter 6, the problem-based curriculum seemed to have induced more desirable approaches to studying. Chessell (1986) and Mårtenson (1986) employed the same instrument to monitor approaches to studying in medical students taking traditional curricula in Scotland and Sweden, respectively.

In a study mentioned in Chapter 5, Wilson *et al.* (1996) gave the 30-item version of the ASI, together with Biggs's (1985, 1987) SPQ, to two cohorts of students in the first year of a psychology programme at a campus-based university in Australia. There were modest correlations in both cohorts between the achieving orientation subscale in the ASI and the achieving approach scale in the SPQ, between the meaning orientation subscale in the ASI and the deep approach scale in the SPQ, and between the reproducing orientation subscale in the ASI and the surface approach scale in the SPQ. This suggested that there was a moderate degree of correspondence between the two instruments. However, the second cohort also produced statistically significant, negative correlations between the meaning orientation subscale of the ASI and the surface approach scale of the SPQ and between the reproducing orientation subscale of the ASI and the deep approach scale of the SPQ. Wilson *et al.* took this to mean that there were theoretical differences between the two instruments. Even so, no such discrepancies were found in the first cohort, and so the problematic effects may not be reliable. Consistent with the results that they had obtained with the SPQ, Wilson *et al.* found no sign of any gender difference in the scores obtained on the ASI in either of the two cohorts.

Fogarty and Taylor (1997) carried out a postal survey of 503 students using the 30-item version of the ASI. The students were taking a mathematics unit by distance learning as part of a preparatory skills course to qualify them for admission to an Australian university. As in the previous research by Watkins (1984; Watkins *et al.* 1986), the internal consistency of the seven subscales was rather low. There was some evidence for two factors corresponding to Entwistle's measures of versatile approach and pathological symptoms, although the level of fit to this theoretical model was not satisfactory. Nevertheless, when the students' scores on the seven subscales were combined into two scales corresponding to these factors, their level of internal consistency was much higher. Moreover, although the students' grades in the mathematics unit showed no sign of any relationship with their scores on the first factor, they did show a highly significant negative relationship with their scores on the second factor.

The 18-item version of the ASI

Gibbs *et al.* (1988) described an even shorter version of the ASI consisting of just the 18 items in the three subscales of Entwistle's (1981) inventory that measured different orientations to studying: meaning, reproducing and achieving. Gibbs *et al.* themselves specifically commended this instrument for lecturers to use in evaluating their own teaching. In the UK, it was subsequently used to assess innovative forms of course design and delivery in the national programme, mentioned in Chapter 2, which aimed at improving the quality of student learning in institutions whose courses were validated by the Council for National Academic Awards. The report on this programme published by Gibbs (1992) contains accounts of ten case studies, together with evaluative data obtained from students taking the relevant course units using the 18-item version of the ASI as well as structured interviews and open-ended questionnaires.

One of the case studies in this programme concerned a unit on oceanography that was being taken by both undergraduate students and postgraduate students. In their responses to the ASI, both groups obtained high scores on meaning orientation, but the postgraduate students showed much higher scores than the undergraduate students on reproducing orientation. This result was attributed to a heavier curriculum and the pressure of examinations on the diploma course. This raises the question whether these factors are endemic to taught postgraduate courses or whether the findings were idiosyncratic to the particular unit that was being assessed in this case study. I therefore compared undergraduate and postgraduate students taking four different course units in my own department using the 18-item version of the ASI (Richardson 1998). The results did not replicate the pattern obtained in the case study: if anything, the postgraduate students tended to obtain slightly higher scores on meaning orientation and slightly lower scores on reproducing orientation than the undergraduate students. In other words, postgraduate students appear to be just as capable as undergraduate students of adopting appropriate orientations to studying, and there is no support for the idea that postgraduate students on taught courses are more likely to adopt a reproducing orientation to studying than undergraduate students on the same courses.

Previously, I had obtained responses to the 18-item version of the ASI from a large number of other students at my own (campus-based) university (Richardson 1992, 1993). Two successive cohorts of students had been asked to complete this version of the ASI at two sessions 1 week apart. In this situation, the test–retest reliability of the three scales proved to be satisfactory and their internal consistency was rather better than in the study by

Watkins (1984), who had used the 30-item version of the ASI. Moreover, there was no sign of a gender difference on any of the three scales (Richardson 1993). However, the results of a factor analysis carried out on the students' responses to the 18 items implied that the three scales were tapping relatively specific aspects of studying rather than more global orientations.

Newstead (1992) carried out a similar study at another campus-based university in the UK. He found that the three scales in the 18-item version of the ASI had moderate levels of internal consistency, and also that there was a weak but statistically significant correlation between the students' scores on meaning orientation and their performance in their end-of-year examinations. Newstead, too, carried out a factor analysis of his students' responses to the individual items and this led him to recommend this version of the ASI as a 'quick and easy' method of assessing the quality of student learning. However, his detailed results did not actually confirm the intended structure of this instrument. Subsequently, colleagues working with campus-based students in the South Pacific obtained further evidence to support my negative evaluation of the 18-item version of the ASI (Richardson *et al.* 1995).

The 32-item version of the ASI

An alternative solution to the problem of the questionable status of some of the subscales in the 64-item version of the ASI is to focus on the items or the subscales that define the constructs of meaning orientation and reproducing orientation. In order to evaluate the effectiveness of a course on learning skills aimed at first-year students at a campus-based university in Australia, Ramsden *et al.* (1986, 1987) constructed an inventory that consisted mainly of items from the meaning orientation and reproducing orientation scales of the ASI and yielded measures of both deep and surface approaches to learning. Students showed a slight decrease in their scores on deep approach during the year, whether or not they had actually attended the learning skills course. The students who had attended the course also showed a modest increase in their scores on surface approach. Thus, the course did not induce more desirable approaches to studying (and it also did not improve the students' academic performance). Nevertheless, the instrument used in this study was not wholly satisfactory because other investigators consistently failed to reproduce the intended structure of these two scales in terms of the constituent subscales or the constituent items. For instance, 'extrinsic motivation' – one of the subscales taken to define a reproducing orientation – fails to load on the same factor as the other subscales that supposedly define this orientation to studying (Harper and Kember 1989; Meyer and Parsons 1989a; see also Chapter 6).

Because of time constraints in their own research, Trigwell and Prosser (1991a, b) reduced the ASI to just three subscales: the four items in the deep approach scale, the four items in the interrelating ideas scale and four of the six items in the surface approach scale. They gave this shortened questionnaire to different groups of students taking a campus-based nursing course in Australia. In each of the groups, the scores on deep approach were correlated with the scores on interrelating ideas, but both were essentially independent of the scores on surface approach. In other words, as in the case of the Study Process Questionnaire, individual students might score high or low on both deep approach and surface approach (see Chapter 5). Trigwell and Prosser noted the practical implication of this finding, that interventions aimed at improving the quality of student learning should be concerned specifically with encouraging a deep approach and not necessarily with discouraging a surface approach. Moreover, in each of the groups, the scores on deep approach and interrelating ideas were positively correlated with the students' level of understanding of the syllabus, assessed using a taxonomy devised by Biggs and Collis (1982). However, Trigwell and Prosser's use of this very short instrument was dictated by expediency, and it may provide only a very superficial glimpse of students' approaches to learning.

In fact, Entwistle and Ramsden (1983: 51–3) carried out factor analyses on the data from their main study involving 2208 campus-based students, both on the entire sample and, separately, on the students taking each of six different academic disciplines (English, history, economics, psychology, physics and engineering). These factor analyses consistently identified a meaning orientation factor measured by deep approach, comprehension learning, interrelating ideas and use of evidence. They equally consistently identified a reproducing orientation factor measured by surface approach, improvidence, fear of failure and syllabus-boundness. It should be noted that this factor structure does not represent the intended composition of the two orientations to studying in the 64-item version of the ASI (see Box 6.1, p. 90). I therefore proposed that it was more appropriate instead to shorten the ASI by focusing upon these eight subscales, because they had been empirically identified with meaning orientation and reproducing orientation across the six different academic disciplines studied by Entwistle and Ramsden. This generates an inventory that contains 32 items and has the following structure:

Meaning orientation
Deep approach (4 items)
Comprehension learning (4 items)
Interrelating ideas (4 items)
Use of evidence (4 items)

Reproducing orientation
Surface approach (6 items)
Improvidence (4 items)
Fear of failure (3 items)
Syllabus-boundness (3 items)

The items in question can be found in an appendix to my published report (Richardson 1990). I administered this shortened instrument to two successive cohorts of campus-based students at two sessions 2 weeks apart. I was able to show that both the eight subscales and the two main orientations to studying could be reproduced by a factor analysis of their responses. In addition, this version of the ASI was found to have levels of internal consistency and test–retest reliability that were both satisfactory and superior to those of the 30-item version of the ASI. Subsequent analyses of the same dataset showed that there was no gender difference on either orientation to studying (Richardson 1993), but that the older students obtained both higher scores on meaning orientation and lower scores on reproducing orientation than the younger students (Richardson 1995b). Moreover, despite the fact that the students had completed the ASI during the first few weeks of the first year of a 4-year degree course, there was a significant positive correlation between their scores on the use of evidence and the probability that they completed the course nearly 4 years later. There was also a significant negative correlation between the scores on syllabus-boundness and the standard of degree obtained by students who completed the course.

In Chapter 6, I mentioned a review paper by Severiens and ten Dam (1994) that suggested that any gender differences in scores on the 64-item version of the ASI were more likely to arise on the motivational aspects of studying than the cognitive aspects of studying. The 32-item version of the ASI includes only one of the original motivational subscales (fear of failure), and so the fact that I found no gender differences on the 32-item version of the ASI is entirely consistent with Severiens and ten Dam's suggestion. However, their review found considerable heterogeneity from one study to another, which suggests that gender differences in both directions can arise in particular contexts. I also mentioned in Chapter 6 the findings of interview-based research concerning the gendered nature of the arts and sciences in higher education. Thomas (1988, 1990) found that men taking arts degrees had little difficulty maintaining their status, partly because of their dominant position in society and partly because of the encouragement of individualism within their chosen disciplines. In contrast, the experiences of women taking science degrees proved to be highly problematic, not simply because they were in a numerical minority but more because of the uncongenial culture of their chosen disciplines and academic departments.

This raises the question of whether women are disadvantaged by the co-educational nature of higher education. Hayes and I addressed this by obtaining responses to the 32-item version of the ASI from students at three Oxbridge colleges (Hayes and Richardson 1995). The first was a single-sex college at which all of the students and members of academic staff were female. The second had been a women's college but, at the time of our study, admitted both men and women, in roughly equal numbers, to be taught by both male and female tutors. The third college had been a men's college but at the time of our study admitted both men and women, in a proportion of 2:1, to be taught by an almost entirely male academic staff. We found that the scores obtained by male students on the ASI were similar in the last two colleges, except that those taking science courses produced much higher scores on syllabus-boundness in the third college (the more 'male' environment) than in the second college (the more 'female' environment). This suggests that in a predominantly male environment men rely more on staff to define their learning tasks. However, the female students obtained higher scores on meaning orientation if they were taking arts courses in the first college (in a 'female' environment) or science courses in the third college (in a 'male' environment). We came to the conclusion that female students adopted more desirable approaches to studying when the gendered nature of their academic discipline accorded with the gendered quality of their learning environment.

More recently, colleagues and I used the 32-item version of the ASI to evaluate the impact of a multimedia variant of the Personalized System of Instruction (or 'Keller Plan') in the context of a mathematics course (Hambleton *et al.* 1998). We noted the evidence that students will adopt different approaches to studying in different contexts in response to the perceived demands of the learning situation (see Chapter 2). Most of this evidence comes from structured interviews with students taking different courses, except for the investigation by Eley (1992) mentioned in Chapter 5, which involved the SPQ. In all these studies, any differences in the approaches to studying adopted in different learning situations were essentially fortuitous because no attempt had been made to manipulate the courses that were being taken. This left it unclear whether desirable changes in approaches to studying could be brought about by the use of specific interventions. The Personalized System of Instruction (PSI) is a kind of programmed instruction that employs a highly structured, student-centred approach to course design and it might, therefore, be expected to bring about a shift towards a meaning orientation to studying.

We asked mathematics and computer science students to complete the 32-item version of the ASI on two separate occasions about two different courses. One course had been constructed in accordance with the features of PSI and was additionally supported by an interactive hypertext software package with video feedback on the students' solutions to problem-based coursework. The other course was delivered in a conventional manner by means of two lectures and a group tutorial each week. Overall, the scores on meaning orientation were significantly higher for the PSI-based course than for the conventionally delivered course. This effect was mainly apparent in the subscales concerned with comprehension learning and the use of evidence. There was no difference in the scores on reproducing orientation between the two courses. These results show that desirable changes in approaches to studying can be brought about by specific interventions. However, the effect was small and was statistically significant only in the computer science students and not in the mathematics students. Paradoxically, then, the intervention had failed to induce the desired changes in those students who were intended to be its chief beneficiaries.

In Chapter 6, I pointed out that the constituent structure of the original, 64-item ASI had been confirmed in factor analyses carried out on data obtained in many different countries around the world. However, these analyses were based on students' subscale scores and hence they took for granted the empirical integrity of the subscales themselves. Indeed, the findings of the investigation by Speth and Brown (1988) suggested that the underlying structure of the ASI might not transfer well to the US. I had an opportunity to obtain data with the 32-item ASI from students at a campus-based university in that country (Richardson 1995a). The results of a factor analysis carried out on their responses to the 32 items indicated the presence of eight factors. Several of these factors were broadly analogous to some of the original subscales, and a higher-order factor analysis demonstrated that they could be subsumed within two overarching dimensions that could be recognized as a meaning orientation and a reproducing orientation. However, the exact composition of the first-order factors differed considerably from that which had originally been specified by Ramsden and Entwistle (1981), and I concluded that these two orientations to studying were interpreted in a manner that was distinctive to the cultural context.

Together with colleagues at another campus-based university in the US, I found very similar results in a study of deaf and hearing students who were taking the same courses (Richardson *et al.* 2000). In this case, the 32-item version of the ASI had the following structure:

Meaning orientation	Reproducing orientation
Comprehension learning	Academic anxiety
Critical approach	Needing external structure
Seeking internal structure	Relating ideas (scored in reverse)
Strategic memorization	Time pressure

There were statistically significant differences between deaf students and hearing students on four of these subscales. On the one hand, the deaf students showed more anxiety about their academic work and found it more difficult than the hearing students to relate ideas on different topics; the latter effect was more marked in deaf students who preferred to communicate by sign language. On the other hand, the deaf students were more likely than the hearing students to adopt a critical approach and to analyse the internal structure of topics they were studying.

Cultural contexts can obviously vary geographically, from country to country, but they can also differ from one institution to another. Colleagues and I had an opportunity to obtain data with the 32-item ASI from students taking 'Access' courses at several colleges of further education (Hayes *et al.* 1997). These courses are intended for older students who are returning to formal education but who lack the normal entrance qualifications that are required by most institutions of higher education in the UK. They are similar to the foundation courses studied by Meyer *et al.* (1990b, 1992) in South Africa (see Chapter 6) and to the 'preparatory' programmes organized by some Australian universities, but they embody values and goals that are educationally and socially radical and different from those of most mainstream programmes in higher education (see Brennan 1989). The

results of a factor analysis carried out on the responses given by 241 participants once again indicated the presence of eight factors, but there was an
extremely poor fit to the original structure of the ASI. The first-order factors could in turn be subsumed within three higher-order factors that were
described as meaning orientation, dependent orientation and mature orientation. The second of these was essentially independent of the other two
and could be construed as a form of reproducing orientation; the first and
third were correlated with each other and could be loosely construed as
different aspects of meaning orientation. However, the important point was
that these orientations were distinctive to the context of Access courses and
qualitatively different from those that tend to be exhibited by conventional
university students.

Provost and Bond (1997) administered the 32-item version of the ASI to
187 students who were starting the second year of an undergraduate course
in psychology at a campus-based university in Australia. They did not report
the results of any factor analyses, but the internal consistencies of the students' scores on the eight subscales were generally low and, in most cases,
poorer than the values that I had obtained in my original study in the UK
(Richardson 1990). The internal consistencies of the students' scores on
the two overall scales (meaning orientation and reproducing orientation)
were more acceptable, although the scores showed few significant relationships with students' performance in different academic assessments. Provost
and Bond suggested that the ASI was insufficiently grounded in actual
studying behaviour and that it was vulnerable to a social desirability bias:
that is, students' responses to the items in the ASI reflect their perceptions
of desirable approaches to studying rather than their actual studying practices. However, a different possibility is that the detailed constituent structure of the 32-item version of the ASI (and also, by implication, of other
versions) simply does not transfer very well, even to the superficially similar
cultural context of Australian higher education.

Woodley and I employed the 32-item version of the ASI to compare
distance-learning students with and without hearing loss at the Open University in the UK (Richardson and Woodley 1999). In this study, 382 students with varying degrees of self-reported hearing loss were compared with
190 students who were taking the same courses and had no declared form
of disablement. The results of a factor analysis of the students' subscale
scores produced two factors: one measured deep approach, interrelating
ideas, use of evidence and comprehension learning; the other measured
surface approach, syllabus-boundness, improvidence and fear of failure.
This confirms the intended structure of this version of the ASI when it is
used with a distance-learning population. These two factors were essentially
independent of one another, which implies that individual students might
score high or low on both meaning orientation and reproducing orientation. I discussed the implications of this result earlier in connection with
the short version of the ASI that was devised by Trigwell and Prosser (1991a;
see also Chapter 5).

Woodley and I found no difference between the two groups of students in terms of their scores on meaning orientation. This demonstrates that students with a hearing loss are just as capable as other students of engaging with the underlying meaning of learning materials. Nevertheless, there was a slight tendency for the students with a hearing loss to obtain higher scores than the students with no hearing loss on reproducing orientation, and this was associated in particular with increased scores on fear of failure. Informal comments appended to the questionnaire by many of the students with a hearing loss indicated that the latter finding could be attributed to negative experiences in tutorials and in other encounters with members of academic staff. We therefore concluded that academic staff needed to be appropriately trained to ensure that they encouraged a positive self-concept in students with a hearing loss.

The Revised Approaches to Studying Inventory

In 1992, a Revised Approaches to Studying Inventory (RASI) was devised by Entwistle and his colleagues. This contained 60 items in 15 subscales measuring five main constructs: deep approach, surface approach, strategic approach, apathetic approach and academic aptitude. It was then reduced to an inventory containing 38 items in 14 subscales that measured five major dimensions (see Tait and Entwistle 1996). The subscales are listed in Box 7.1 and the individual items can be found in an appendix to an article by Waugh and Addison (1998). In each case, respondents are instructed to indicate the extent of their agreement or disagreement with a statement along a five-point scale between 'definitely agree', scoring 4, and 'definitely disagree', scoring 0. The responses given to the relevant items are summed to obtain a score on each subscale and the scores on the relevant subscales are then summed again to obtain a score on each scale. As in the case of the ASI, all the items reflect the meaning of the corresponding subscales and so the RASI, too, is vulnerable to a response bias either to agree or to disagree with all of the items.

Sadler-Smith (1996) obtained responses to the RASI from 245 students on a course in business studies at a campus-based institution in the UK. The internal consistencies of the major dimensions were high, except for the 'lack of direction' scale, which was extremely low. A factor analysis carried out on the students' subscale scores yielded five independent factors that showed a good fit to the intended structure of the RASI. Moreover, academic performance on the course in business studies showed modest positive correlations with the scores on deep approach and strategic approach. The older students obtained higher scores on deep approach but lower scores on surface approach and lack of direction than the younger students. The men obtained higher scores on deep approach and academic self-confidence but lower scores on surface approach than the women. As mentioned earlier with regard to the 32-item ASI, such differences may reflect the specific situation or context in which the course was being taught.

Box 7.1 **Subscales contained in the Revised Approaches to Studying Inventory**

Deep approach
Looking for meaning (2 items)
Active interest/critical stance (2 items)
Relating and organizing ideas (3 items)
Using evidence and logic (3 items)

Surface approach
Relying on memorizing (2 items)
Difficulty in making sense (2 items)
Unrelatedness (2 items)
Concern about coping (4 items)

Strategic approach
Determination to excel (2 items)
Effort in studying (2 items)
Organized studying (3 items)
Time management (3 items)

Lack of direction (4 items)

Academic self-confidence (4 items)

Source: Tait and Entwistle 1996: 107

Duff (1997) carried out a similar study with business studies students at another campus-based institution in the UK using only the 30 items in the RASI that measured the three main approaches to studying. Once again, the internal consistencies of the main scales were high and a factor analysis conducted on the students' subscale scores yielded three factors that could clearly be identified with the three approaches to studying. The 'deep approach' factor was highly correlated with the 'strategic approach' factor but both were independent of the 'surface approach' factor. Another factor analysis was carried out on the students' responses to the 30 individual items. On the one hand, this too generated three factors that could also be identified with the different approaches to studying; once again, the 'deep approach' factor was highly correlated with the 'strategic approach' factor but both were independent of the 'surface approach' factor. Nevertheless, on the other hand, the factor solution provided no support for the existence of any identifiable subscales within these three factors.

Sadler-Smith and Tsang (1998) administered the RASI to 183 students taking a general degree course in business studies at a campus-based institution in Hong Kong and compared the results with those obtained from 225 of the British students described by Sadler-Smith (1996). In the Hong Kong sample, the internal consistencies of the lack of direction and academic self-confidence scales were unsatisfactory and so these scales were omitted from further analysis. Factor analyses carried out on the students' subscale scores yielded three factors in both of the samples that could be readily identified with deep approach, surface approach and strategic approach. One interesting anomaly was that the 'relying on memorizing' subscale produced a positive loading on the 'strategic approach' factor in the British sample but a positive loading on the 'deep approach' factor in the Hong Kong sample. This fits with the different notion of the role of the memorization among Chinese students that was discussed in Chapters 2 and 3.

Sadler-Smith and Tsang found that there were relatively few correlations between the students' scores on the subscales of the RASI and their academic performance. For Hong Kong students, scores on organized studying were positively related to their current and cumulative grade point averages, and scores on difficulty in making sense were negatively related to their current grade point averages. For the British students, none of the subscales was significantly related to their marks on the module in which the RASI was administered, but their aggregate marks across 12 modules were positively correlated with their scores on using evidence and logic, relating and organizing ideas, active interest/critical stance and effort in studying, and negatively correlated with their scores on difficulty in making sense. The British students tended to produce higher scores than the Hong Kong students on all of the subscales except unrelatedness and concern about coping. Among the Hong Kong students, older students tended to produce higher scores on deep approach and strategic approach in the case of the men, whereas older students tended to produce lower scores on deep approach and strategic approach in the case of the women. No explanation was offered for these findings, or for the disparity with the findings in British students.

Waugh and Addison (1998) administered the RASI to 346 students in their first year of courses in business studies at a campus-based university in Australia. In this study, the middle response category ('only to be used if the item doesn't apply to you or if you really find it impossible to give a definite answer') was omitted from the response scale to ensure that the participants were using an ordered response format. Waugh and Addison then applied the analytic model devised by Rasch (1960) to assess whether the items in the RASI defined a single coherent scale. They concluded that the psychometric properties of the RASI were broadly satisfactory but that there was some scope for improvement in the selection and wording of the constituent items. In a subsequent study, Waugh (1999) obtained similar results when he asked another sample of 369 students from the same institution to respond to the 38 items, first with regard to their attitudes to studying and then again with regard to their actual studying practices.

There is, however, a fundamental problem, in that the method devised by Rasch was originally intended to assess whether a test of ability or intelligence containing a series of different items was measuring a single ability (see, for instance, Wright and Stone 1979). It therefore assesses whether the empirical data can be fitted by a single dimension and, to achieve this, Waugh and Addison had to score items on the surface approach and lack of direction scales in reverse, as if they simply measured the converse of the remaining scales. Nevertheless, the results that were obtained by Sadler-Smith (1996) and by Duff (1997) show that the surface approach scale is actually independent of both the deep approach scale and the strategic approach scale, as one might well have expected from research using the SPQ (see Chapter 5) or short versions of the ASI (Trigwell and Prosser 1991a; Richardson and Woodley 1999). It follows that the use of a uni-dimensional model to capture the structure of the RASI is misleading and inappropriate. (It is interesting, in this regard, that the items Waugh found to be most problematic in both of his studies tended to come from the surface approach scale.) Having said this, the individual scales of the RASI *are* intended to be uni-dimensional and the reservations expressed by Waugh and Addison with regard to their item composition will need to be addressed in future research.

In short, the RASI does not appear to represent an improvement on earlier versions of the ASI. At the time of writing (September 1999), no research studies have been published in which the RASI was administered to students taking courses by distance learning. It is, however, being used by a number of researchers at the Open University in the UK. For instance, Calder *et al.* (1995) used an extended version to compare vocational training courses being run by colleges of further education and those being run in-house at various companies. Students on company schemes tended to obtain higher scores on academic self-confidence and lower scores on surface approach than students at colleges of further education, but there were no significant differences between the scores obtained by students taking traditionally designed courses and those obtained by students taking courses designed on open-learning principles (see Chapter 1). A fundamental problem, however, is that the RASI is a substantively different instrument from the ASI and thus it will not be possible to compare findings obtained using the RASI with the established body of research literature obtained using different versions of the ASI.

Concluding summary

- The 30-item version of the ASI consists of seven subscales measuring a versatile approach to learning (associated with success) and pathological symptoms (associated with failure). The three subscales measuring achieving, meaning and reproducing orientations are correlated in an appropriate manner with the achieving, deep and surface scales of the SPQ.

The 18-item version of the ASI consists solely of the subscales measuring different orientations to studying. The 32-item version of the ASI consists of the eight subscales that have been shown to be most consistently related to meaning and reproducing orientation in campus-based students. Finally, the RASI is a relatively new instrument intended to measure the same constructs.

- The 30-item and 32-item versions of the ASI have been shown to be sensitive to the nature of the curriculum (traditional versus innovative), and the 32-item version has been shown to be sensitive to differences between individual students related to their age. Typically, men and women produce similar scores on these instruments, although gender differences can be obtained in particular disciplines and in overtly gendered academic environments. Finally, the 32-item version of the ASI has been used to investigate the impact of hearing loss upon approaches to studying in higher education.

- The factor structures of the 30-item and 32-item versions of the ASI have been reproduced in research studies carried out with distance-learning students. However, there are problems in transferring these instruments to different cultures and different systems of higher education. Evidence from two research studies in the US confirms the existence of two broad orientations underlying the 32-item version of the ASI but indicates that they are interpreted differently in this context. In addition, the factor structure of the 32-item version of the ASI appears to be different when it is administered to 'Access' students in the UK.

- The 30-item and 18-item versions of the ASI are not adequate from a psychometric point of view and cannot be recommended as research instruments, although the 30-item version can be used to generate global measures of a versatile approach and of pathological symptoms. The 32-item version of the ASI appears to possess satisfactory psychometric properties and can be recommended as a useful instrument for both research and practice. In the case of the RASI, the three main scales appear to be psychometrically sound but there is little support for the underlying subscales and doubts have been expressed about the selection of items.

8

The Distance Education Student Progress Inventory

Chapters 5, 6 and 7 were concerned with the SPQ and the ASI. Both of these instruments were originally devised to measure approaches to learning among students who were taking courses at campus-based institutions of higher education. The obvious research question in both these cases is whether or not it is valid and appropriate to employ the same instruments in exploring approaches to studying in distance education. In fact, with both questionnaires, the answer seems to be in the affirmative, although research with distance-learning students has tended to confirm fundamental problems with the design and construction of these instruments that had previously been identified in research with campus-based students. In contrast, in this chapter and the next, I shall discuss two other instruments that were specifically intended from the outset to measure approaches to learning in students who were taking courses by distance education.

The first of these instruments, the Distance Education Student Progress (DESP) inventory, was devised by Kember *et al.* (1991) in the light of the findings of Kember and Harper (1987b) with regard to the relationships between students' scores on the various subscales of the ASI and different measures of academic outcome. It will be remembered from Chapter 6 that the precise nature of these relationships depended: (a) upon the relevant measure of academic outcome (completing a course versus obtaining a credit or better); and (b) upon the mode of course delivery (internal versus external, or campus-based versus distance education). The latter aspect of these findings indicates that adopting particular approaches to studying has different implications for academic attainment in campus-based and distance education. This, in turn, is potentially important if one wishes to maximize student attainment within either system of education and especially if one wishes to maximize student retention.

Student retention in campus-based education

Course completion or student persistence (as opposed to attrition, withdrawal or 'drop-out') has always been a concern for researchers, administrators and policy makers in higher education. Tinto (1982) presented figures that suggested that course completion at institutions of higher education in the US (defined as the proportion of students who completed bachelor's degrees on schedule 4 years after their initial enrolment) had consistently been around 55 per cent over the period from 1880 to 1980. Some of the students in the remaining 45 per cent may have taken longer to obtain their degrees or they might have transferred to other institutions of higher education. However, Tinto subsequently claimed that there was a substantial residual number of students who withdrew for academic or nonacademic reasons and would never obtain a degree:

> Of the nearly 2.8 million students who in 1986 will be entering higher education for the first time, over 1.6 million will leave their first institution without receiving a degree. Of those, approximately 1.2 million will leave higher education altogether without ever completing a degree program.
>
> (Tinto 1987: 1)

A theoretical analysis of student attrition was provided by Spady (1970, 1971), who referred to Durkheim's ([1897] 1952) account of suicide. Durkheim had argued that people were disposed towards suicide when two kinds of integration were lacking: value or moral integration, which was based upon sharing similar values and beliefs with the community; and collective or social integration, which was based upon social interactions and the formation of personal affiliations. Spady suggested that the predicament of students deciding whether to continue their studies or to withdraw was broadly analogous to the situation of the individual contemplating suicide. He elaborated this into a detailed descriptive account of the various factors influencing a student's decision either to persist with their studies or to withdraw. Spady (1971) presented results from 683 students at a campus-based university in the US that supported his account.

Tinto (1975) built upon Spady's account in attempting to develop a predictive model of student retention. He argued that it was necessary to distinguish between a student's integration into the academic structure of an institution of higher education and their integration into its social life. Tinto proposed that the first kind of integration would be reflected in the congruency between the students' expectations and the norms and practices of their institutions, whereas the second kind of integration would be reflected in the quality of the social interactions with their teachers and with other students (Figure 8.1). In a later account, Tinto (1987: chapter 4) suggested that a critical factor determining the quality of a students' academic and social integration was how they negotiated the transition from

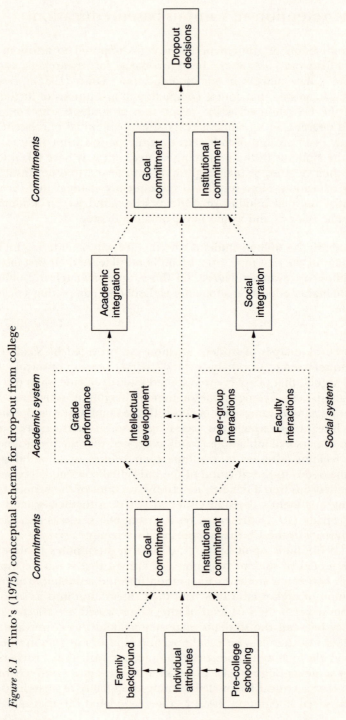

Figure 8.1 Tinto's (1975) conceptual schema for drop-out from college

Source: Tinto 1975: 95. Reprinted by permission of the American Educational Research Association. Copyright 1975

secondary education to higher education. Here, he borrowed from the ideas of the anthropologist, van Gennep ([1908] 1960), concerning the 'rites of passage' that regulated people's access and admission to different social communities.

Clearly, there are important processes at work in the transition to higher education – and not just for students who come directly from secondary education but for adult returners as well. There is limited empirical support for Tinto's analysis, at least in the case of campus-based education (for instance, Christie and Dinham 1991), and it has been used to study other kinds of outcome, such as students' self-reports and personal development (Pascarella and Terenzini 1991: 51–3). However, other researchers have criticized Tinto's use of anthropological analogies as inappropriate (see, for example, Tierney 1992). In the present context, the main problem with his account is that it is based upon a very narrow and traditional view of the 'typical' student. Indeed, Tinto (1982: 693) acknowledged that his primary goal was to account for variations in attrition across a particular type of institution: 4-year residential institutions where membership of a specific community was an essential element of an individual's educational experience.

In elaborating this point, Tinto suggested that the notions of academic or social integration were much less relevant in the case of urban colleges, where most students did not live in the vicinity of the institution itself. In fact, this suggestion was not borne out by subsequent research on the experience of students at such 'commuting colleges', and this led Tinto to amend his proposal:

> But it does not follow . . . that social contact with other persons on campus may not be important to persistence of students in two-year and nonresidential colleges . . . Quite the contrary, there are reasons to suspect that social and intellectual contact beyond the classroom may be as important, if not more important, to persistence in commuting colleges as it is in residential ones . . . But it may apply less for the average student than for those who are marginal with regard to college completion.
>
> (Tinto 1987: 75)

Tinto's original suggestion ignores the fact that students can create their own social networks and it ignores the social relationships and interactions that students have outside the institution with their families and friends. Bean and Metzner (1985) suggested that the latter relationships were particularly important in the case of students who were 'non-traditional' (in other words, students who were older, who lived outside the institution or who studied on a part-time basis), and they put forward an alternative model of student attrition to accommodate these additional factors. Tinto himself agreed that, in this context, social systems outside educational institutions (such as students' families, peer groups or local communities) could have a substantial impact upon their decisions whether to persist with their studies or to withdraw (Tinto 1987: 108, 124). This is of obvious relevance for understanding the situation of students in distance education.

Student retention in distance education

It is sometimes claimed that retention and completion rates in distance education are low, both in absolute terms and when compared with those of campus-based courses. (The figures quoted above with regard to course completion in the US between 1880 and 1980 obviously should be borne in mind when evaluating such claims.) One problem is that accounts of student retention in distance education have focused on the completion of individual course units rather than entire degree programmes (see Bernard and Amundsen 1989). It would appear that many students who take individual course units by distance learning are not expecting to complete a degree or, at least, are not expecting to complete a degree by distance learning. For instance, von Prümmer (1990) found that nearly a quarter of all students taking courses by distance learning in the former West Germany had enrolled in order to test whether they were capable of studying at a campus-based university. This motive was endorsed by an even higher proportion of those students who subsequently discontinued distance education. Other students stated that they had discontinued their studies because they had achieved their personal goals without proceeding to a degree. It is therefore not clear whether 'non-completion' means the same thing in the context of distance education or, indeed, whether it is necessarily undesirable (see Coldeway 1982).

Woodley and Parlett (1983) analysed student retention in distance education at the level of the individual course unit. For one single year at the Open University in the UK they found that the withdrawal rate was 24 per cent of all students who had completed their course registration. In their analyses, they combined cases of student drop-out with those of academic failure into an overall 'wastage rate', of which student withdrawal accounted for nearly 80 per cent. Woodley and Parlett quoted figures from other institutions in Europe and North America that indicated that the wastage rate in distance education varied between 20 and 70 per cent. Within the Open University, some variation in wastage rate could be ascribed to characteristics of the students taking different courses: in particular, their lack of prior experience of studying with the Open University and the number of courses that they were currently taking. Additional variation in wastage rate could be attributed to characteristics of the courses themselves: here, the age of a course, its academic level and the involvement of a mathematics component in the syllabus were positively associated with the wastage rate, whereas the credit value of the course and the inclusion of a residential school were negatively associated with the wastage rate.

In the late 1970s and 1980s, a number of attempts were made to apply Tinto's (1975) model of student retention and attrition to the context of distance learning, with only limited success. Sweet (1986) found that measures of academic and social integration, combined with students' demographic characteristics, were statistically significant predictors of whether students would successfully complete their coursework assignments and examination at a Canadian institution. A much larger study by Taylor *et al.* (1986) encompassed students who were taking courses at distance-learning institutions in five different countries. This attempted to build upon an earlier finding by Rekkedal ([1973] 1984) that reducing the time to return marked assignments could lead to a marked improvement in the course completion rate. Unfortunately, there was no consistent relationship across the five institutions between course completion and any of the variables that were used to try to predict student persistence, including the time to return marked assignments. However, Bernard and Amundsen (1989) criticized this investigation because it did not reflect the major dimensions of Tinto's model and did not include the full range of relevant variables. Bernard and Amundsen themselves examined course completion in three courses delivered by distance education in Canada; they found that all the components in the model were important in predicting course completion but that their relative importance varied from course to course.

In these studies, researchers attempted to explain attrition in terms of students' stated reasons for dropping out, basic demographic data and information about the courses and institutions in question. With hindsight, the main limitation of these studies is that they made little attempt to explore the actual nature and experience of learning in distance education (see Cookson 1989). Indeed, Tinto (1987: 211) made a similar criticism of research into student retention at two-year and non-residential colleges in the US. (Two-year colleges are institutions whose programmes last for two years and are usually intended for high-school graduates in the immediate locality. On satisfactory completion of these programmes, students may receive the qualification of associate of arts or associate of science and may then transfer to some other institution to undertake the final two years of a bachelor's degree.) Nevertheless, several studies conducted during the 1980s repeatedly confirmed that course completion in distance education depended less on academic factors than on non-academic ones, such as students' intentions, goals and approaches to learning and personal support from teachers, counsellors and family members (for example, Rekkedal 1983; Gatz 1986; Siqueira de Freitas and Lynch 1986; Billings 1987).

The DESP inventory

Kember (1989b) argued that it was necessary to build on the accounts devised by Spady (1970), Tinto (1975, 1987) and Bean and Metzner (1985) to produce a model of student retention that was linked to the distinctive context of distance education (Figure 8.2). In this situation, he proposed

Figure 8.2   Kember's (1989b) model of student drop-out from distance education

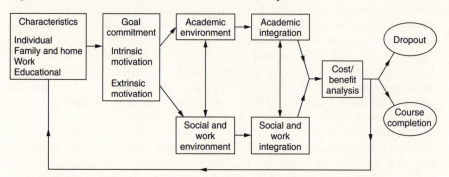

Source: Kember 1989b: 286. From 'A longitudinal model of drop-out from distance education' by David Kember, *The Journal of Higher Education*, Volume 60, Number 3 (May/June 1989). Copyright 1989 by Ohio State University Press. All rights reserved

that 'academic integration' encompassed all of the different facets of course delivery and that 'social integration' depended upon the extent to which students were able to reconcile the demands of their course with the continuing commitments of their work, their families and their social lives (compare this with Hezel and Dirr 1990; see also Kember 1995: 50). Kember went on to refer to the results obtained by Kember and Harper (1987b) regarding the prognostic value of scores on the ASI in internal and external students (see Chapter 6). He argued that, for distance-learning students, adopting a deep approach or a surface approach to studying would be a potential determinant of academic integration, whereas intrinsic motivation and extrinsic motivation represented different aspects of goal commitment which would in turn have consequences for both their academic integration and their social integration.

Initially, Kember (1989a) supported his model by reference to illustrative quotations taken from published case studies of students taking courses by distance learning in the UK (Kennedy and Powell 1976) and Papua New Guinea (Kember 1981), as well as an unpublished case study of distance-learning students in Tasmania. This led him to derive a number of recommendations for ways in which distance-learning institutions might try to reduce attrition (Kember 1990; see also Kember 1995: chapters 13–15). In particular, the roles of support staff could include:

- building collective affiliation through the use of tutoring programmes
- helping students to reorientate their conceptions of knowledge and adapt to the demands and conventions of higher education
- enhancing collective affiliation by helping students with administrative problems
- counselling students on how to integrate their study demands with their work, family and social commitments.

Figure 8.3 Kember's (1995) model of student progress in distance education

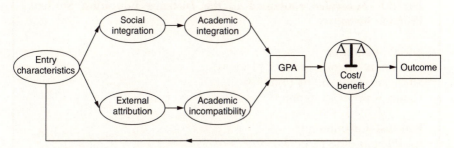

Source: Kember 1995: 64. Reprinted by permission of Educational Technology Publications Inc. Copyright 1995

Further support came from the findings of interview-based investigations in Australia (Roberts *et al.* 1991) and Hong Kong (Kember *et al.* 1990, 1992; see also Kember 1995: chapters 6–10).

Nevertheless, in the light of these findings some key changes were made to the original model and a revised version was presented by Kember (1995) (Figure 8.3). This was based around the two key dimensions of academic integration and social integration. Students who have the appropriate entry characteristics and achieve satisfactory social and academic integration would normally be expected to achieve satisfactory performance in the form of a grade point average or some other measure of attainment. This is represented in the upper (that is, positive) track in Figure 8.3. However, students who fail to achieve satisfactory social integration tend to blame competing work, family and social pressures: that is, they make external attributions for their predicament. Equally, students who fail to achieve satisfactory academic integration tend to be insufficiently integrated into the academic structure of their institution: that is, they demonstrate academic incompatibility. Students who lack the appropriate entry characteristics or who fail to achieve satisfactory social and academic integration would not be expected to achieve satisfactory performance. This is represented in the lower (that is, negative) track in Figure 8.3.

Within this account, the dimensions of goal commitment (intrinsic and extrinsic motivation) are subsumed under the constructs of academic integration and incompatibility. Moreover, there is an explicit assumption that students make the decision either to proceed with their studies or to withdraw in the light of their actual performance in academic assessments. Among other things, this means that the model can be tested not only against measures of persistence or attrition but also against measures of performance such as grade point averages. In other words, it is not just an account of student drop-out but also a model of student progress. Finally, there is a recycling loop to reflect the fact that students continuously reappraise their situation in the light of their changing academic and personal

---

Box 8.1 **Subscales contained in the Distance Education Student Progress inventory**

Social integration
Enrolment encouragement (4 items)
Study encouragement (4 items)
Family support (3 items)

External attribution
Insufficient time (4 items)
Events hinder study (3 items)
Distractions (7 items)
Potential drop-out (3 items)

Academic integration
Deep approach (4 items)
Intrinsic motivation (4 items)
Positive course evaluation (5 items)
Positive telephone counselling (4 items)
Reading habit (3 items)

Academic incompatibility
Surface approach (6 items)
Extrinsic motivation (4 items)
Negative course evaluation (6 items)
Potential drop-out (3 items)
English ability (4 items)

Source: Kember 1995: 232–6

---

circumstances. (In principle, this could also be a feedback loop in which a decision to persist or withdraw had consequences for students' entry characteristics, but this was apparently not considered by Kember.) To test this account against data from large numbers of students it was necessary to develop a quantitative instrument that could be used to measure the various constructs in the model. This was the purpose of the DESP inventory.

In its final version, the DESP inventory consisted of 68 items in 16 subscales (Box 8.1); these were published as an appendix to the book by Kember (1995: 233–6). The subscales were subsumed within four higher-order scales: 'social integration', 'external attribution', 'academic integration' and 'academic incompatibility'. (The 'potential drop-out' subscale is included within both the external attribution scale and the academic incompatibility scale:

Kember 1995: 138.) As in the ASI, respondents are asked to indicate for each item the extent of their agreement or disagreement with a statement along a five-point scale between 'definitely agree', scoring 4, and 'definitely disagree', scoring 0. Once again, the middle category on this scale was 'only to be used if the item does not apply to you or if you find it impossible to give a definite answer' (Kember 1995: 231). For four items, these responses have to be coded in reverse; however, the remaining 64 items all reflect the meanings of the corresponding scales. Finally, the coded responses are summed to obtain a score on each subscale and the scores on the relevant subscales are then summed again to obtain a score on each scale.

Four of the 16 subscales were adapted from the 64-item version of the ASI with changes in wording to make them suitable for use in a distance-learning context: the subscales relating to deep approach and intrinsic motivation contributed to the measurement of academic integration, and the subscales relating to surface approach and extrinsic motivation contributed to the measurement of its converse, academic incompatibility. The instrument was developed and validated with large numbers of distance-learning students at several institutions in Hong Kong (for whom it was translated into Chinese, as English was their second language). The subscales exhibited satisfactory levels of internal consistency and factor analyses carried out on the subscale scores confirmed the existence of the four main scales. Moreover, the DESP inventory achieved a fairly high degree of success in predicting both the students' current grade point average and the proportion of courses that students had failed to complete (Kember *et al.* 1991, 1992, 1994; see also Kember 1995: chapters 5, 11 and 12).

Further research using the DESP inventory in distance education

Joughin *et al.* (1992) administered a version of the DESP inventory to 1843 students who were taking distance-learning courses with an Australian university. They focused on the responses given to the 18 items in the four subscales that had been taken from the ASI. They conducted a factor analysis of these responses and extracted four factors. Although these broadly corresponded to the four subscales that had originally been defined by Entwistle and Ramsden (1983: see Box 6.1, p. 90), there were some discrepancies. In particular, one item from the subscale relating to a surface approach, 'When I am reading I try to memorize important facts which may come in useful later', showed a significant loading on the 'deep approach' factor. This led Joughin *et al.* to argue that even Australian students might combine memorizing and understanding, an approach to studying previously found only among students in China and Hong Kong (see Chapter 2). Moreover, one item from the subscale relating to a deep approach, 'I often find myself questioning things that I hear in lectures or read in books', did *not* generate a significant loading on the factor in question.

Joughin *et al.* raised the idea that distance education failed to promote a critical or questioning attitude on the part of students.

Potentially, this should be a matter of some concern to distance educators. A subsequent study by Anderson and Garrison (1995), which used an *ad hoc* questionnaire, identified two different models of instructional design in the delivery of distance-learning courses by teleconferencing. In one model, the teleconference sessions were employed to support discussion and interaction among the students in a 'community of learners'. In the other model, the sessions were simply employed as 'independent learner support' to monitor the progress of individual students and ensure that they were satisfying the institutional demands for passing their courses. Anderson and Garrison suggested that the first model was far more likely to foster critical thinking skills than the second model. This is consistent with the idea that approaches to studying depend on the context of learning, in so far as for all students (but especially for those studying by distance learning) the 'context' of learning encompasses the educational technology available to support their learning and how it is used in practice (Brown 1982; Moore 1989; Hezel and Dirr 1990).

Nevertheless, there are two basic reasons for questioning the validity of the inference drawn by Joughin *et al.* The first has to do with the phrasing of the relevant item. According to their own account, Joughin *et al.* used the original wording of the item, 'I often find myself questioning things that I hear in lectures or read in books', as used by Entwistle and Ramsden (1983: 228). The inclusion of a reference to 'lectures' in this item might have led students taking courses by distance learning to respond that the item simply did not apply to them. This would have led to a reduction in the amount of variance to be explained on this item and this, in turn, would have reduced its loading on any of the factors obtained in the factor analysis. In contrast, Kember *et al.* (1991) employed the modified wording, as used by Harper and Kember (1986), 'I often find myself questioning things that I read in books or study materials' (Kember 1995: 234), which would have caused no problems for students taking courses by distance learning.

A different reason for rejecting the inference made by Joughin *et al.* is that they did not obtain any comparison data from campus-based students. This makes it very difficult to interpret their findings because one simply does not know whether a similar factor solution would have been produced if campus-based students were asked to complete the DESP inventory. In fact, few studies have reported the results of factor analyses carried out on responses to the individual items in the ASI. There is, however, one precedent for the pattern of results obtained by Joughin *et al.* in my very first study using the 32-item version of the ASI (Richardson 1990) with campus-based students in the UK (see Chapter 7). Here, too, the item, 'I often find myself questioning things that I hear in lectures or read in books', failed to show a significant loading on the factor identified with deep approach. In short, there is no evidence at all from the study by Joughin *et al.* that distance-learning students lack a critical or questioning attitude. Indeed, the most that one could infer is that both campus-based and distance-learning students might, on occasion, fail to produce significant loadings on some of the individual items that constitute the DESP inventory. This simply provides further confirmation of the general conclusion that was reached in Chapters 6 and 7 – that the different versions of the ASI exhibit the same factor structure in distance-learning and campus-based students.

Thompson (1999) used the DESP inventory to try to predict persistence or attrition in external students in the fourth year of an education programme at an Australian university. Responses were obtained from 197 students who completed the units for which they registered during the relevant semester and from 61 students who withdrew from at least one unit during the semester. Thompson calculated their scores on 15 of the subscales, omitting the subscale concerned with English ability, and used the subscale scores in discriminant analyses to predict whether or not each respondent had completed the course units for which they were registered. (In the absence of any information, it would of course be possible to make correct predictions for 50 per cent of the students simply by random guessing.) Thompson found that the academic outcome could be correctly predicted in 67.5 per cent of the students using the scores on all 15 subscales. This suggests that the DESP inventory was moderately useful in determining which students persisted with the courses for which they were registered.

However, the detailed findings of Thompson's study were less promising. Only four of the 15 subscales showed a statistically significant relationship with the relevant outcome: withdrawal from one or more units was positively related to the students' scores on the subscales concerned with insufficient time, events hinder study, potential drop-out and negative course evaluation. Inspection of Box 8.1 reveals that three of these subscales come from the 'external attribution' scale and, indeed, this was the only one of the four scales to show a significant relationship with the outcome in question. Conversely, none of the four subscales taken from the ASI showed a statistically significant relationship with student withdrawal. In a separate discriminant analysis, Thompson found that the academic outcome could be correctly predicted in only 56.1 per cent of the students when using the scores on these four subscales alone, which is not very different from what could be achieved by random guessing. This suggests that approaches to studying are not, in fact, of much importance in predicting student persistence or withdrawal.

I mentioned earlier that it is not clear whether 'non-completion' means the same thing in campus-based education and distance education. One issue in the case of Thompson's study (which she herself acknowledged) is that the student population and the outcome measure were both different from those employed in the investigations carried out by Kember and his colleagues. Thompson's respondents were experienced students who had already obtained a bachelor's degree and who were in their fourth year of academic study towards a professionally relevant qualification. It is quite possible that their decisions to discontinue a unit reflected their lack of interest in the particular course content rather than academic failure in any sense. (Thompson did not specify whether the units in question were 'core' or optional courses.) Consequently, such decisions are likely to depend upon idiosyncratic factors rather than upon their academic integration or social circumstances.

Another point is that any effects of the four ASI subscales upon student withdrawal might have been mediated by other factors being tapped by the DESP inventory. In this case, Thompson's statistical analyses would simply have 'controlled out' any contribution they might have made to predicting the relevant academic outcome. There is some evidence for this in the results of a factor analysis that she carried out on the students' scores on the 15 subscales. The primary factor was positively related to students' scores on surface approach and extrinsic motivation and was negatively related to their scores on deep approach and intrinsic motivation. However, it was also related to their scores on six other subscales, four of which also came from the scales concerned with academic integration and academic incompatibility. This suggests that student attrition is related to a single dimension in which approaches to studying play a central role.

Concluding summary

- Course completion or student attrition is a serious problem in campus-based education. The theoretical accounts devised since the 1970s suggest that it depends on the integration of the student into the academic structure and social life of an institution of higher education.
- Student attrition is also regarded as a problem in distance education. However, it is not at all clear whether 'non-completion' means the same thing in campus-based education as it does in distance education, or whether it should be regarded as something that is undesirable at all.
- Kember's (1995) model of student retention, based on similar notions of academic and social integration, appears to provide a useful account of persistence and withdrawal in distance education that is linked to prevalent ideas about approaches to studying in higher education.
- The DESP inventory seems to provide an adequate measure of the constructs underlying this model and is useful in predicting different measures of outcome. The DESP subscales drawn from the ASI show the same factor structure in campus-based and distance-learning students.

9

The Inventory of Learning Styles

In Chapter 8, I mentioned that the SPQ and the ASI were developed for use in investigations into student learning in campus-based institutions of higher education and were not specifically intended to characterize students who were taking courses in distance education. In contrast, the DESP inventory was designed to measure relevant characteristics of distance-learning students. Nevertheless, the subscales in the DESP inventory concerned with approaches to studying were simply borrowed from the existing ASI with minor alterations to their wording to render them suitable for use in a distance-learning context. In this regard, the DESP inventory was essentially parasitic upon research tools that had been designed to measure approaches to studying in campus-based students.

A different research strategy was adopted by Vermunt and van Rijswijk (1988), who set out to develop a valid, reliable and usable instrument that would measure differences in approaches to learning among students taking courses for the first time with the Dutch Open University. This institution delivers courses primarily through specially prepared correspondence materials with tutorial support available at regional study centres. In developing their instrument, Vermunt and van Rijswijk built on the results of a qualitative investigation in which first-year students who had recently embarked on courses with the Dutch Open University were interviewed about their approaches, conceptions and orientations towards studying. As explained in detail in Chapter 4, Vermunt and van Rijswijk distinguished between: (a) the processing activities used by students to learn specific materials; and (b) the regulation activities used by students to coordinate their own processing activities. In addition, whether and how students are able to regulate their own learning activities depends upon their conceptions (or 'mental models') of learning and upon their motivation or orientation towards their studies (see also Vermunt 1996).

The 144-item version of the Inventory of Learning Styles

On the basis of the different comments made by their interviewees, Vermunt and van Rijswijk (1988) assembled a list of 241 statements concerning study activities, motives and conceptions to construct a new instrument, the Inventory of Learning Styles (ILS). The first section of this instrument was concerned with the study activities involved in the processing of course content (50 items) and the regulation of learning (50 items). For each item, respondents were instructed to indicate how often they engaged in the relevant study activity using a five-point scale from 'I seldom or never do this', scoring 1, to 'I (almost) always do this', scoring 5. The second section was concerned with study orientations (50 items) and with students' conceptions of learning, education and cooperation (91 items). Here, respondents were instructed to indicate the extent of their agreement or disagreement with each listed motive or attitude using a five-point scale from 'totally disagree', scoring 1, to 'totally agree', scoring 5. Responses were obtained from a total of 211 students who had taken at least one course with the Dutch Open University.

Vermunt and van Rijswijk used factor analysis to identify those items that were most strongly associated with each of the four components of the ILS (processing, regulation, orientations and conceptions). On the basis of the results, they constructed a revised version of their instrument, which contained just 144 items in 16 subscales, grouped in turn under four main scales. These scales and subscales are listed in Box 9.1. Vermunt and van Rijswijk then calculated the scores obtained by their respondents on these 16 subscales and carried out a further factor analysis on these scores. This yielded four independent factors:

- One factor showed positive loadings on the subscales concerned with self-regulation, the construction of knowledge, a deep approach, an elaborative approach and a personally interested orientation. This was taken to represent a self-regulated and 'meaning directed' learning style.
- A second factor showed positive loadings on the subscales that were concerned with external regulation, the intake of knowledge, a surface approach, a certificate directed orientation and a self-test directed orientation. This was taken to represent an externally regulated and 'reproduction directed' learning style.
- A third factor showed positive loadings on the subscales concerned with a vocation directed orientation, the use of knowledge, an elaborative approach and a certificate directed orientation, together with a negative loading on the subscale concerned with a personally interested orientation. This was taken to represent an 'application directed' learning style.
- The fourth factor showed positive loadings on the subscales concerned with a lack of regulation, an ambivalent orientation, cooperation and a

Box 9.1 **Subscales contained in the 144-item version of the Inventory of Learning Styles**

Processing of subject matter
Surface approach (12 items)
Deep approach (12 items)
Elaborative approach (6 items)

Regulation of learning
External regulation (12 items)
Self-regulation (12 items)
Lack of regulation (6 items)

Study orientations
Certificate directed (6 items)
Self-test directed (6 items)
Vocation directed (6 items)
Personally interested (6 items)
Ambivalent (6 items)

Conceptions of learning, education and cooperation
Intake of knowledge (12 items)
Construction of knowledge (12 items)
Use of knowledge (6 items)
Stimulating education (12 items)
Cooperation (12 items)

Source: Vermunt and van Rijswijk 1988: 661, 663

stimulating education. This was taken to represent an unregulated or 'problematic' learning style.

In Chapter 4, I described the four qualitatively different learning 'styles' that Vermunt (1996) arrived at on the basis of the accounts given by campus-based and distance-learning students in structured interviews (see, in particular, Box 4.2, p. 58). The detailed specification of the four learning styles is remarkably close to the composition and interpretation of the four factors obtained by Vermunt and van Rijswijk on the basis of the responses given by distance-learning students to the ILS. This is an excellent example of 'triangulation' in educational and social research: that is, the crossvalidation of one's findings by the use of both quantitative and qualitative methods.

Vermunt and van Rijswijk went on to examine the relationship between their students' scores on these 16 subscales and their educational experience. First, the respondents were divided into those who had already completed a course in higher education before studying with the Dutch Open University and those who had not. Those students who had previous experience of higher education obtained lower scores on the subscales that were concerned with a self-test directed orientation, the intake of knowledge, a certificate directed orientation, external regulation and a lack of regulation. In other words, they were less likely to exhibit an externally regulated and reproduction directed learning style than those students with no previous experience of higher education. This is consistent with the proposal by Säljö (1979a,b), which was mentioned in Chapter 3, that learning may become 'thematic' in the light of experience of higher education.

Next, Vermunt and van Rijswijk identified amongst their respondents those who had relatively little experience of studying with the Dutch Open University (at most 50 hours of study time), and those who had studied more than two complete units (typically representing at least 200 hours of study time). The more experienced students obtained higher scores on the subscales that were concerned with a certificate directed orientation, a vocation directed orientation and external regulation but lower scores on the subscales that were concerned with an ambivalent orientation, a lack of regulation, an elaborative approach and cooperation. In other words, although the more experienced students were less likely to exhibit an unregulated or problematic learning style, they were also more likely to exhibit an externally regulated and reproduction directed learning style than students with less experience of the Open University.

Of course, groups of students with more or less experience of studying in distance education may differ on a number of other variables that might in principle influence their approaches to studying and hence their responses to instruments such as the ILS. Thus, these latter conclusions need to be interpreted with some caution as they were based upon simple pairwise comparisons that failed to control for the confounded effects of other variables. Nevertheless, they indicate that the Dutch Open University was conspicuously unsuccessful in fostering more appropriate approaches and orientations to studying on the part of its students. In this respect, it is far from unique: in Chapter 5 I mentioned that a very similar observation had been made with respect to campus-based institutions on the basis of the findings of research using the SPQ (Biggs 1987; Gow and Kember 1990; Volet *et al.* 1994). However, in Chapter 6, I cited evidence obtained using different versions of the ASI, which suggested that this trend was not observed at the Open University in the UK (Richardson *et al.* 1999) and that it could be avoided and even reversed by the introduction of a problem-based curriculum (Coles 1985; Newble and Clarke 1986, 1987).

The 120-item version of the ILS

Another difficulty in interpreting the findings obtained by Vermunt and van Rijswijk is that they did not include in their study any comparison group of campus-based students. This was remedied in a subsequent invest-igation by Vermunt (1998), who obtained responses to the 144-item ver-sion of the ILS from a further 443 students at the Dutch Open University. Vermunt then pooled these with the responses produced by the 211 stu-dents who had participated in the original study by Vermunt and van Rijswijk. From the 654 sets of responses, Vermunt devised a revised version of the ILS that contained just 120 items in 20 subscales. There is currently no published source for either this or the earlier versions of the ILS, but copies of the 120-item version in Dutch or English together with a scoring guide can be obtained from the author: Professor Jan Vermunt, Department of Educational Research and Development, Maastricht University, P.O. Box 616, 6200 MS Maastricht, The Netherlands.

Vermunt and van Rijswijk (1988) had used the 144-item version of the ILS as the basis for a self-instructional package designed to help distance-learning students develop their learning skills and their conceptions of learning. Vermunt (1995) extended this package, incorporating the 120-item version of the ILS. It was then evaluated in a cohort of psychology students who had enrolled at a campus-based university in the Netherlands. In the course of this evaluation, Vermunt compared the students' subscale scores on the ILS with those of other students who had used the package in the course of their studies with the Dutch Open University. He found that the two groups differed significantly in their scores on eight of the subscales:

- The distance-learning students tended to obtain higher scores than the campus-based students on the subscales concerned with the analytic processing strategy, the external regulation strategy directed at learning processes and the personally interested learning orientation.
- The campus-based students tended to obtain higher scores than the distance-learning students on the subscales concerned with memorizing and rehearsing, a lack of regulation, the mental model or conception devoted to stimulating education, the mental model or conception devoted to cooperative learning, and the vocational learning orientation.

Vermunt concluded that in general the campus-based students were more likely to exhibit an undirected learning style than the distance-learning students. It is, however, difficult to give a clear interpretation of these findings. Vermunt noted that the campus-based students and the distance-learning students were different both in their mean ages (25.1 years and 34.0 years, respectively) and in their gender distribution (67 per cent women versus 33 per cent women, respectively). More important, the two groups had also been exposed to different versions of the self-instructional package and the campus-based students had additionally received two tutorials at which the contents of the package had been discussed. Although the campus-based students rated their programme more favourably than did the distance-learning students, one possibility is that the extended pro-gramme tended to undermine their existing learning styles.

Table 9.1 Mean scores obtained on the 120-item version of the Inventory of Learning Styles by distance-learning and campus-based students

Subscales	Distance learning	Campus based	Effect size
Processing strategies			
Deep processing: relating and structuring	3.56	3.36	+0.17**
Deep processing: critical processing	3.16	2.81	+0.28**
Stepwise processing: memorizing and rehearsing	2.63	2.83	−0.15**
Stepwise processing: analysing	2.92	2.73	+0.16**
Concrete processing	3.03	2.81	+0.18**
Regulation strategies			
Self-regulation: learning process and results	2.45	2.54	−0.07
Self-regulation: learning content	2.50	1.87	+0.54**
External regulation: learning process	3.45	3.08	+0.29**
External regulation: learning results	3.51	3.38	+0.10*
Lack of regulation	2.15	2.40	−0.21**
Mental models of learning			
Construction of knowledge	3.69	3.52	+0.17**
Intake of knowledge	3.47	3.53	−0.05
Use of knowledge	3.75	3.91	−0.16**
Stimulating education	2.85	3.13	−0.23**
Cooperative learning	2.25	3.01	−0.63**
Learning orientations			
Personally interested	3.69	3.17	+0.47**
Certificate oriented	3.09	3.28	−0.15**
Self-test oriented	2.59	2.83	−0.18**
Vocation oriented	3.11	3.79	−0.54**
Ambivalent	1.75	2.07	−0.30**

Source: Vermunt 1998: 161
$*p < 0.05$, two-tailed test; $**p < 0.005$, two-tailed test

Vermunt (1998) then administered the 120-item version of the ILS to first-year students drawn from all of the subject areas taught at a campus-based university in the Netherlands, with minor changes in wording to render certain items appropriate for campus-based students. Table 9.1 shows the mean scores obtained on the 20 subscales by the 654 distance-learning students and by 795 campus-based students. From the information provided in Vermunt's article, I compared the two sets of data using two-tailed Student's t tests; the comparisons that are statistically significant at the 5 per cent level are indicated in Table 9.1 by asterisks. However, as mentioned in Chapter 6, Harper and Kember (1986) argued that a more stringent significance level should be used to guard against the increased probability of making Type I errors (that is, of obtaining spuriously significant results) when carrying out large numbers of independent statistical tests. Consequently, those comparisons that are significant using the more stringent criterion of 0.5 per cent are indicated by two asterisks. There are significant differences between the groups on 18 of the 20 subscales, and 17 of the differences remain significant at this more stringent level.

A separate issue is that comparisons may be statistically significant and yet be of little practical importance, which is especially likely if the groups in question are very large. This issue can be addressed by deriving a measure of the size of the relevant effect (see Richardson 1996). When two separate groups are being compared, the most common measure of effect size is computed by standardizing the difference between their respective means against the pooled within-group standard deviation; thus, an effect size of 0.5 means that the two groups differ on average by an amount equal to one-half of their standard deviation. The standardized mean difference obtained from two samples is known to overestimate the standardized mean difference in the populations from which the samples have been drawn. However, the former can be adjusted by multiplying it by a simple correction factor and the bias is quite small with very large samples (Hedges and Olkin 1985: 76–85). Table 9.1 shows the standardized mean differences for the 20 subscales of the ILS, corrected for sampling bias. Any effect sizes that are smaller than 0.2 in their absolute magnitude might in principle be dismissed as being of little practical importance (Cohen 1969: 22–4) but this still leaves nine differences that represent effect sizes larger than this.

Vermunt went on to confirm that the internal consistency and the test–retest reliability of each of the 20 subscales were broadly satisfactory. Factor analyses that were carried out separately on the scores obtained by the campus-based students and the distance-learning students led to solutions that were very similar to each other. As in Vermunt and van Rijswijk's (1988) earlier study, there were four factors representing styles of learning that were described as meaning directed, reproduction directed, application directed and undirected. In general, the distance-learning students tended to obtain higher scores than the campus-based students on the subscales that were associated with a meaning directed learning style, but they tended to obtain lower scores than the campus-based students on the subscales that were associated with an application directed learning style and an undirected learning style. The differences on the subscales associated with a reproduction directed learning style were inconsistent in direction.

These findings suggest that students in distance education exhibit learning styles that are more desirable than those shown by campus-based students, in the sense that they are more consistent with the avowed aims of institutions of higher education. Nevertheless, one should be cautious about drawing the inference that these differences in learning style are actually the consequence of differences in the mode of course delivery. As always, one must remember the demographic differences that exist between campus-based and distance-learning students and which may, in principle, lead to differences in their approaches to studying. In the case of Vermunt's

(1998) study, an obvious confounded variable was that of the participants' ages: the average age of the distance-learning students was 36.5 years, whereas that of the campus-based students was only 22.5 years (Vermunt, personal communication, November 10, 1997).

As I mentioned in Chapter 4, Gibbs *et al.* (1984) claimed on the basis of interview data that an intrinsic or personal orientation was common both in distance-learning students and in older campus-based students. Thus, the apparent difference in learning styles obtained by Vermunt might have been due to the fact that the distance-learning students in his study were older than the campus-based students. However, Vermunt and van Rijswijk (1988) had examined the role of age as a predictor of scores on the ILS and their findings do not support this interpretation:

- The ages of the 211 participants varied between 20 and 75 years, and so their study should have been able to detect any effects of practical importance. Nevertheless, age did not show a statistically significant correlation with their scores on four of the five subscales measuring a meaning directed learning style, and there was only a weak positive relationship with their scores on the fifth subscale. It is therefore implausible that the tendency for distance-learning students to obtain higher scores than campus-based students on the subscales measuring this learning style could be due to confounded differences in age.
- Conversely, Vermunt and van Rijswijk found that there was a significant positive correlation between age and the scores on three of the five subscales measuring a reproduction directed learning style, yet there was no consistent pattern of differences between campus-based and distance-learning students on the subscales measuring this learning style. If distance-learning students were more likely to exhibit a meaning directed learning style just because they were older, why were they not more likely to exhibit a reproduction directed learning style, too?
- Vermunt and van Rijswijk found that there was a statistically significant negative correlation between age and the scores on four of the five subscales measuring an application directed learning style. Vermunt found, correspondingly, that distance-learning students obtained lower scores than campus-based students on the subscales measuring this learning style. In this case, the apparent differences between campus-based and distance-learning students in their subscale scores could in principle be ascribed to the confounded difference in their age.
- Finally, Vermunt and van Rijswijk found no significant relationship between age and their participants' scores on three of the four subscales measuring an undirected learning style; there was a weak positive relationship with their scores on the fourth subscale. In other words, older students are, if anything, more likely to exhibit this style than younger students. Nevertheless, the (older) distance-learning students actually tended to obtain lower scores than the (younger) campus-based students on the subscales measuring this learning style.

Figure 9.1 Vermunt's (1998) model of the regulation of constructive learning processes

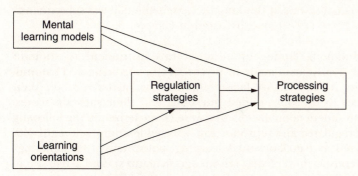

Source: Vermunt 1998: 153. Reproduced with permission from the *British Journal of Educational Psychology*, © The British Psychological Society 1998

Finally, Vermunt showed that, in both groups of students, their scores on the five subscales measuring different regulation strategies could be predicted by their scores on the subscales measuring different mental models of learning and different learning orientations. Moreover, their scores on the five subscales measuring different processing strategies could be predicted by their scores on the subscales measuring different regulation strategies, mental models and learning orientations. These findings were taken as evidence for Vermunt and van Rijswijk's original assumption that the influence of students' mental models and learning orientations on their processing strategies was largely mediated by their use of different regulation strategies (Figure 9.1). The general pattern of predictive relationships was similar in these two groups of students and this implies that the findings are highly generalizable between campus-based education and distance education.

Further research in campus-based education

Lonka and Lindblom-Ylänne (1996) constructed a composite instrument containing open-ended questions and items from a number of previous inventories:

- the 14 items constituting the subscales of the ASI concerned with deep approach, surface approach and achievement motivation (see Chapter 6);
- 50 items selected from the subscales of the 144-item version of the ILS concerned with the regulation of learning (external regulation, self-regulation and lack of regulation) and with conceptions of learning, education and cooperation (intake of knowledge, construction of knowledge, use of knowledge, stimulating education and cooperation);

- seven items selected by Ryan (1984) from the Checklist of Educational Views (CLEV), which had been designed by Perry *et al.* (1968) to measure adherence to dualist ways of thinking in the scheme that was subsequently described by Perry (1970) and discussed in Chapter 3.

Lonka and Lindblom-Ylänne administered this instrument to students in their first or final year of study in psychology or medicine at a campus-based university in Finland. A factor analysis was carried out on their coded responses to the open-ended questions and their subscale scores. This yielded four independent factors that were characterized in the following way: externally regulated and reproduction directed learning; self-regulated, meaning directed and goal-oriented learning; constructivist epistemology (involving the construction of new knowledge structures); and active use of knowledge. The first and second factors were very similar to Vermunt and van Rijswijk's (1988) reproduction directed and meaning directed learning styles. The researchers then computed the respondents' scores on these four factors and examined the possible effects of discipline (medicine versus psychology) and academic level (first-year versus fifth-year).

The medical students obtained higher scores than the psychology students on the first factor and the fourth factor, but the psychology students obtained higher scores than the medical students on the third factor. Thus, medical students were more active yet reproduction directed, whereas psychology students were more likely to exhibit constructive ideas of learning and knowledge. This was thought to reflect the more factual demands of the curriculum in medicine as opposed to a more constructivist approach in teaching and learning psychology. The effects of academic level were largely confined to constructivist epistemology, where the fifth-year students tended to obtain higher scores than the first-year students. Adherence to dualism on the CLEV varied with both discipline and academic level: medical students were more dualist than psychology students and first-year students were more dualist than fifth-year students. When the students were classified as dualists or relativists according to their responses to the CLEV, the dualists were more likely to exhibit a reproduction directed learning style and less likely to exhibit a constructivist epistemology than the relativists; however, there was no significant difference between the dualists and the relativists in terms of their scores on meaning directed learning.

Severiens and ten Dam (1997) obtained responses to the ILS from a total of 432 students of 'adult secondary education' in the Netherlands. A factor analysis carried out on the students' subscale scores identified four factors. Three of these corresponded to the meaning-directed, reproduction-directed and undirected learning styles described by Vermunt (1998). However, the fourth factor did not reflect the application-directed learning style. Instead, it represented high scores on the mental models concerned with use of knowledge and stimulating education and on the self-test directed and vocation directed study orientations. Severiens and ten Dam argued that this learning style was typical of secondary adult education, and they called it the 'prove yourself' directed learning style.

In Chapter 3, I referred to another study by Severiens and ten Dam (1998) in which they sought to confirm the developmental scheme devised by Baxter Magolda (1992) through interviews conducted with a further 53 students of adult secondary education in the Netherlands. Severiens and ten Dam noted that there was a broad parallel between this developmental scheme and the classification of learning styles described by Vermunt (1996), which was discussed in Chapter 4. They gave their students the subscales from the 120-item version of the ILS concerned with conceptions or mental models of learning and compared the scores obtained by students who were classified as demonstrating 'absolute knowing', 'transitional knowing' and 'independent knowing' in Baxter Magolda's scheme. Unfortunately, none of the comparisons was statistically significant. Severiens and ten Dam concluded that the apparent conceptual similarity between these two theoretical frameworks could not be confirmed empirically.

However, Baxter Magolda (1998) pointed out a different possibility: that respondents who were at different developmental levels had given similar ratings to ILS items in accordance with their different interpretations of the items themselves. As Strack and Schwarz (1992) pointed out, the responses given to standardized questionnaires are communicative and collaborative acts. In the absence of any additional guidance, respondents will endeavour to make sense of the items in questionnaires about learning and knowledge in terms of their own conceptions of learning and knowledge. One might argue that the apparent discrepancy was not between the two theoretical frameworks but rather between the use of quantitative and qualitative research methods. Indeed, the results obtained by Lonka and Lindblom-Ylänne (1996) showed that students' scores on the subscales of the ILS do correlate with their intellectual development when the latter is assessed using a quantitative instrument. Conversely, one would expect to find empirical confirmation of the relations between Baxter Magolda's scheme and Vermunt's (1996) classification of learning styles if both frameworks were assessed by means of qualitative methods. It is, in fact, puzzling why Severiens and ten Dam chose to use the ILS at all, as Vermunt's model had been based upon students' accounts in structured interviews rather than their ratings of the items in the ILS.

Busato *et al.* (1998) used the 120-item version of the ILS to explore whether there were any systematic changes in learning styles during the undergraduate programme in psychology at one campus-based institution in the Netherlands. They obtained responses to the ILS from 329 first-year students who had attended an obligatory test session. They also carried out a postal survey of samples of students in Years 2–5 of the same programme and obtained responses to the ILS from between 32 and 45 students in each cohort. Although there were statistically significant fluctuations in the scores obtained by students in different cohorts on the scale measuring a meaning directed learning style, there was no systematic trend on any of the scales

over the 5 years of the programme. In three of the five cohorts, the scores
on the scale measuring an undirected learning style showed a significant
negative correlation with the number of study points (or course credits)
obtained towards their degree; however, there were no statistically significant relationships involving any of the other three scales in the ILS.

Unfortunately, there are serious problems of sampling bias in this study.
The collection of data from an obligatory test session ensured a response
rate of 94 per cent from the students in Year 1. In passing, it should be
noted that, in other countries such as Australia and the US, requiring
psychology students to serve as research participants is nowadays generally
regarded as ethically questionable unless appropriate and equitable alternative activities are available for those students who do not wish to participate
(Coulson 1999). In contrast, the use of a postal survey for the other four
cohorts yielded at best a response rate of 22.5 per cent. In Chapter 6,
I pointed out that students who respond to surveys are known to be different from those students who do not on many variables, including their
approaches to studying (see Watkins and Hattie 1985). In the study by Busato
et al., the effects of sampling bias might have counteracted any genuine
differences between the first-year students and the other cohorts in their
scores on the scales of the ILS. A separate problem is that the relatively
small size of the groups sampled from the other four cohorts would have
made it more difficult to obtain significant results using a cross-sectional
research design (that is, a design comparing different groups of students).

Busato *et al.* also reported two sets of data obtained using a longitudinal
design (that is, one that compared the same group of students assessed on
different occasions). Of the students sampled from Year 2 of the programme,
32 had completed the ILS during an obligatory test session held 14 months
previously during their first year of study. A comparison of the scores they
obtained on the two occasions revealed no significant differences on any of
the four scales. In a similar manner, of the students sampled from Year 3 of
the programme, 26 had in fact completed the ILS on two different occasions during their first year of study in connection with another research
project. In this case, there was a statistically significant trend for their scores
on the scale measuring a meaning directed learning style to increase between Year 1 and Year 3. Unfortunately, there is no guarantee that this
(relatively modest) trend was not peculiar to the small proportion of the
cohort who chose to respond to the postal survey containing the ILS.

In Vermunt's (1998) model, Vermetten *et al.* (1999a) suggested that learning orientations and mental models were relatively stable but that the students' choice of processing or regulation strategies might well depend upon
the content, context and assessment of a particular course. They assessed
two successive cohorts of students who were each taking four different
courses in the second semester of the first year of the law degree at a
campus-based university in the Netherlands. Vermetten *et al.* compiled a
questionnaire consisting of 50 items from the subscales of the ILS concerned with processing and regulation strategies, which were amended so

as to refer to a specific course. (They collapsed together the two sub-scales concerned with self-regulation and the two subscales concerned with external regulation.) These items were supplemented by 25 other items about problems that students might encounter while studying.

The questionnaire was then employed in a postal survey of students taking all four courses. The data analyses were confined to those students who had returned questionnaires about all of the courses and partly for this reason the overall response rates were quite low (29 and 22 per cent, respectively, for the two cohorts). However, the key question was whether there would be significant differences among the scores obtained by the same students across the four courses. There were in fact significant differences on six of the eight subscales in the first cohort and on seven of the eight subscales in the second cohort. The greatest variation across the four courses was apparent in the students' ratings of concrete processing and lack of regulation: two courses, in particular, seemed to receive more positive ratings than the other two courses as the result of the teachers' use of vivid material, practical examples and clear organization.

Nevertheless, Vermetten *et al.* (1999b) argued that there was genuine intellectual development as students proceeded through higher education and that this should be exhibited in changes in scores on other subscales of the ILS. They added to the 50 items in their previous questionnaire another 50 items concerned with mental learning models and study orientations. Moreover, they modified the instructions so that the respondents were asked to report specifically about the past semester. Vermetten *et al.* administered the resulting instrument to students in four departments of a campus-based university in the Netherlands at the end of their first and third semesters. It was distributed on both occasions in a postal survey and completed copies were returned from both surveys by 276 students.

Separate factor analyses conducted on the students' subscale scores in the two semesters tended to confirm the intended scale structure of the four major learning styles, though this was clearer after the third semester than after the first. All the correlation coefficients computed from the two scores obtained on each subscale were greater than 0.50, reflecting reasonable stability over a period of 1 year. Nevertheless, there were also statistically significant changes on eight of the scales between the two occasions:

- With regard to their processing strategies, the students showed a significant increase on the two subscales concerned with deep processing (relating and structuring, critical processing) and a significant increase on the subscale concerned with concrete processing.
- With regard to their regulation strategies, the students showed a significant increase on the subscale concerned with self-regulation.
- With regard to their mental models of learning, the students showed a significant decrease on the subscale concerned with intake of knowledge.
- With regard to their learning orientations, the students showed a significant increase on the subscales concerned with vocational orientation and

personal interest, and a significant decrease on the subscale concerned with certificate orientation.

Vermetten *et al.* concluded that the students as a group showed higher scores on the subscales defining a meaning-directed learning style and that, in this respect, they showed improvement in their reported quality of learning within the early years of university study. However, it should be noted that the response rates to the two postal surveys were only 42 per cent and 31 per cent, respectively, and in principle it is possible that the improved quality of learning occurred only in those students who complied with the request to participate in this study on both occasions. Vermetten *et al.* in fact had the data to investigate this notion, as they could have carried out a between-subjects comparison based on the students who had responded to only one of the surveys. If they had found a similar improvement in the reported quality of learning of these students, one might be more confident that this was a general phenomenon. However, they reported only the within-subjects comparison based on the students who responded to both of the surveys.

Concluding summary

- The ILS was constructed by Vermunt and van Rijswijk (1988) on the basis of students' accounts of their activities, motives and conceptions of learning in distance education and especially at the Dutch Open University. It was motivated by the idea that the influence of students' conceptions and orientations on their processing activities was mediated by their use of different regulation activities. It appears to measure four basic 'learning styles'.
- Using the 144-item version of the ILS, Vermunt and van Rijswijk found that students with previous experience of higher education were less likely to show an externally regulated and reproduction directed learning style. However, students with more experience of studying in distance education were more likely to show such a learning style. This indicates that the Dutch Open University fails to promote the adoption of appropriate approaches to studying.
- Vermunt (1998) found differences between campus-based and distance-learning students on most subscales in the 120-item version of the ILS. In general, the distance-learning students showed more desirable approaches to studying, and some differences were sufficiently large to be of practical significance. In principle, the differences could be due to confounded age differences, but Vermunt and van Rijswijk's detailed results do not support such an account.
- The pattern of relationships between students' scores on the subscales measuring different mental models of learning, orientations, regulation strategies and processing strategies tends to support the original theoretical

assumptions underlying the derivation of the ILS. However, they also imply that essentially the same mechanisms are at work both in campus-based education and in distance education.

- Students' scores on the subscales of the ILS that are concerned with processing activities and regulation activities demonstrate variability dependent upon the content, the context and the demands of particular courses. Their scores on the subscales that are concerned with learning orientations and mental models seem to be more stable, but it has been possible to show genuine improvement in the quality of learning during the early years of higher education.

10

Other Inventories and Questionnaires

I shall conclude my account of approaches to studying in campus-based and distance education by describing some other inventories and questionnaires that have been employed to investigate differences in how students go about learning in higher education. These are of less importance than the SPQ and the ASI and have been used less often in distance education than the DESP inventory or the ILS. However, the findings of research using these inventories and questionnaires serve to highlight some of the themes discussed in previous chapters and provide further examples of the problems in developing quantitative instruments for use in this field.

The Inventory of Learning Processes

In Chapter 2, I mentioned the notion of 'levels of processing' in human memory put forward by Craik and Lockhart (1972). They claimed in particular that the use of 'deeper' or more abstract levels of processing during learning would lead to better retention than the use of shallow levels of processing. Craik and Tulving (1975) set out to test the latter claim in a series of experiments in which participants made judgements about each of a series of individual words. For example, they might be asked to say whether a word was printed in upper-case letters, whether it rhymed with a particular word, whether it was the name of a particular kind of thing or whether it fitted into a particular sentence in a sensible way. These tasks were assumed to induce progressively deeper levels of processing. Subsequently, the participants received an unexpected test on their memory for the words that had been presented and Craik and Tulving found that the level of performance varied directly with the depth of processing that they assumed had been induced.

There were, however, some anomalous results that could not be readily handled by assumed variations in depth of processing. First, words that had yielded positive responses were better remembered than words that had yielded negative responses, particularly with deeper levels of processing, though presumably they had been processed at the same level. Second, there were considerable variations in retention even among tasks that involved only semantic processing. In particular, performance was better when the participants judged whether words fitted into more complicated sentences than when they judged whether words fitted into simple sentences. Finally, the more abstract tasks led to better performance even when the participants had been forewarned of the retention test and were free to try to remember the words just as they wished. To handle these findings, Craik and Tulving argued that learning depended partly on the depth of processing but more on the 'spread' or degree of elaboration of the processing at any level.

In fact, the notion that the elaboration of material to be learned would enhance its subsequent memorability was widely accepted in theories of human memory at that time. Schmeck *et al.* (1977) set out to construct a new questionnaire, the Inventory of Learning Processes (ILP), on the basis of these and other ideas in experimental psychology concerning human learning and remembering. They compiled a list of 121 statements concerning different aspects of studying and asked 503 students at a campus-based university in the US to say whether each statement was true or false as a description of how they generally learned (rather than how they learned within any particular course or academic discipline). In the light of the results of a factor analysis of their responses, Schmeck *et al.* reduced the list to 62 items in four scales, which can be found in Tables 1 and 2 of their paper. The four scales were defined as follows:

- Synthesis–Analysis (assessing deep, as opposed to superficial, information processing);
- Elaborative Processing (assessing elaborative, as opposed to verbatim, information processing);
- Fact Retention (assessing attention to details and specifics as opposed to generalities); and
- Study Methods (assessing repetitive, drill-and-practice habits of processing information).

(Schmeck and Grove 1979: 43)

To reduce the influence of response bias, for some items the response 'true' was in accordance with the meaning of the scale in question, whereas for other items the response 'false' was in accordance with the meaning of the scale. A respondent's score on each scale was calculated simply by counting the number of responses that were in accordance with the meaning of the scale. Schmeck *et al.* found that the scales had satisfactory internal consistency and test–retest reliability, and that there were no significant differences between the scores obtained by male and female students. Schmeck and Grove (1979) found that the current academic performance of campus-based students (measured by their grade point averages) was significantly correlated with their scores on the synthesis–analysis, elaborative processing and fact retention scales, but not with their scores on study methods. Fact retention and elaborative processing seemed to have direct effects on academic performance, whereas the effects of synthesis–analysis were exerted mainly through students' entrance qualifications. Schmeck (1980) subsequently showed that the latter scale was also related to students' scores on vocabulary and comprehension tests.

Of course, the development of the ILP was essentially contemporaneous with a number of other developments in research into student learning in higher education: the work of Marton and his colleagues in Sweden on approaches to studying (see Chapter 2), the development of the SPQ by Biggs in Australia and Canada (Chapter 5) and the development of the ASI by Entwistle and his co-workers in the UK (Chapter 6). Moreover, Ribich and Schmeck (1979) found that there was a modest amount of overlap between the dimensions measured by the ILP and those measured by Biggs's (1970a) SBQ. In the light of these developments, Schmeck (1983) relabelled the first two of the scales in the ILP 'deep processing' and 'methodical study', respectively.

Schmeck claimed that his notion of deep processing was distinct from that which had been put forward by Marton and Säljö (1976a) because it was concerned not with a student's intention or approach to a specific task but rather with the underlying cognitive processes. As explained in Chapters 2 and 5, it is true that Marton and Säljö used the expression 'levels of processing' to refer to students' strategies when performing the specific task of reading isolated passages of text. There is, however, a far closer relationship between Schmeck's notion of deep processing and Marton and Säljö's notion of a 'deep approach', which referred to a general way in which students' might set about their academic studies. Subsequently, indeed, Schmeck and Geisler-Brenstein (1989) acknowledged the parallels between the following pairs of constructs:

- deep processing versus shallow processing (Schmeck 1983)
- deep approach versus surface approach (Marton and Säljö 1976a)
- internalizing versus utilizing (Biggs 1979; see also Chapter 5)
- meaning orientation versus reproducing orientation (Entwistle *et al.* 1979; see also Chapter 6).

This seemed to demonstrate the convergent validity of the different research methods by which these constructs had been measured. However, it should be pointed out that in interview-based research the first two pairs are mutually exclusive: individual students cannot employ *both* deep processing *and* shallow processing, and they cannot exhibit *both* a deep approach *and* a surface approach. However, as I pointed out in Chapters 5 and 7, in questionnaire-based research, the latter pairs of constructs turn out to be essentially independent, so that individual students can score high or low on *both* internalizing *and* utilizing in the SPQ and on *both* meaning orientation *and* reproducing orientation in the ASI (Trigwell and Prosser 1991a). Finally, Schmeck and Geisler-Brenstein noted that a distinction between deep and elaborative processing had also been made by Vermunt (see Chapter 9).

The ILP was extensively validated in research carried out at several campus-based institutions of higher education across the US (Schmeck 1983, 1988) but it has had only a very limited use outside that country and apparently none at all in distance education. Watkins and Hattie (1981a) used the ILP in a comparison of students in Australia and the Philippines. Some of the scales did not generate satisfactory measures of internal consistency and factor analyses failed to replicate the ILP's intended constituent structure, although the students' scores on the different scales of the ILP were significantly related to their cumulative grade point averages (see also Watkins and Hattie 1981b; Watkins *et al.* 1983). Schmeck (1983) suggested that the discrepancies between his own results and those obtained by Watkins and Hattie (1981a) could be ascribed to cultural and linguistic differences between the various student populations.

Subsequently, however, Schmeck (1988) described an unpublished study where 269 students at a campus-based university in the US had completed the ASI in addition to the ILP (see chapter 6). Entwistle (1988) provided a table of correlation coefficients between their scores on the scales of the ILP and their scores on the 16 subscales of the ASI. As Entwistle commented, there was very little overlap between the deep processing scale of the ILP and any of the ASI subscales defining meaning orientation. In fact, high scores on deep processing were associated with low scores on the subscales relating to fear of failure, improvidence and surface approach; and the ASI subscales defining meaning orientation were most closely related to the elaborative processing scale. Even so, the strength of these relationships was relatively modest: perhaps unsurprisingly, the strongest relationship was that between the scores on methodical study and disorganized study methods ($r = -0.49$).

A factor analysis carried out on the students' responses to the total set of 126 items was said to have yielded 'six clearly interpretable factors and a "hint" of two additional factors' (Schmeck 1988: 178). I mentioned in Chapter 6 that these factors were based on groupings of items that corresponded to the scales in the ILP rather than to the subscales in the ASI. There were indeed factors corresponding to deep processing and elaborative processing, respectively, but a third factor subsumed items that were associated with both fact retention and methodical study. The five remaining factors represented different aspects of confidence or self-efficacy (see also Schmeck and Geisler-Brenstein 1989). However, two other studies that had used short versions of the ASI and the ILP at campus-based institutions in Scotland (Entwistle and Waterston 1988; see also Entwistle 1988) and the US (Speth and Brown 1988) yielded factor solutions that failed to represent the constituent scales of either instrument. This tends to suggest that the anomalous findings obtained by Watkins and Hattie (1981a) might have been due to inherent problems with the ILP itself, rather than to cultural or linguistic factors.

Schmeck *et al.* (1991) supplemented the four original scales of the ILP with seven other scales that examined broader aspects of self-concept and personality, to produce a Revised Inventory of Learning Processes (ILP-R). In completing this instrument, respondents indicated the extent of their agreement or disagreement with each of 160 statements along a six-point scale between 'strongly agree', scoring 5, and 'strongly disagree', scoring 0. Schmeck and Geisler-Brenstein (1989: 100) had mentioned an unpublished study in which an earlier version of the ILP-R had been administered to students at campus-based institutions in both the US and China. They commented that 'a similar factor structure was obtained for both groups', but they did not present any quantitative results. Nevertheless, it is clear from their brief discursive account that the factor solutions failed to replicate the scale structure of the original ILP.

Subsequently, Schmeck *et al.* (1991) reported the correlation coefficients among the different scale scores that had been produced by the American students in this study. While the scales of the original ILP had earlier been stated to be 'relatively independent' (Schmeck *et al.* 1977: 420), their scores on the scales of the ILP-R exhibited substantial associations among the deep processing, fact retention and elaborative processing scales. Henson and Schmeck (1993) used the original ILP in an investigation involving 89 students at two campus-based institutions in the US and obtained similar results. It would therefore appear that the scales of the ILP and the ILP-R do not provide distinctive, independent and homogeneous measures of the constructs on which these instruments were originally based and, accordingly, neither can be recommended as a useful instrument for investigating student learning in higher education.

It should be also be pointed out that doubts had already been raised about Craik and Lockhart's (1972) idea of 'levels of processing' even before the ILP had been developed (Baddeley 1976: 167–8) and more extended critiques were published shortly thereafter (Baddeley 1978; Eysenck 1978). Some problems were basically factual. For instance, I mentioned in Chapter 5 that under certain circumstances shallow processing could lead to relatively good retention; in fact, Biggs (1978b) himself obtained results along these lines. Again, people with memory problems due to brain damage often do not show any impairment of semantic processing (Baddeley 1976: 167). However, other problems were conceptual. In particular, Baddeley (1978) and Eysenck (1978) claimed that no satisfactory independent criterion of either the 'depth' or the 'elaboration' of processing had been devised, in which case they argued that explanations in terms of levels of processing were at best *post hoc* and at worst entirely circular. Schmeck (1983) claimed to have taken such issues into consideration when developing the ILP but, even so, Craik and Lockhart's account is no longer regarded by psychologists as a useful framework for understanding human memory (see, for example, Eysenck and Keane 1990: 148–55; Baddeley 1996: 115–24).

The Learning and Study Strategies Inventory

In Chapter 5, I mentioned Biggs's (1970a) early finding that differences in how students went about their learning consisted of a number of distinct components that could not be reduced to one single dimension of 'good' versus 'bad' in their implications for subsequent attainment. Biggs himself took this finding as evidence against the idea that there was a determinate set of 'study skills' that somehow guaranteed effective academic performance. Weinstein *et al.* (1988) arrived at a similar conclusion by comparing several inventories published in the US that claimed to measure study skills. In Chapters 3 and 7, I mentioned research carried out by Martin and Ramsden (1987) and by Ramsden *et al.* (1986, 1987), which suggested that students' participation in study skills programmes did not give rise to any improvement in their approaches to studying or their conceptions of learning.

As a result, in the UK at least, the attitudes of teachers and researchers concerning the value of study skills programmes are nowadays very sceptical (see, for example, Ford 1980; Gibbs *et al.* 1980; Gibbs 1981: chapter 4; Cowan 1989; Entwistle 1992). This may be somewhat unfair: a meta-analytic review of previous studies carried out by Hattie *et al.* (1996) found that study skills programmes typically produce clear improvements in measures of performance and in students' self-concepts and attitudes though only very slight improvements in students' reported study skills. Nevertheless, in the case of studies conducted with university students, Hattie *et al.* found that the effects upon academic performance were much more modest. At this educational level, Hattie *et al.* concluded that study skills interventions were relatively ineffective, except in improving students' attitudes to learning or in reducing their levels of experienced anxiety.

Despite this conclusion, it is clear from research in experimental psychology on human learning and memory that people differ from each other in the kinds of strategies that they use when they engage in learning tasks, and that this strategic variation has implications for the quality of their subsequent performance (Weinstein *et al.* 1979). On the basis of this research, Weinstein *et al.* (1988) devised the Learning and Study Strategies Inventory (LASSI), which in its final version contained 77 items within ten scales that were related to different aspects of studying. Brief definitions of the ten scales are given in Box 10.1. For each item, respondents are asked to indicate the extent of their agreement or their disagreement with a particular statement along a five-point scale, and the responses are then coded so that higher scores reflect more desirable patterns of studying. (In particular, the 'anxiety' scale as a whole is coded so that higher scores represent *lower* levels of anxiety.) Using data from 96 students taking an introductory course in educational psychology at a campus-based university in the US, it was found that the ten scales achieved satisfactory levels of both internal consistency and test–retest reliability.

Cano-Garcia and Justicia-Justicia (1994) administered a battery of questionnaires including the ASI, the ILP and the LASSI to 991 students who

Box 10.1   **Scales contained in the Learning and Study Strategies Inventory**

Scale	Meaning
Anxiety	Often worries about school; may worry so much that it is hard to concentrate; easily discouraged about grades; tense about school and studying for tests; nervous even when well prepared (coded so that higher scores represent *lower* levels of anxiety)
Attitude	Attitude about and interest in college
Concentration	Ability to concentrate, pay close attention, listen carefully and think about what is being said; not easily distracted
Information processing	Uses imaginal and verbal elaboration; thinks about how new information fits with what is already known; interrelates new information; creates comparisons; thinks about the meaning of what is read and heard; translates information into one's own words; uses logic
Motivation	Willingness to work hard; level of motivation for college; has a considerable degree of incentive; diligent; stays 'on top of' work; self-disciplined
Selecting main ideas	Seems to be able to pick out key ideas and critical points in information read or heard; focuses on important points in what has been read
Self-testing	Reviews information learned; reviews regularly; prepares for classes and learning
Study aids	Makes use of a broad approach to learning, makes good use of aids to help learning; supplements learning with helpful techniques; makes good use of key words, practice exercises, sample problems, examples, headings, diagrams, etc., to help learning
Test strategies	Approach toward taking tests and exams; generally prepares appropriately; reviews right materials; ties materials together well; flexible when necessary
Time management	Uses time well, is well organized, systematic in planning the use of time; productive in using time to the best advantage

Source: Weinstein *et al.* 1988: 36–9

were taking courses in ten academic subjects at a campus-based university in Spain. A factor analysis was carried out on their scores on the ten scales of the LASSI, and this produced just two factors. One reflected the students' scores on test strategies, concentration, selecting main ideas, (low) anxiety and attitude, which seemed to relate to the specific goal of succeeding at university. The other factor reflected the students' scores on self-testing, motivation, time management and study aids, which all seemed to relate more to a constant, responsible and organized approach to studying. A second factor analysis was carried out on the students' scores on the 16 subscales of the ASI, the four scales of the ILP and the ten scales of the LASSI; this produced just three factors:

- one factor reflected the students' scores on information processing (LASSI), interrelating ideas (ASI), elaborative processing (ILP), deep approach (ASI) and use of evidence (ASI)
- a second factor reflected the students' scores on surface approach (ASI), fear of failure (ASI) and improvidence (ASI) and was negatively related to their scores on deep processing (ILP), (low) anxiety (LASSI) and test strategies (LASSI)
- the third factor reflected the students' scores on time management (LASSI), motivation (LASSI), concentration (LASSI) and methodical study (ILP) and was negatively related to their scores on disorganized study methods (ASI).

These results seem to support the convergent validity of the ASI, the ILP and the LASSI at the level of their constituent scales and subscales. The first two factors appear to correspond quite closely to Ramsden and Entwistle's (1981) concepts of meaning and reproducing orientations. However, the third factor is concerned specifically with an organized approach to studying.

Köymen (1992) compared 375 distance-learning students and 329 campus-based students who were taking courses in economics and business administration at two institutions in Turkey in their responses to a Turkish translation of the LASSI, which had been modified to ensure that all of the items were appropriate for both groups of students. Table 10.1 shows the mean scores obtained by the two groups of students on the ten scales of the LASSI. It will be noted that the distance-learning students obtained higher scores than the campus-based students on all but one of the scales. Köymen described the differences as 'only moderate' and finally concluded that there was 'no important difference' between the two groups in terms of their learning and study strategies (Köymen 1992: 111, 116). However, these assertions need to be properly assessed by means of appropriate statistical analyses.

From the information provided in Köymen's article, I compared the two sets of mean scores by means of two-tailed Student's t tests. The comparisons that are statistically significant at the 5 per cent level are indicated in Table 10.1 by asterisks. However, in Chapters 6 and 9 I noted the argument that one should use a more stringent significance level in order to guard

Table 10.1   Mean scores obtained on the Learning and Study Strategies Inventory by distance-learning and campus-based students

Scales	Distance learning	Campus based	Effect size
Anxiety	24.429	22.027	+0.35**
Attitude	31.753	29.388	+0.49**
Concentration	24.385	23.297	+0.16*
Information processing	30.391	30.603	−0.04
Motivation	27.057	25.559	+0.29**
Selecting main ideas	19.260	19.142	+0.03
Self testing	28.287	25.881	+0.45**
Study aids	28.123	26.419	+0.35**
Test strategies	27.968	27.293	+0.11
Time management	28.194	24.778	+0.56**

Source: Köymen 1992: 112
*$p < 0.05$, two-tailed test; **$p < 0.005$, two-tailed test

against an increased likelihood of making Type I errors (that is, of obtaining spuriously significant results) when carrying out large numbers of independent statistical tests (see also Harper and Kember 1986). Therefore, those comparisons that are significant using the more stringent criterion of 0.5 per cent are indicated in Table 10.1 by two asterisks. There are significant differences between the two groups of students on seven of the ten scales and six of these differences remain significant even at this more stringent level.

However, Köymen's claim that the differences are 'only moderate' and unimportant needs to be assessed against measures of the size of the relevant effects (see Richardson 1996). This matter was discussed in detail in Chapter 9 in connection with the data obtained by Vermunt (1998) in campus-based and distance-learning students using the ILS. The index of effect size used was the difference between the mean scores of the two groups, standardized against the pooled within-group standard deviation; thus, an effect size of 0.5 means that the two groups differ on average by an amount equal to one-half of their pooled standard deviation. Table 10.1 shows the standardized mean differences for the ten scales of the LASSI, corrected for sampling bias. Once again, effect sizes that are smaller than 0.2 in their absolute magnitude might be dismissed as being of little practical importance (Cohen 1969), but all the differences that are significant at the 0.5 per cent level are associated with effect sizes larger than this.

In other words, Köymen was in error in concluding that there was no important difference between the learning and study strategies of the two groups of students. On the contrary, differences that were statistically highly significant and of potential practical importance were obtained on six of the ten scales in the LASSI: the distance-learning students produced higher scores than the campus-based students in terms of their attitude, their motivation, their self-testing, their use of study aids and their time management; they also exhibited lower anxiety than the campus-based students. Köymen was disposed to ascribe these differences to the nature of the distance-learning system itself but acknowledged that the two groups of students differed in terms of their educational experience and in their previous qualifications. (They were, however, matched in terms of their academic disciplines, as they were all taking courses in economics and business administration.)

Perhaps more important, Köymen did not mention whether these two groups of students were similar or different in the distributions of their ages. In many national systems, students taking courses by distance learning are on average older than students at campus-based institutions, and the pattern of findings obtained in this study would certainly be consistent with the general trend noted in Chapters 5, 6 and 7 for older students to demonstrate more desirable approaches to studying than younger students (see also Richardson 1994b). It is worth adding that Trueman and Hartley (1996) obtained responses to a time-management inventory from 293 students at a campus-based university in the UK. They found that students over the age of 25 years gave higher ratings of their time-management skills than did younger students. This is scarcely surprising, because many of the older students will have been successfully juggling their various domestic and occupational responsibilities for several years before embarking on their university course. In the absence of further information, however, it is simply not possible to arrive at an unambiguous interpretation of Köymen's findings.

Learning style inventories

From time to time in previous chapters I have used the expression 'learning style'. This may be used to describe students' preferences for particular kinds of learning activities and perhaps also for particular kinds of teaching or instruction (see, for instance, Jonassen and Grabowski 1993: 5). However, it is used in a wide variety of other ways to describe individual differences in the way that people learn. There is also an even broader literature concerned with 'cognitive styles', which was well reviewed by Riding and Rayner (1998). In a widely cited paper, Curry (1983) tried to make sense of the ways in which 'learning style' had been used by grouping them under three headings. The different notions varied in terms of the extent to which they could be directly observed and modified as a result of environmental influences and, as a metaphor to capture this idea, Curry likened them to progressively deeper layers of an onion:

- Instructional Preference. 'This is the individual's choice of environment in which to learn. We would expect this choice to be modulated by all person–environment interactions. Examples would be a preference for attending lectures versus small group learning situations . . . As this is the layer that interacts most directly with learning environments, learner expectations, teacher expectations and other external features, we would expect instructional preference to be the least stable, the most easily influenced level of measurement in the learning styles arena.'

- Information Processing Style. 'This is the individual's intellectual approach to assimilating information ... An example would be whether better retention occurred in an individual given one or other approach to hierarchies among concepts (i.e. processing generalizations followed by details, or detailed examples followed by generalized principles) ... Because this processing does not directly involve the environment we would expect that measures of this Information Processing Style would be a good deal more stable than Instructional Preference, and yet still be modifiable by learning strategies.'

- Cognitive Personality Style. 'This is defined as the individual's approach to adapting and assimilating information, but this adaptation does not interact directly with the environment, rather this is an underlying and relatively permanent personality level dimension that becomes manifest only indirectly and by looking for universals within an individual's behavior across many learning instances.'

(Curry 1983: 3, 8–9)

This is a useful categorization for many practical purposes. Nevertheless, it might be noted that Vermunt's notion of learning style, which was discussed in Chapters 4 and 9, serves more as an overarching construct that appears to straddle all three 'layers' or categories in Curry's scheme. In Vermunt's account, students' learning orientations and their conceptions (or mental models) of learning are assumed to be relatively stable, and so these probably belong to the third layer. In contrast, students' choice of processing and regulation strategies is contextually determined, and so these belong to the first or second layers (see Vermunt and van Rijswijk 1988; Vermunt 1996, 1998; Vermetten *et al.* 1999a).

The Learning Style Inventory

In noneducational contexts, the concept of learning styles is most commonly associated with the ideas of Kolb (see, for instance, Kolb *et al.* 1971; Kolb and Fry, 1975; Kolb 1984). Kolb devised the Learning Style Inventory (LSI) to evaluate a person's orientation towards each of four learning modes that were believed to represent successive stages in experiential learning:

- concrete experience (CE)
- reflective observation (RO)
- abstract conceptualization (AC)
- active experimentation (AE).

In its original version, the LSI consisted of nine sets of four words and respondents were asked to rank the four words in each set as they described their own preferred mode of learning (with the best scored as 4), inserting the appropriate number beside the corresponding word. One set of adjectives, for instance (and the one that perhaps best captures the gist of the four different learning modes), was

_____feeling   _____thinking   _____watching   _____doing

(Kolb and Fry 1975: 37)

Six words had been chosen to represent each of the four learning modes, whilst the remaining words were distractors and were ignored in the scoring procedure. The score on each mode was obtained by summing the ranks assigned to the six words relevant to that mode. The difference between the scores obtained on AC and CE was taken to reflect different ways of perceiving the world (that is, emphasizing abstractness over concreteness), whereas the difference between the scores obtained on AE and RO was taken to reflect different ways of processing information (that is, emphasizing active experimentation over reflection). Comparisons between these two difference scores were taken to be diagnostic of four basic learning styles:

- 'The *convergent* learning style relies primarily on the dominant learning abilities of abstract conceptualization and active experimentation. The greatest strength of this approach lies in problem solving, decision making, and the practical application of ideas.'
- 'The *divergent* learning style has the opposite learning strengths from convergence, emphasizing concrete experience and reflective observation. The greatest strength of this orientation lies in imaginative ability and awareness of meaning and values.'
- 'In *assimilation*, the dominant learning abilities are abstract conceptualization and reflective observation. The greatest strength of this orientation lies in inductive reasoning and the ability to create theoretical models, in assimilating disparate observations into an integrated explanation.'
- 'The *accommodative* learning style has the opposite strengths from assimilation, emphasizing concrete experience and active experimentation. The greatest strength of this orientation lies in doing things, in carrying out plans and tasks and getting involved in new experiences'.

(Kolb 1984: 77–8).

The instructions, the items and the scoring procedure for the LSI can be most conveniently found in the book by Kolb *et al.* (1991: 56–7).

I have not located any published research in which the original version of the LSI was given to students taking courses by distance learning and so the following account is based on evidence from campus-based students. Freedman and Stumpf (1978) collected responses on the LSI from 1179 students taking courses in business administration. A factor analysis of their responses to the individual items identified two factors that corresponded to the (AC–CE) and (AE–RO) dimensions. Similar results were obtained by Certo and Lamb (1980) with students of business studies, by Merritt and Marshall

(1984) with nursing students and by Katz (1986) with students in nine different disciplines. In contrast, Ferrell (1983) tested students from both high schools and community colleges and obtained four factors that were claimed to match the four learning modes in the LSI, while Newstead (1992) failed to obtain a coherent factor solution in students of psychology. Freedman and Stumpf also found that the two factors that they had identified explained only 20.6 per cent of the variance in responses to the LSI and that the scores on the four scales showed poor internal consistency and test–retest reliability. They argued that these results cast doubt on the practical usefulness of the LSI in measuring students' learning styles. The LSI's poor measurement qualities were confirmed by Geller (1979) and Sims *et al.* (1986).

Because the original LSI used a response procedure based upon forced ranking, Freedman and Stumpf noted that the respondents' scores on the four scales were not statistically independent of one another and that this artefact might itself generate data that tended to confirm the LSI's intended scale structure. In agreement with this proposal, Lamb and Certo (1978) showed that the strongest relationships among the words that defined the two scales reflecting each of the two major dimensions of the LSI (that is, AC and CE, on the one hand, and AE and RO, on the other hand) tended to occur between pairs of words that had to be ranked against each other within the same set. To eliminate these mathematical constraints, Lamb and Certo constructed a modified version of the LSI in which respondents rated themselves on each of the 36 adjectives separately, using a seven-point rating scale. A factor analysis of the responses produced by 450 students of business studies on this modified LSI yielded very little support for the existence of two bipolar dimensions, and Lamb and Certo therefore concluded that the results obtained with Kolb's original version mainly reflected instrument bias (see also Certo and Lamb 1980).

Certo and Lamb (1979) explored this idea further by generating artificial data representing 1000 sets of totally random responses to the original version of the LSI. The correlation coefficients among the scale scores computed from these artificial data varied between -0.11 and -0.35. In the data obtained from real students by Lamb and Certo (1978), the corresponding correlation coefficients varied between $+0.05$ and -0.55. Certo and Lamb argued that the predominantly negative direction of these correlation coefficients resulted from the forced ranking procedure and not the underlying nature of the students' learning styles. In addition, when they examined the correlation coefficients among the responses given to the individual words, they found the same pattern that they had identified in the responses given by genuine students: the strongest relationships tended to occur between pairs of words that had to be ranked against each other within the same set. All of this evidence implied considerable instrument bias within the LSI.

Certo and Lamb demonstrated that the ranking procedure would ensure that even random data were in certain respects in accordance with Kolb's model. However, they did not demonstrate that the randomly generated data would give rise to the appropriate factor solution for the LSI. To test this idea, I generated an artificial data set equivalent to Certo and Lamb's. The pattern of correlations among the scales and the individual items was very similar to that described in the previous paragraph. However, a factor analysis on the ratings given to the 24 critical words showed that there were 15 factors with eigenvalues greater than one, and the scree test (Cattell 1966) confirmed that this number of factors should be extracted from the data set. Inspection of these factors showed that they reflected all possible statistically orthogonal (or independent) comparisons among the words in each of the different sets. Let me spell this out in more detail:

- In five of the nine sets of words there were two distractors and only two words contributed to the scale scores on the LSI. There is only one way of comparing ratings to two words and these comparisons were represented in five of the factors obtained in this analysis.
- In two of the nine sets of words there was one distractor and three words contributed to the scale scores on the LSI. There are two possible statistically orthogonal comparisons that can be made among ratings to three words and these comparisons were represented in another four of the factors obtained in this analysis.
- In the two remaining sets of words there were no distractors and all four words contributed to the scale scores on the LSI. There are three possible statistically orthogonal comparisons that can be made among ratings to four words and these comparisons were represented in the six remaining factors obtained in this analysis.

In short, the factor analysis faithfully retrieved the underlying structure of this artificial data set. However, when the analysis was constrained to extract just two factors, these seemed to reflect the ratings given to an arbitrary group of just eight words and they certainly did not represent the two main dimensions that the LSI is assumed to measure. In short, although Kolb's ranking procedure can explain some of the properties of data obtained using the LSI, it is not possible to extract two factors representing the (AC–CE) and (AE–RO) dimensions from artificial data sets. It follows that the identification of two such factors in ratings obtained from real students (see Freedman and Stumpf 1978; Certo and Lamb 1980; Merritt and Marshall 1984; Katz 1986) cannot be dismissed as an artefact due to the use of a forced ranking procedure.

Earlier in this chapter, I referred briefly to a study by Ribich and Schmeck (1979) in which the ILP and Biggs's (1970a) SBQ were administered to students taking an introductory psychology course at a campus-based university in the US. In fact, the students also completed the LSI. Ribich and Schmeck carried out canonical correlation analyses among all possible pairs of these questionnaires to assess the degree of overlap in the constructs they were measuring. As I mentioned earlier, there was a modest amount of overlap between the ILP and the SBQ, but there was much less overlap between the LSI and either the ILP or the SBQ. In both the latter questionnaires, certain subscales appeared to be positively related to abstract conceptualization and (to a lesser extent) negatively related to reflective observation and concrete experience. Ribich and Schmeck concluded that the LSI was sensitive to variations in depth of processing. In general, however, the LSI does not seem to be a measure of differences in approaches to studying, as reflected in the ILP and the SBQ.

A similar approach was adopted by Newstead (1992), who obtained responses from 188 psychology students at a campus-based university in the UK on both the LSI and the 18-item version of the ASI. The correlations between their scale scores on the two instruments were uniformly weak, the largest coefficients being those between AC and meaning orientation (+0.20), between CE and meaning orientation (+0.23), and between (AC–CE) and meaning orientation (+0.23). This pattern is somewhat strange, given that there was a strong negative relationship between AC and CE (−0.52). However, as Newstead himself commented, in terms of the underlying theory it is not clear why those students with a meaning orientation should tend to score more highly on the concrete experience scale. In this case, the poor overlap between the LSI and the 18-item version of the ASI could be ascribed to the basic methodological problems with the latter instrument that were discussed in Chapter 7.

The revised version of the LSI

Because of the poor psychometric properties of the original version of the LSI, Smith and Kolb (1986) produced a revised version. This consists of 12 incomplete sentences, for each of which four alternative endings are given. Respondents are asked to rank the endings for each sentence as they describe their own preferred mode of learning. Sims *et al.* (1986) obtained responses to the revised version of the LSI from students taking undergraduate and postgraduate courses in business studies at a campus-based university in the US. They found that the internal consistency of the revised version of the LSI was better than that of its predecessor but that its test–retest reliability over a 5-week period was just as poor. Even with only a 9-day follow-up, Atkinson (1988) found that the test–retest reliability of this instrument was far from satisfactory.

In discussing their results, Sims *et al.* suggested that their students 'may have been measured at a time when they were in the process of developing a particular learning style and therefore this study's finding may be due to a lack of a fully developed approach to problem solving' (Sims *et al.* 1986: 757–9). Indeed, in response to criticisms based on the poor test–retest reliability of the original LSI, Kolb (1981) argued that learning styles were sensitive to situational influences, in which case scores on the LSI might be expected to change over a period of time. Curry (1983) endorsed this view by placing the LSI in the second 'layer' of her account of learning styles. To test this idea, Veres *et al.* (1987) gave the revised version of the LSI to 230 people employed in industry, whose learning styles were expected to be more stable than those of the students in the study by Sims *et al.* In fact, the test–retest reliability of their scale scores remained poor.

A criticism of the revised version of the LSI that was acknowledged by Smith and Kolb (1986: 10) themselves is that it is vulnerable to response bias. To simplify the scoring of responses, the sentence endings that reflect a particular learning style are arranged in the same column on the response sheet. As a consequence, 'The first available choice of responses to each question has to do with feelings. The second deals with watching and listening, the third focuses on thinking and logic, while the fourth emphasizes working hard, being active and getting things done' (Sims *et al.* 1986: 759). This could lead to a response bias in two different ways. On the one hand, the participants might stereotype themselves as people who prefer one kind of response over another. On the other hand, they might acquire a response 'set' simply to assign the same ranks to the sentence endings in particular columns regardless of their actual content.

In both cases, this kind of response bias would artificially increase the internal consistency of this instrument, in spite of its poor test–retest reliability (see Sims *et al.* 1986; Veres *et al.* 1987; Atkinson 1988). Ruble and Stout (1990, 1991) tested this possibility by devising a scrambled form of the revised LSI in which the four alternative endings for each sentence were arbitrarily reordered. The scrambled form and the standard form were given to students taking courses in business studies at several campus-based institutions across the US. The internal consistency of the scrambled form was lower than that of the standard form but its test–retest reliability was actually higher. Similar results were found by Veres *et al.* (1991) with a sample of campus-based students and employees. This indicates that the revised LSI is vulnerable to a response set that inflates its internal consistency but suppresses its test–retest reliability.

As I mentioned earlier, the factor structure of the original version of the LSI seemed to be fairly robust, and this could not be attributed to the mathematical constraints that are inherent in the use of a forced ranking procedure. In the revised version of the LSI, these constraints become particularly acute because there are no distractor items and all of the rankings contribute to the resulting scale scores. This means that the revised version of the LSI is an 'ipsative' instrument: that is, one in which the total score is the same for all respondents. In this case, the total score for each sentence will be $(1 + 2 + 3 + 4)$, or 10, and the total score on the instrument as a whole will be $(1 + 2 + 3 + 4) \times 12$, or 120. This gives rise to problems in the interpretation of factor analyses, as bipolar factors can emerge simply as an artefact (Dunlap and Cornwell 1994).

Ruble and Stout (1990) carried out factor analyses on the ratings given to individual items in both the standard and the scrambled form of the revised LSI. Both two-factor and four-factor solutions were obtained for comparison. Analysis of the standard form generated a two-factor solution in which one factor reflected the AC scale and the other factor reflected the CE scale. A four-factor solution contained factors reflecting the AC, AE and RO scales, respectively, but the CE items were spread across two different factors. Analysis of the scrambled form led to a two-factor solution in which one factor compared AE with CE and the other factor compared RO with CE. The four-factor solution was similar to but less distinct than that obtained with the standard form and this was taken as further evidence that the latter was vulnerable to response bias. In short, there was very little support for the intended structure of either instrument.

Subsequent investigations using the standard form of the revised LSI reached essentially the same conclusion: there was, indeed, a consistent trend for factors to emerge that contrasted AC with AE and CE with RO (Cornwell *et al.* 1991; Geiger *et al.* 1992, 1993; Loo 1996). This may be an interesting pattern but it is not in accord with Kolb's theoretical model. Loo (1999) reanalysed the ratings that he had obtained from 200 students at a campus-based university in Canada. Instead of using exploratory factor analysis on the instrument as a whole, he used confirmatory factor analysis on the items defining each of the four scales and the two underlying dimensions (AC–CE) and (AE–RO). In each case, the data were a very poor fit to these scales and dimensions on a number of different statistical criteria.

To eliminate the ipsative property of the instrument, Geiger *et al.* (1993) devised an alternative, 'normative' form of the revised LSI in which respondents rated 48 randomized sentences along a seven-point scale from 'not like me', scoring 1, to 'very much like me', scoring 7. This was given to students taking courses in business administration at two campus-based universities in the US, along with the standard, 'ipsative' form of the instrument. Both the normative and the ipsative forms demonstrated satisfactory internal consistency and there were moderate correlations between their corresponding scales. A factor analysis carried out on the students' ratings of the 48 sentences produced four factors that could be readily identified with the four scales, but a two-factor solution did not support the intended relationships among these scales. Geiger *et al.* concluded that these were worth exploring as distinct learning abilities.

Geiger and Pinto (1991) gave the revised version of the LSI to 40 students of business studies at a campus-based university in the US during the fall semesters of their sophomore, junior and senior years (in other words, in Years 2–4 of the undergraduate programme). The test–retest reliabilities of the four learning modes were all greater than 0.50, except for those on concrete experience, which were very low. There were small changes in the students' mean scores on the four scales over the 3 years, which were not in themselves statistically significant, but there was a significant change in the classification of their learning styles (assimilator, accommodator, converger and diverger). In particular, 17 of the 40 students were assigned to different learning styles in their senior year compared with their sophomore year. This is consistent with the idea that the experience of higher education (and, presumably, other environmental influences, as well) can lead to changes in students' learning styles.

Dille and Mezack (1991) administered the revised version of the LSI to 151 students who were embarking on distance-learning courses delivered by television programmes with support from study guides, textbooks and other printed materials. They then compared the students who were academically successful (in that they completed their course with a grade of C or better during their first semester of enrolment) with those who were unsuccessful (in that they withdrew from their course or failed to obtain a grade of C or better) in their scale scores on the revised version of the LSI. The unsuccessful students tended to have higher scores on concrete experience (CE) and consequently lower scores on (AC–CE) than the successful students. Dille and Mezack argued that people with high scores on CE had a greater need to relate to other people, and that this was frustrated by the social isolation that was inherent in distance education.

Canfield's Learning Style Inventory

Canfield (1980) devised a similar instrument to Kolb's LSI that was also named the 'Learning Style Inventory' (CLSI). This consisted of 30 sets of four words and in each case respondents once again ranked the words to describe their preferred mode of learning. This generated scores on 21 measures: eight scales represented 'conditions' or different dynamics of learning, four scales represented 'content' or major areas of interest, four scales represented 'mode' or the general preferred modality for learning and the remaining scales represented 'expectation' or the anticipated level of academic performance (Canfield 1980: 22).

Alsagoff (1985, 1986) obtained responses to the CLSI from a total of 629 students taking one of four different degree programmes by distance learning in Malaysia. There were statistically significant differences on some of the scales across the four degree programmes and there were significant correlations between the students' scores on certain of the scales and their current academic performance. In particular, performance was higher in students who affiliated with their peers rather than their instructors, higher in students who preferred to learn by reading rather than by listening and higher in students who expected to achieve good performance.

Coggins (1988; Gibson and Graff 1992) found that scores on the CLSI could be used to predict course completion in 153 students on distance-learning courses at a university in the US. A discriminant analysis showed that course completion versus non-completion could be correctly predicted in 70 per cent of these students on the basis of their scores on the scales of the CLSI alone. In particular, course completion was higher in students who expected to obtain outstanding results and lower in students who expected to obtain average or satisfactory results. Completion was also higher in students who preferred to learn about people rather than about inanimate things. There were no statistically significant differences associated with conditions of learning or with modalities of learning, although satisfactory course completion tended to be associated with a lower preference for peer affiliation.

The Learning Style Questionnaire

Because of possible problems due to mathematical constraints in the forced ranking procedure employed in Kolb's LSI, Marshall and Merritt (1985, 1986) developed another instrument, the Learning Style Questionnaire (LSQ-MM), which incorporated three different modifications to the LSI. First, the respondents were asked to rate themselves on individual words along a five-point scale. Second, the ends of the scale were labelled with pairs of words that were polar opposites (for instance, accepting–questioning). Third, the items intended to measure the four learning modes were reconstructed afresh by selecting 40 pairs of words from a sample of 100 pairs.

Earlier in this chapter, I mentioned an investigation by Cano-Garcia and Justicia-Justicia (1994) in which a battery of questionnaires was administered to students at a campus-based university in Spain. The battery included the ASI, the ILP and the LASSI and a factor analysis indicated that there was considerable overlap in the constructs being measured by these three instruments. In fact, the battery also included the LSQ-MM and Cano-Garcia and Justicia-Justicia also carried out a factor analysis on the scores on all four instruments. Scores on the four scales in the LSQ-MM defined two factors that reflected the (AC–CE) and (AE–RO) dimensions, respectively.

This provides confirmation of the underlying structure of this instrument in terms of Kolb's experiential learning theory. However, the factors that reflected the dimensions underlying the LSQ-MM were related only marginally to the students' scores on the other three instruments. In addition, their scores on the LSQ-MM showed no significant loadings on the factors that were defined by the other three instruments. These results are wholly consistent with the implication of the study carried out by Ribich and Schmeck (1979), that whatever the LSI measures is not related to individual differences in approaches to studying.

The Learning Styles Questionnaire

Honey and Mumford (1982) adopted a different approach to measuring four learning styles that were intended to be broadly equivalent to the stages in Kolb's account of experiential learning. Their Learning Styles Questionnaire (LSQ-HM) was mainly intended as a pedagogical tool for use by staff developers working in the area of management training. It consists of 80 statements describing learners' beliefs, preferences and behaviour and, in each case, respondents are asked to indicate whether they agree or disagree with the relevant statement. There are 20 statements relevant to each of four learning styles:

- '*Activists* will learn best from activities where they can engross themselves in short here-and-now activities such as business games and competitive teamwork tasks.'
- '*Reflectors* learn best from activities where they are able to stand back from events and listen and observe.'
- '*Theorists* learn best from activities where what is being offered is part of a system, model, concept or theory.'
- '*Pragmatists* learn best from activities where there is an obvious link between the subject matter and the problem or opportunity on the job.'
  (Mumford 1993: 4)

The respondents' score on each of the four learning styles is obtained by counting the number of 'agree' responses. Honey and Mumford presented results from 29 participants who had completed both the LSI and the LSQ-HM. These showed that there were moderately strong associations between the corresponding scales of the two instruments, except that the concrete experience scale of the LSI was only weakly correlated with the activist scale of the LSQ-HM.

Allinson and Hayes (1988) presented results from 95 managers from developing countries who were taking a Master of Business Adminstration (MBA) programme at a British campus-based university and from 127 managers from British industry. In both samples, a factor analysis of the participants' scale scores on the LSQ-HM identified two factors: an 'analysis' factor that measured scores on theorist and pragmatist, and an 'action' factor that contrasted scores on activist and reflector. Allinson and Hayes therefore calculated scores on these two dimensions and found that they had satisfactory internal consistency and test–retest reliability. They argued that the LSQ-HM might be preferable to the LSI as a measure of learning style.

Allinson and Hayes (1990) obtained a similar factor structure in the scores obtained by 138 students taking courses in management at a campus-based university in the UK. In a second study, involving 21 MBA students from developing countries, they found no difference in the scores obtained by those who preferred to be taught in a conventional lecture format and those who preferred a 1-day simulation exercise. However, in a third study involving 29 male managers from a British-based multinational corporation, they found that participants who had been identified by their employers as 'high fliers' obtained higher scores on both the 'analysis' factor and the 'action' factor. This was taken to support the construct validity of the LSQ-HM.

Sims *et al.* (1989) obtained responses to both the LSQ-HM and the revised version of the LSI from 279 students who were taking courses in business studies at a campus-based university in the US. The scales of the LSQ-HM showed levels of internal consistency that were satisfactory, although inferior to those of scales of the LSI. Nevertheless, the associations between the corresponding scales of the two instruments were relatively weak, the highest correlation coefficient being 0.28. Sims *et al.* concluded that there was little evidence of any convergence between the two instruments, although this might be partly because there were problems with the ways that both instruments attempted to operationalize the construct of learning styles.

Goldstein and Bokoros (1992) argued that comparisons of this sort were inappropriate because in Kolb's LSI learning styles (that is, converger, diverger, assimilator and accommodator) were captured by particular combinations of scores on the scales rather than by the scales themselves. They obtained responses on both the original version and the revised version of the LSI and on the LSQ-HM from 44 campus-based students in the US. When these participants were classified in terms of their learning styles on the three different instruments, only 41 per cent were assigned to equivalent styles on the original LSI and the LSQ-HM, and only 30 per cent were assigned to equivalent styles on the revised LSI and the LSQ-HM. Goldstein and Bokoros concluded that the degree of coincidence between the different classifications was only modest.

Sadler-Smith (1997) administered a battery of questionnaires to 245 business studies students at a campus-based university in the UK. The battery included the LSQ-HM and the RASI (see Chapter 7). Sadler-Smith found several statistically significant correlations between the students' scale scores on these two instruments:

- activists tended to produce lower scores on strategic approach
- reflectors tended to produce higher scores on deep, surface and strategic approach
- theorists tended to produce higher scores on deep and strategic approach and lower scores on lack of direction
- pragmatists tended to produce higher scores on deep approach, strategic approach and academic self-confidence.

In addition, the students' scores on both of these instruments showed some relationships with their overall academic performance: specifically, good performance was associated with higher scores on the theorist scale from the LSQ-HM and on the deep approach, strategic approach and self-confidence scales from the RASI. Sadler-Smith concluded that there might be some overlap between the LSQ-HM and the RASI, and he speculated that this included 'constructs such as motivation, learning process and degree of learning activity' (Sadler-Smith 1997: 61). Provided that this pattern can be replicated, it would seem that in this respect the LSQ-HM is different from other measures of learning styles, such as the LSI and the LSQ-MM, which tend to show little overlap with instruments intended to measure approaches to studying (Ribich and Schmeck 1979; Cano-Garcia and Justicia-Justicia 1994; see also Murray-Harvey 1994).

Concluding summary

- The ILP was developed on the basis of prevalent notions in psychological research into human memory during the 1970s. However, its psychometric properties are questionable, and several studies have failed to replicate its intended structure. The 'levels of processing' framework on which it was based is no longer regarded as useful for understanding human memory and so the ILP has no advantage by virtue of its supposed theoretical underpinning.
- Many writers are sceptical about the idea of study skills and the value of study skills courses. Nevertheless, the LASSI seems to provide a useful way of assessing learning strategies and shows convergence with both the ASI and the ILP. Distance-learning students have better learning and study skills than campus-based students taking similar courses but this may be due to confounded differences in age, educational experience or previous qualifications.
- The LSI was designed to measure a person's orientation towards four learning modes. It is subject to several methodological criticisms, despite having undergone revision in the 1980s. The revised LSI and the CLSI may be useful in predicting outcomes in distance education. However, with the possible exception of the LSQ-HM, learning style inventories show little overlap with questionnaires designed to measure approaches to studying in higher education.

11

Conclusions and Implications

In this final chapter, it is obviously appropriate and necessary for me to try to draw out some of the main issues and themes that I have been discussing in this book. Indeed, I will in due course review the main findings from research into approaches to studying in campus-based education and distance education and identify their practical, theoretical and heuristic implications. What I want to do first, however, is to stand back from the substantive issues that have been discussed and consider the general nature of the research that I have been describing. In this regard, I want to make certain comments about the quality of research in campus-based and distance education and about the quality of the literature through which that research is disseminated. I shall then focus upon the key issue of whether campus-based and distance-learning students go about their studies in a similar manner, before considering the relationship between approaches to studying and academic attainment. Finally, I will discuss the contributions and limitations of qualitative and quantitative methods in understanding approaches to studying before making some final comments concerning research in campus-based education and research in distance education.

The quality of research in campus-based and distance education

In this book, I have provided an account of research that has been carried out into approaches to studying in both campus-based and distance education. From time to time, I have made critical comments about some of the studies that I have reviewed or about the inferences that have been drawn by their authors. This is both appropriate and inevitable in a book of this kind. Research in education (as in any other area of scientific or scholarly inquiry) must never be taken at face value but needs to be subjected to a continuing process of critical scrutiny and evaluation. It is, I think, fair to say that research into campus-based education is nowadays an established field, with explicit research standards and recognized means for the discussion and dissemination of findings through a number of respected academic journals. A brief scrutiny of the bibliography that follows this chapter will readily identify the journals in question.

In comparison, I also think that it is fair to say that research into distance education is less well established and that there are several issues to be raised concerning the quality of that research and how it is disseminated, especially with regard to research on approaches to studying. Bååth (1982: 13) bemoaned 'the severe lack of scientifically validated knowledge' on the subject of approaches to learning in distance-learning students. It is obvious from the amount of material reviewed in this book that this kind of complaint could not be made today and, in a moment, I shall describe some tentative conclusions that one can draw from that material. However, to say this is not to imply that the available research evidence and the available research literature is entirely lacking in flaws. Indeed, one could debate at some length precisely how 'scientifically validated' the research on approaches to studying in distance education has really been.

One issue is that some researchers have adopted conceptual frameworks or research methods designed for use with campus-based students and have used them uncritically in the context of distance education. This kind of unreflective 'borrowing' in research on distance education was criticized by Gibson (1990). In the choice of research methods, it could perhaps be justified by the need to ensure that the same instrument was being used in different situations. However, in some cases, questionnaires were not sufficiently modified (or else were not modified at all) for the distinctive context of distance education, so that some items were really quite inappropriate. Examples include the research by Ekins (1992a, b) using the SPQ (see Chapter 5) and the research by Joughin *et al.* (1992) using the DESP inventory (see Chapter 8): in both cases, distance-learning students were asked to rate items that referred to face-to-face lectures. Of course, this is merely a special case of the general issue in cross-cultural research of ensuring that instruments are properly translated so that they can be used in different cultural contexts (see Van de Vijver and Hambleton 1996).

A different issue is that some researchers have drawn inferences concerning distance-learning students without including any comparison group of campus-based students, while others have compared the approaches to studying of distance-learning students and campus-based students without taking into account the many differences that exist between these two populations of students apart from their mode of study or course delivery. I have emphasized these differences at various points in this book. The most obvious ones are in:

• age: in most national systems, students taking courses by distance learning are on average older (and also show a greater range of ages) than students at campus-based institutions

- prior academic qualifications: students taking courses by distance learning may lack the entrance qualifications that are normally required of students at campus-based institutions, especially if distance-learning institutions operate an 'open' admissions policy
- recent academic experience: distance-learning students may have returned to education after many years, whereas most students attend campus-based institutions within a few years of having completed their secondary education.

Obviously, the third of these factors is likely to be confounded with the other two factors but in principle any or all of them may influence students' approaches to learning in higher education.

Recently, there has been a wider debate in the US concerning the general adequacy of research carried out in distance education. Russell (1999) had for some years been compiling an ongoing bibliography of research studies that failed to show a statistically significant difference in various measures of outcome as the consequence of employing different kinds of educational technology. Russell himself inclined to the view that one should use cheaper and simpler forms of technology, as these were apparently just as effective as more sophisticated and expensive ones (Russell 1999: xiii, xx). A more cynical view, however, is that there is simply a good deal of bad research in distance education. This view was taken in one report, which concluded that

- 'there is a relative paucity of true, original research dedicated to explaining or predicting phenomena related to distance learning,'
- 'the overall quality of the original research is questionable and thereby renders many of the findings inconclusive.'

(Phipps and Merisotis 1999: 2–3)

However, the latter report has itself come under attack for its uncritical assumption that it is possible to make straightforward comparisons between academic outcomes in campus-based and distance education and for adopting a simple-minded and contradictory view of the basic nature of educational research (Brown and Wack 1999). Similar issues have been mentioned earlier in this book: for instance, whether student retention means the same thing in campus-based and distance education (see Chapter 8). In their report, Phipps and Merisotis said little about the process of learning and based their conclusions primarily on North American research. Even so, some of their points are worth mentioning because they have cropped up from time to time in previous chapters as criticisms of research on approaches to studying in both campus-based and distance education:

- 'Much of the research does not control for extraneous variables and therefore cannot show cause and effect.'
- 'Most of the studies do not use randomly selected subjects.'
- 'The validity and reliability of the instruments used to measure student outcomes and attitudes are questionable.'

(Phipps and Merisotis 1999: 3–4)

Apart from the quality of research in distance education, there must also be a question mark over the quality of the relevant literature. A substantial proportion of the existing publications on distance education (and not merely on approaches to studying in distance education) take the form of in-house publications, institutional technical bulletins, research students' dissertations or proceedings of academic conferences. This, too, can be readily confirmed by a brief scrutiny of the bibliography following this chapter. In such cases, it is often not clear what kind of editorial review (if any) was imposed before these publications were released. One cannot deny that this 'grey' literature contains a great deal of useful information and provides many valuable insights, but there is clearly a possibility that it lacks the full academic rigour of materials that have been properly subjected to the formal processes of independent peer review. Of course, as Suen and Stevens (1993) demonstrated in the case of one journal in distance education, even articles that are published in peer-reviewed journals may turn out to be flawed in key respects.

In the past, the research literature on distance education has been described as being dominated by speculation, opinion and anecdotal reports based on the authors' own personal experiences; where studies have attempted to provide genuinely new evidence about distance learning they have been characterized as largely descriptive and empirical in nature, rather than analytical or theoretical (Coldeway 1982, 1988; Moore 1985; Cookson 1989; Phipps and Merisotis 1999: 27). In addition, this literature has often tended to focus on institutional issues of organization or policy, rather than on pedagogical issues relevant to the practical business of studying in distance education (Villegas Grijalba 1995). Fortunately, in the previous chapters, I have been able to provide a good many counterexamples to these trends from the research on approaches to studying in distance education carried out during the 1980s and 1990s.

Another issue is the relative insularity of research on campus-based and distance education. In my preface, I mentioned that there had in the past been little dialogue between the communities of researchers in campus-based and distance education. Coldeway (1988), in particular, noted that researchers in distance education seemed to be reluctant to link their work to existing areas of scholarship and inquiry in mainstream educational research. In fact, research on approaches to studying has proved to be an exception to this trend, in that researchers in distance education have been at the forefront of some of the key theoretical developments in the field (see Chapters 4 and 9, in particular). Even so, there is also an insularity within the field of distance education, as Calvert (1995) noted from an analysis of articles published in the four main journals:

- *American Journal of Distance Education* (US)
- *Distance Education* (Australia)
- *Journal of Distance Education* (Canada)
- *Open Learning* (UK).

Calvert showed that each of the journals was dominated by articles from authors in the country in which the journal was based; that most authors cited other articles that had been published in the same journal and that most authors cited articles by authors from their own country, even when their own article was published in a journal based in a different country. Calvert described these trends as evidence of parochiality in research on distance education. One might, of course, find similar trends in other areas of inquiry. However, Calvert also noted that issues and debates did not cross over from one journal to another and this is not a sign of healthy, open discourse.

Approaches to studying in campus-based and distance education

With these caveats in mind, the evidence and arguments that have been reviewed in this book can be summarized as follows.

First, qualitative investigations based upon semi-structured interviews with individual students have identified certain study approaches, conceptions, orientations and learning styles in higher education (see Chapters 2–4). These have all been identified both in campus-based students and in distance-learning students, which implies that the two populations of students are at the very least commensurable in their approaches to studying. There is very little information, however, about whether the distributions of such study approaches, conceptions, orientations and learning styles differ between campus-based and distance-learning students, and even less about whether any differences of this kind should be attributed to the different modes of course delivery. The chief exception is that distance-learning students tend not to show a social orientation, but this is not surprising given the physical separation from teachers and other students that is inherent in distance education. Instead, distance-learning students appear to be more likely to exhibit a personal orientation. In this regard, they resemble older students at campus-based institutions and differ from younger campus-based students. There must therefore be a strong presumption that differences in personal orientation depend upon age rather than mode of course delivery.

Second, quantitative investigations have used a variety of formal inventories and questionnaires to assess approaches to studying in large groups of students (see Chapters 5–10). Although these have not proved entirely satisfactory as research instruments, they have served to identify some important constructs that seem to underlie students' accounts of their approaches to learning in higher education. The most important and most general example is the distinction between an orientation towards the underlying meaning of the course materials and an orientation towards simply being able to reproduce those materials for the purposes of academic assessment. There is, in contrast, very little support for any 'strategic' approach to assessment of the sort that was posited by Ramsden (1979), nor equivalently for any 'achieving' orientation towards studying. There is, in addition, little unambiguous support for the various learning styles and pathologies that were described by Pask (1976), except as components of the two fundamental orientations.

In the course of confirming the existence of these two basic study orientations, investigations have found all of the major inventories to be wanting, in so far as it has not proved possible to confirm their intended constituent structure through the application of factor analysis. The one exception is the 32-item version of the ASI (Richardson 1990), which appears to possess satisfactory psychometric properties, at least when used with either campus-based or distance-learning students in the UK (see Chapter 7). However, the application of factor analysis has produced similar solutions in campus-based and distance-learning students on both the 64-item version of the ASI and the ILS. This means that these two instruments have a similar constituent structure (albeit not the one that they were intended to have) in both campus-based students and distance-learning students. This in turn confirms the implication of the findings from qualitative investigations that these two populations are commensurable in their approaches to studying. In other words, it makes sense to compare them in terms of the same dimensions, though this then leaves open the question of whether they are different in their distributions on these dimensions.

Third, researchers have found statistically significant differences between campus-based and distance-learning students in the scores obtained on the individual subscales of the ASI, the ILS and the LASSI. Most typically, distance-learning students tend to obtain higher scores than campus-based students on those aspects of studying that are more desirable in the sense of being more appropriate to the avowed aims of higher education, and they tend to obtain lower scores than campus-based students on those aspects of studying that are less desirable or appropriate. This is of practical importance to distance educators and of political importance in demonstrating the value of distance education. As I explained in my Preface, national governments are likely to become increasingly interested in the establishment or expansion of distance education. This may be motivated solely by economic considerations; but governments and institutions need have few qualms about such developments with regard to the quality of the students' learning.

Fourth, however, as I mentioned earlier, distance-learning students differ from campus-based students on a number of characteristics that are likely to influence their approaches to studying. In particular, distance-learning students tend to be older than campus-based students, and it is well established that older students tend to obtain higher scores than younger students on those aspects of studying that are more desirable or appropriate and lower scores than younger students on those aspects of studying that are less desirable or appropriate (for a comprehensive review, see Richardson 1994b). This would suggest that the differences in approaches to studying between campus-based and distance-learning students can be attributed at least in part to the confounded effects of differences in the students' ages.

Some researchers have also confounded effects of the mode of course delivery with differences in students' previous academic qualifications or experience. In campus-based students, these are typically unrelated to their approaches to studying (Biggs 1970b; Entwistle and Ramsden 1983: 48; but compare Schmeck and Grove 1979). However, this may be because such students have a relatively narrow range of previous academic experience. As I mentioned in Chapter 8, Vermunt and van Rijswijk (1988) found that students joining the Dutch Open University who had prior experience of higher education were less likely to exhibit an externally regulated and reproduction-directed learning style than students without prior experience of higher education. In a survey of students at the Open University in the UK, my colleagues and I similarly found that scores on reproducing orientation were inversely related to the students' level of education before joining the Open University (Richardson *et al.* 1999).

Other researchers have confounded effects of the mode of course delivery with differences in students' academic disciplines, their levels of study or their response rates. The possible role of academic discipline was assessed by Ramsden and Entwistle (1981) in campus-based students. Students taking arts courses were more likely than students taking science courses to exhibit a deep approach and other aspects of meaning orientation, whereas the opposite was true in the case of syllabus-boundness and other aspects of reproducing orientation (see also Entwistle and Ramsden 1983: 181–4). Biggs (1987: 50) obtained similar results in campus-based students, as did Harper and Kember (1986) in both campus-based students and distance-learning students. These effects are often attributed to the substantial knowledge base that science students need to learn but they might also be due to different teaching practices in departments responsible for providing courses in the arts and sciences (see Kember and Gow 1994).

The effect of a student's level of study is potentially interesting, in so far as most teachers in higher education would hope that they were bringing about genuine intellectual development in their students during the course of a degree. In fact, there is evidence from several studies that campus-based students are likely to adopt *less* desirable approaches to studying as they proceed through their degree programme (see Watkins and Hattie 1985; Biggs 1987; Gow and Kember 1990; Volet *et al.* 1994) and even within the first year of study (Coles 1985). Vermunt and van Rijswijk (1988) noted a similar trend in distance-learning students. There is evidence that this pattern can be avoided and even reversed in campus-based education (Vermetten *et al.* 1999b), especially by the introduction of a problem-based curriculum (Coles 1985; Newble and Clarke 1986, 1987), as well as in distance education (Richardson *et al.* 1999). However, extrapolating from these results suggests that exposure to higher education could turn out to be disastrous for students intending to enter professions (such as medicine) in which practitioners are expected to engage in a continuous process of maintaining and updating their knowledge and skills.

Newble *et al.* (1990) investigated this notion by comparing approaches to studying in medical students and in practising physicians. The physicians obtained much lower scores on surface approach than the medical students and they also tended to obtain higher scores on deep approach. Newble *et al.* noted that the causal relationship here was not clear because physicians tended to be recruited from amongst the more successful medical students, who might in turn be those with more desirable approaches to studying. Moreover, the difference appeared to lie not in the physicians' level of seniority or their amount of clinical experience but in whether or not they had undertaken additional postgraduate academic training. The causal relationship was once again not clear, because it might be that the physicians with more desirable approaches to studying were those who were more likely to choose to undertake additional academic training. Nevertheless, the results suggest that in some physicians inappropriate patterns of learning are entrenched during their medical education and can persist through their subsequent careers.

The effect of response rate has been well discussed at a number of points in this book, where I pointed out that students who respond to postal surveys differ from non-respondents in many characteristics, including their approaches to studying. It follows from this that it is not valid to make comparisons between samples of students that differ in the proportion of respondents to nonrespondents. One example is the study by Wong (1992) discussed in Chapter 6, where the internal or campus-based students produced a response rate of 74 per cent, whereas the external or distance-learning students produced a response rate of only 19 per cent. Another example is the study by Busato *et al.* (1998) discussed in Chapter 9, where students in their first year of a campus-based programme yielded a response rate of 94 per cent whereas those in subsequent years yielded at best a response rate of only 22.5 per cent. From a research point of view, it is obviously desirable to try to maximize response rates to student surveys. However, there is also an ethical issue in requiring students to take part in activities that are of no direct benefit to the participants themselves. In the study by Busato *et al.*, the requirement to participate might have been justified by its supposed benefits to the participants as students of psychology but it can be argued that any coercion to participate in research is unethical (see Coulson 1999).

One study that used appropriate statistical techniques to take account of the possible effects of age, gender and discipline found no significant differences between campus-based students and distance-learning students taking the same courses in terms of their reported approaches to studying (Harper and Kember 1986). Accordingly, the safest conclusion that one might reach from the available evidence is that students who are taking courses by distance learning show different approaches to studying from campus-based students, but that these differences are more likely to be due to the effects of background variables (most notably, age, previous qualifications or experience, academic discipline and level of study) than to the effects of different modes of course delivery.

So, are there no differences between campus-based and distance-learning students that could be linked to the different modes of course delivery? From the research discussed in this book, there seem to be two possible candidates:

- One is the finding by Vermunt (1998) that distance-learning students exhibit learning styles that are more desirable than those exhibited by campus-based students according to their scores on the subscales of the ILS. Distance-learning students tended to obtain higher scores on the subscales associated with a meaning directed learning style but lower scores on the subscales associated with an application directed learning style and an undirected learning style. In Chapter 9, I argued that these results were qualitatively different from the effects of age upon students' responses to the ILS, and thus that they could not be attributed to the confounded difference between campus-based and distance-learning students in terms of their mean age. Nevertheless, in principle, it is possible that these results are simply due to other confounded differences in uncontrolled demographic variables.
- The other candidate is the finding by Kember and Harper (1987b) that the implications for students' subsequent academic performance of adopting particular approaches to studying appear to be somewhat different in campus-based students and in distance-learning students. Kember and Harper had taken into account the possible effects of age, gender and academic subject in making direct comparisons between campus-based and distance-learning students in terms of their approaches to studying. However, their inference that the two populations of students were different in terms of the prognostic implications of approaches to studying was not based upon any formal statistical procedure and there is a strong possibility that it confounds the differences in the mode of course delivery with differences in demographic variables. Even so, this is an area of concern that deserves more attention in future research.

Approaches to studying and academic performance

There is, in fact, a body of research evidence from campus-based education that is worth citing in this connection. First, in interview-based research, a deep approach and a strategic approach tend to be associated with good academic performance, whereas a surface approach tends to be associated with poor academic performance (see Miller and Parlett 1974: 55; Svensson 1977; Ramsden 1979, 1981; Entwistle and Ramsden 1983: 176–8). Moreover, students' performance also varies with the sophistication of their conceptions of learning (Martin and Ramsden 1987). Second, a number of studies have found that success in subsequent academic assessments can be predicted on the basis of the students' scores on the subscales of the ASI. In particular, academic performance tends to be positively related to scores on deep approach, intrinsic motivation and strategic approach but negatively related to scores on surface approach, disorganized study methods and negative attitudes to studying (Entwistle *et al.* 1979; Ramsden and Entwistle 1981; Watkins 1982, 1983; Clarke 1986; Miller *et al.* 1990).

When they were developing the ILP, Schmeck and Grove (1979) found that students' current grade point averages were positively correlated with their scores on the synthesis–analysis, fact retention and elaborative processing scales, though not on the study methods scale. Similar results were obtained by Miller *et al.* (1987, 1990), by Gadzella *et al.* (1987) and by Watkins and Hattie (1981a; Watkins *et al.* 1983). However, Watkins and Hattie (1981a) found that the magnitude of these correlations varied across different faculties, while Lockhart and Schmeck (1984) found that the pattern of relationships depended on the demands of particular forms of academic assessment. Moreover, Moss (1982) failed to find any positive correlations between scores on the ILP and grade point average in a sample of students who had been referred for remedial study skills tuition.

Nevertheless, Kember and Harper (1987b) found that the aspects of studying that were most important in predicting academic outcomes depended on the outcome being predicted (course completion versus final performance) (see also Richardson *et al.* 1999). A further example of this comes from studies using Canfield's LSI (see Chapter 10). Alsagoff (1985, 1986) found that current performance was higher in students who affiliated with their peers rather than their instructors, whereas Coggins (1988) found that the likelihood of course completion was actually lower in such students. As Kember and Harper pointed out, all these findings suggest that academic achievement should not be characterized as a single continuum running from excellence to failure to non-completion.

Moreover, the relationship between approaches to studying and any single measure of academic attainment is by no means a simple one. For instance, Trigwell and Prosser (1991a) found that even a surface approach could be associated with good performance in academic assessments if the teacher demonstrated the relevance of the subject matter, made opportunities for students to ask questions and provided clear assessment criteria. Indeed, several investigations have found that academically unsuccessful students do not just exhibit 'poorer' approaches to studying but fail to exhibit any coherent approaches at all. This outcome was obtained in two studies where the data were processed using multi-dimensional unfolding analysis (Meyer *et al.* 1990a,b) and in two further studies where the data were processed using factor analysis (Entwistle *et al.* 1991; Meyer and Dunne, 1991). In short, poor academic performance appears to be associated with a disintegration or fragmentation of the normal patterns of studying.

Qualitative and quantitative research into student learning

In research on approaches to studying in campus-based and distance education, qualitative and quantitative methods have proved to be complementary in their strengths and their weaknesses (Coldeway 1988; and see the more general discussion by Hammersley 1996). On the one hand, students' approaches, conceptions, orientations and learning styles can be investigated directly through their individual accounts provided in semi-structured interviews. However, qualitative investigations have often involved relatively small samples of students and they have generally provided no concrete findings about the distributions of approaches, conceptions, orientations or learning styles or about how those distributions might vary with other variables of interest, such as age, gender, academic subject or educational level. In fact, the published accounts of qualitative research into student learning typically provide little or no information about how the samples of students were selected, recruited or rewarded, and in principle they might well be unrepresentative of the populations from which they have been drawn. One counterexample illustrating good practice in research on distance learning is an article by Kember *et al.* (1990).

On the other hand, students' approaches, conceptions, orientations and learning styles can also be studied through the responses that they give to quantitative instruments such as inventories and questionnaires. In this case, the identification of approaches, conceptions, orientations and learning styles can only be carried out indirectly, by inference from the patterns of responses to those instruments that are given by large groups of students. This process rests upon technically sophisticated procedures, such as factor analysis or multi-dimensional unfolding analysis, whose detailed implementation remains highly contentious. Nevertheless, the published accounts of quantitative research are typically more careful and explicit about the mechanisms by which the samples of students have been obtained; they often provide precise information concerning the distributions of scores in particular samples; and they can evaluate particular hypotheses about the relationships between individual differences in studying and background variables.

Most of the research focusing on the role of student characteristics in determining approaches to studying has focused on three variables:

- *Gender.* I have argued in earlier chapters that there are no overall differences in approaches to studying between men and women in higher education (for a review, see Richardson and King 1991). However, it would seem that differences may arise in particular situations and it would be of interest in future research to determine which properties of situations lead to such an outcome. Severiens and ten Dam (1997) proposed that apparent gender differences are actually due to differences in gender identity, which varies among both men and women.

- *Age.* Earlier, I referred to the general finding that older students tend to obtain higher scores than younger students on measures of deep approach and meaning orientation, whereas they obtain lower scores than younger students on measures of surface approach and reproducing orientation (for a review, see Richardson 1994b). This is contrary to the stereotypes held by many people in higher education, according to which the predicament and the experience of older students in higher education are inherently problematic (Richardson and King 1998).
- *Culture.* In Chapter 7, I argued that the basic distinction between meaning orientation and reproducing orientation appeared to emerge across all national systems of higher education but that it tended to receive a specific interpretation in each system or culture (for a review, see Richardson 1994a). The word 'culture' can be understood broadly, so that it includes the culture of the US (Richardson 1995a), the culture of Access courses (Hayes *et al.* 1997) and the culture of people who are deaf (Richardson *et al.* 2000).

This is an interesting starting point for understanding the ways in which people differ from one another in their approaches to studying. Nevertheless, it is also worth adding that other characteristics (such as ethnicity, disablement and social class) may be just as important but have so far been largely ignored in research on student learning in higher education.

The fact that the responses given to formal questionnaires can be encoded and aggregated in a quantitative manner does not mean that they can be regarded as objective or unbiased measures of some underlying psychological reality. To be sure, the respondents are highly constrained by the predetermined format of any particular questionnaire and this means that they are unable to calibrate their understanding of the individual items against the meanings that were intended by the person who originally devised the questionnaire or by the person who actually administers it to them. Nevertheless, as Strack and Schwarz (1992) demonstrated, responses to questionnaires are communicative and collaborative acts that are based upon the same principles of everyday conversation as responses to an interview. In the absence of any explicit feedback, respondents will use cues that allow them to make pragmatic inferences about the intended meaning, such as the content of neighbouring items or the range of response categories available.

Accordingly, the responses given to questionnaires on student learning always stand in need of analysis and interpretation. As will have become apparent, the most common analytic technique is that of factor analysis, which endeavours to reduce the data generated by a very large sample of individuals to a few coherent and consistent constructs. This kind of technique should always be carried out when a questionnaire is employed in a situation different from that in which it was originally developed, in order to check that the instrument's intended constituent structure can be reconstructed in this new situation. Examples would include the use of a questionnaire initially devised to study campus-based undergraduate students in research on Access students, disabled students, mature students or postgraduate students, or the use of a questionnaire that was developed in Australia or the US in research carried out in the UK.

Although the results of factor analyses carried out upon responses to questionnaires have been broadly consistent with those of interview-based studies in demonstrating two basic approaches or orientations to learning, they are discrepant in one fundamental respect. The accounts that have been derived from interviews indicated the existence of two distinct categories or forms of understanding (Marton 1975; Entwistle and Marton, 1984; Marton and Säljö 1984) or a single bipolar dimension along which individual students might vary (Marton 1976c). Nevertheless, in questionnaires, deep and surface approaches are operationalized as separate scales that turn out to be orthogonal to each other, so that an individual student might score high or low on both (Biggs and Rihn 1984; O'Neil and Child 1984; Biggs 1985, 1987: 16; Trigwell and Prosser 1991a; Richardson and Woodley 1999). As Trigwell and Prosser (1991a) pointed out, this has the implication that interventions aimed at improving student learning should be concerned more with encouraging a deep approach than with necessarily discouraging a surface approach.

A productive *rapprochement*?

In this chapter, I have so far come to two conclusions, and to these I wish to add a third. The *practical* conclusion is that students in distance education exhibit approaches to studying that tend to be more desirable than those of campus-based students, in the sense that they are more appropriate to the avowed aims of institutions of higher education. The *theoretical* conclusion is that these differences are probably due to the effects of background variables and that students in distance education show no intrinsic differences in their approaches to studying attributable to the mode of course delivery. Finally, my *heuristic* conclusion is that this should mean that a productive *rapprochement* can be achieved between the two previously separate research communities of those studying campus-based education and those studying distance education.

On the one hand, if students in distance education are qualitatively similar to campus-based students in their approaches to studying then, as Morgan *et al.* (1980) commented, the findings in the mainstream research literature concerned with approaches to studying in campus-based education will be broadly valid for understanding approaches to studying in distance education. In particular, these research findings can in the future be fully exploited by academic staff in distance education when seeking new ways in which to develop and to evaluate their courses. Moreover, there will be no excuse for the insularity in research on distance education of which Coldeway

(1988) complained, at least with regard to future research on students' approaches to learning in distance education.

On the other hand, there is also an insularity (or perhaps 'ignorance' would be a more accurate word) in mainstream educational research with regard to the findings of research into distance education. If campus-based students are qualitatively similar to distance-learning students in terms of their approaches to studying, then the previously separate literature on approaches to studying in distance education can be used to illuminate the processes at work in campus-based higher education. To reiterate the example that I put forward in the Preface at the outset of this book, the effects of students' age or educational background upon their approaches to studying might be more apparent in distance education than in campus-based education because in the latter context they are subject to restriction of range due to the application of selective entrance requirements. As a consequence, research on distance education should not remain marginal but should become of interest to everyone involved in mainstream higher education. It is to this end that I dedicate this book.

Concluding summary

- Research into distance education can be criticized for the unreflective borrowing of concepts and methods from research on campus-based students, the lack of attention to differences in background variables between campus-based and distance-learning students and the quality and insularity of the research literature itself.
- Nevertheless, campus-based and distance-learning students are commensurable in so far as the same study approaches, conceptions, orientations and learning styles have been identified in both populations.
- Distance-learning students exhibit approaches to studying that are more desirable than those of campus-based students in the sense that they are more appropriate to the avowed aims of institutions of higher education.
- These differences are probably due to the effects of background variables (such as age, previous qualifications or experience, academic discipline and level of study) rather than to the different modes of course delivery.
- In principle, this should make it possible to achieve a productive *rapprochement* between the two previously separate research communities, whereby research in campus-based students is used to develop courses in distance education and research in distance education is used to illuminate the processes at work in campus-based education.

References

Alcoff, L. and Potter, E. (eds) (1993) *Feminist Epistemologies*. New York: Routledge.

Allinson, C.W. and Hayes, J. (1988) The Learning Styles Questionnaire: an alternative to Kolb's Inventory? *Journal of Management Studies*, 25: 269–81.

Allinson, C.W. and Hayes, J. (1990) Validity of the Learning Styles Questionnaire, *Psychological Reports*, 67: 859–66.

Alsagoff, S.A. (1985) Learning styles of Malaysian distance education students. Paper presented at the 13th World Conference of the International Council for Distance Education, 'Flexible Designs for Learning', Melbourne, Australia, 13–20 August.

Alsagoff, S.A. (1986) A study of learning styles, student characteristics and faculty perceptions of the distance education program at Universiti Sains Malaysia, *Dissertation Abstracts International*, 46: 3566A.

Anderson, R.C. (1970) Control of student mediating processes during verbal learning and instruction, *Review of Educational Research*, 40: 349–69.

Anderson, T.D. and Garrison, D.R. (1995) Critical thinking in distance education: developing critical communities in an audio teleconference context, *Higher Education*, 29: 183–99.

Arger, G. (1993) Australia, in *Distance Education in Asia and the Pacific: Country Papers* (pp. 1–11). Chiba, Japan: National Institute of Multimedia Education.

Ashworth, P. and Lucas, U. (1998) What is the 'world' of phenomenography? *Scandinavian Journal of Educational Research*, 42: 415–31.

Astin, A.W. (1970) The methodology of research on college impact, Part Two, *Sociology of Education*, 43: 437–50.

Atkinson, G., Jr (1988) Reliability of the Learning Style Inventory–1985, *Psychological Reports*, 62: 755–8.

Atkinson, J.W. (1964) *An Introduction to Motivation*. Princeton, NJ: Van Nostrand.

Bååth, J.A. (1982) Distance students' learning: empirical findings and theoretical deliberations, *Distance Education*, 3: 6–27.

Baddeley, A.D. (1976) *The Psychology of Memory*. New York: Basic Books.

Baddeley, A.D. (1978) The trouble with levels: A reexamination of Craik and Lockhart's framework for memory research, *Psychological Review*, 85: 139–52.

Baddeley, A. (1996) *Human Memory: Theory and Practice*, rev. edn. Hove: Psychology Press.

Bandura, A. (1997) *Self-Efficacy: The Exercise of Control.* New York: W.H. Freeman.

Barker, B.O., Frisbie, A.G. and Patrick, K.R. (1989) Broadening the definition of distance education in light of the new telecommunications technologies, *American Journal of Distance Education,* 3(1): 20–9.

Baxter Magolda, M.B. (1987) Comparing open-ended interviews and standardized measures of intellectual development, *Journal of College Student Personnel,* 28: 443–8.

Baxter Magolda, M.B. (1988) Measuring gender differences in ethical development: a comparison of assessment methods, *Journal of College Student Development,* 29: 528–37.

Baxter Magolda, M.B. (1992) *Knowing and Reasoning in College: Gender-related Patterns in Students' Intellectual Development.* San Francisco: Jossey-Bass.

Baxter Magolda, M.B. (1998) Learning and gender: complexity and possibility, *Higher Education,* 35: 351–5.

Baxter Magolda, M. and Porterfield, W.D. (1985) A new approach to assess intellectual development on the Perry scheme, *Journal of College Student Personnel,* 26: 343–51.

Bean, J.P. and Metzner, B.S. (1985) A conceptual model of nontraditional undergraduate student attrition, *Review of Educational Research,* 55: 485–540.

Beaty, E. and Morgan, A. (1992) Developing skill in learning, *Open Learning,* 7(3): 3–11.

Beaty, E., Dall'Alba, G. and Marton, F. (1997) The personal experience of learning in higher education: changing views and enduring perspectives, in P. Sutherland (ed.) *Adult Learning: A Reader* (pp. 150–65) London: Kogan Page.

Belenky, M.F., Clinchy, B.M., Goldberger, N.R. and Tarule, J.M. (1986) *Women's Ways of Knowing: The Development of Self, Voice and Mind.* New York: Basic Books.

Bell, R. and Tight, M. (1993) *Open Universities: A British Tradition?* Buckingham: SRHE and Open University Press.

Bernard, R.M. and Amundsen, C.L. (1989) Antecedents to dropout in distance education: does one model fit all? *Journal of Distance Education,* 4(2): 25–46.

Biggs, J.B. (1970a) Faculty patterns in study behaviour, *Australian Journal of Psychology,* 22: 161–74.

Biggs, J.B. (1970b) Personality correlates of certain dimensions of study behaviour, *Australian Journal of Psychology,* 22: 287–97.

Biggs, J.B. (1973) Study behaviour and performance in objective and essay formats. *Australian Journal of Education,* 17: 157–67.

Biggs, J.B. (1976) Dimensions of study behaviour: another look at ATI, *British Journal of Educational Psychology,* 46: 68–80.

Biggs, J.B. (1978a) Individual and group differences in study processes, *British Journal of Educational Psychology,* 48: 266–79.

Biggs, J.B. (1978b) Levels of processing, study processes and factual recall, in M.M. Gruneberg, P.E. Morris and R.N. Sykes (eds) *Practical Aspects of Memory* (pp. 671–8). London: Academic Press.

Biggs, J.B. (1979) Individual differences in study processes and the quality of learning outcomes, *Higher Education,* 8: 381–94.

Biggs, J.B. (1982) Student motivation and study strategies in university and college of advanced education populations, *Higher Education Research and Development,* 1: 33–55.

Biggs, J.B. (1984) Learning strategies, student motivation patterns and subjectively perceived success, in J.R. Kirby (ed.) *Cognitive Strategies and Educational Performance* (pp. 111–34). Orlando, FL: Academic Press.

Biggs, J.B. (1985) The role of metalearning in study processes, *British Journal of Educational Psychology*, 55: 185–212.

Biggs, J.B. (1987) *Student Approaches to Learning and Studying.* Melbourne: Australian Council for Educational Research.

Biggs, J.B. (1988) Assessing student approaches to learning, *Australian Psychologist*, 23: 197–206.

Biggs, J.B. (1989) Approaches to the enhancement of tertiary teaching, *Higher Education Research and Development*, 8: 7–25.

Biggs, J.B. (1991) Approaches to learning in secondary and tertiary students in Hong Kong: some comparative studies, *Educational Research Journal*, 6: 27–39.

Biggs, J.B. (1993a) From theory to practice: a cognitive systems approach, *Higher Education Research and Development*, 12: 73–85.

Biggs, J. (1993b) What do inventories of students' learning processes really measure? A theoretical review and clarification, *British Journal of Educational Psychology*, 63: 3–19.

Biggs, J. (1999a) *Teaching for Quality Learning at University.* Buckingham: SRHE and Open University Press.

Biggs, J. (1999b) What the student does: teaching for enhanced learning, *Higher Education Research and Development*, 18: 57–75.

Biggs, J.B. and Collis, K.F. (1982) *Evaluating the Quality of Learning: The SOLO Taxonomy (Structure of the Observed Learning Outcome).* New York: Academic Press.

Biggs, J.B. and Rihn, B.A. (1984) The effects of intervention on deep and surface approaches to learning, in J.R. Kirby (ed.) *Cognitive Strategies and Educational Performance* (pp. 279–93). Orlando, FL: Academic Press.

Billings, D.M. (1987) Factors related to progress toward completion of correspondence courses in a baccalaureate nursing program, *Dissertation Abstracts International*, 47: 2846A.

Brennan, J. (1989) Access courses, in O. Fulton (ed.) *Access and Institutional Change* (pp. 51–63). Milton Keynes: SRHE and Open University Press.

Brew, A. and McCormick, B. (1979) Student learning and an independent study course, *Higher Education*, 8: 429–41.

Brown, D.H. (1982) Just one version of reality: using television case-studies in university courses. Paper presented at the 32nd Annual Meeting of the International Communication Association, Boston, MA, 2–5 May (ERIC Document Reproduction Service No. ED 217 497).

Brown, G. and Wack, M. (1999) The difference frenzy and matching buckshot with buckshot, in *Critical Reading* [on-line]. Available: http://horizon.unc.edu/TS/reading/1999–05.asp

Busato, V.V., Prins, F.J., Elshout, J.J. and Hamaker, C. (1998) Learning styles: a cross-sectional and longitudinal study in higher education, *British Journal of Educational Psychology*, 68: 427–41.

Calder, J., McCollum, A., Morgan, A. and Thorpe, M. (1995) *Learning Effectiveness of Open and Flexible Learning in Vocational Education*, Research Series No. 58. London: Department for Education and Employment.

Calvert, J. (1995) Mapping knowledge in distance education, in D. Sewart (ed.) *One World Many Voices: Quality in Open and Distance Learning* (Proceedings of the 17th World Conference for Distance Education, Vol. 1, pp. 384–8). Olso: International Council for Distance Education. Milton Keynes: The Open University.

Canfield, A.A. (1980) *Learning Styles Inventory.* Ann Arbor, MI: Humanics Media Inc.

Cano-Garcia, F. and Justicia-Justicia, F. (1994) Learning strategies, styles and approaches: an analysis of their interrelationships, *Higher Education*, 27: 239–60.

Cattell, R.B. (1966) The scree test for the number of factors, *Multivariate Behavioral Research*, 1: 245–76.

Certo, S.C. and Lamb, S.W. (1979) Identification and measurement of instrument bias within the Learning Style Inventory through a Monte Carlo technique, in D.F. Ray and T.B. Green (eds) *Management for the Needs of Today and the Challenge of Tomorrow* (Proceedings of the 1979 Southern Management Association Meeting, pp. 22–4). Mississippi State, MI: Southern Management Association.

Certo, S.C. and Lamb, S.W. (1980) An investigation of bias within the Learning Styles Inventory through factor analysis, *Journal of Experiential Learning and Simulation*, 2: 1–7.

Chessell, G. (1986) Learning styles in first year medical students, *Medical Teacher*, 8: 125–35.

Chick, J. (1992) The New England model in theory and practice, in I. Mugridge (ed.) *Perspectives on Distance Education: Distance Education in Single and Dual Mode Universities* (pp. 33–48). Vancouver: Commonwealth of Learning.

Christensen, C.A., Massey, D.R. and Isaacs, P.J. (1991) Cognitive strategies and study habits: an analysis of the measurement of tertiary students' learning, *British Journal of Educational Psychology*, 61: 290–9.

Christie, N.G. and Dinham, S.M. (1991) Institutional and external influences on social integration in the freshman year, *Journal of Higher Education*, 62: 412–36.

Clarke, R.M. (1986) Students' approaches to learning in an innovative medical school: a cross-sectional study, *British Journal of Educational Psychology*, 56: 309–21.

Clinchy, B. and Zimmerman, C. (1982) Epistemology and agency in the development of undergraduate women, in P.J. Perun (ed.) *The Undergraduate Woman: Issues in Educational Equity* (pp. 161–81). Lexington, MA: Lexington Books.

Coggins, C.C. (1988) Preferred learning styles and their impact on completion of external degree programs, *American Journal of Distance Education*, 2(1): 25–37.

Cohen, J. (1969) *Statistical Power Analysis for the Behavioral Sciences*. New York: Academic Press.

Coldeway, D.O. (1982) Recent research in distance learning, in J.S. Daniel, M.A. Stroud and J.R. Thompson (eds) *Learning at a Distance: A World Perspective* (pp. 29–37). Edmonton: Athabasca University/International Council for Correspondence Education.

Coldeway, D.O. (1988) Methodological issues in distance educational research, *American Journal of Distance Education*, 2(3): 45–54. Reprinted (1990) in M.G. Moore (ed.) *Contemporary Issues in American Distance Education* (pp. 386–96). Oxford: Pergamon Press.

Coles, C.R. (1985) Differences between conventional and problem-based curricula in their students' approaches to studying, *Medical Education*, 19: 308–9.

Conway, M. and Ross, M. (1984) Getting what you want by revising what you had, *Journal of Personality and Social Psychology*, 47: 738–48.

Cookson, P.S. (1989) Research on learners and learning in distance education: a review, *American Journal of Distance Education*, 3(2): 22–34.

Cornwell, J.M., Manfredo, P.A. and Dunlap, W.P. (1991) Factor analysis of the 1985 revision of Kolb's Learning Style Inventory, *Educational and Psychological Measurement*, 51: 455–62.

Coulson, M. (1999) In at the deep end or still testing the water? Subject pools and required participation in UK psychology departments, *Psychology Teaching Review*, 8: 19–25.

Cowan, J. (1989) Who needs study skills? *British Journal of Educational Technology*, 20: 61–2.

Craik, F.I.M. and Lockhart, R.S. (1972) Levels of processing: a framework for memory research, *Journal of Verbal Learning and Verbal Behavior*, 11: 671–84.

Craik, F.I.M. and Tulving, E. (1975) Depth of processing and retention of words in episodic memory, *Journal of Experimental Psychology: General*, 104: 268–94.

Crawford, M. (1989) Agreeing to differ: feminist epistemologies and women's ways of knowing, in M. Crawford and M. Gentry (eds) *Gender and Thought: Psychological Perspectives* (pp. 128–45). New York: Springer-Verlag.

Crawford, M. and Chaffin, R. (1997) The meanings of difference: cognition in social and cultural context, in P.J. Caplan, M. Crawford, J.S. Hyde and J.T.E. Richardson, *Gender Differences in Human Cognition* (pp. 81–130). New York: Oxford University Press.

Curry, L. (1983) An organization of learning styles theory and constructs. Paper presented at the Annual Meeting of the American Educational Research Association, Montreal, 11–15 April (ERIC Documentation Reproduction Service No. ED235185).

Dahlgren, L.-O. (1975) *Qualitative Differences in Learning as a Function of Content-Oriented Guidance*. Göteborg: Acta Universitatis Gothoburgensis.

Dahlgren, L.O. and Marton, F. (1978) Students' conceptions of subject matter: an aspect of learning and teaching in higher education, *Studies in Higher Education*, 3: 25–35.

Dahlin, B. and Regmi, M.P. (1997) Conceptions of learning among Nepalese students, *Higher Education*, 33: 471–93.

Dall'Alba, G. (1991) Foreshadowing conceptions of teaching, in B. Ross (ed.) *Teaching for Effective Learning* (*Research and Development in Higher Education*, Vol. 13, pp. 293–297). Sydney: Higher Education Research and Development Society of Australasia.

Daniel, J.S. (1996) *Mega-universities and Knowledge Media: Technology Strategies for Higher Education*. London: Kogan Page.

Department of Employment, Education and Training (1993) *National Report on Australia's Higher Education Sector*. Canberra: Australian Government Publishing Service.

Dille, B. and Mezack, M. (1991) Identifying predictors of high risk among community college telecourse students, *American Journal of Distance Education*, 5(1): 24–35.

Duff, A. (1997) A note on the reliability and validity of a 30-item version of Entwistle and Tait's Revised Approaches to Studying Inventory, *British Journal of Experimental Psychology*, 67: 529–37.

Dunkin, M.J. and Biddle, B.J. (1974) *The Study of Teaching*. New York: Holt, Rinehart and Winston.

Dunlap, W.P. and Cornwell, J.M. (1994) Factor analysis of ipsative measures, *Multivariate Behavioral Research*, 29: 115–26.

Durkheim, E. ([1897] 1952) *Suicide: A Study in Sociology* (J.A. Spaulding and G. Simpson, trans.; G. Simpson, ed.). London: Routledge and Kegan Paul.

Ekins, J.M. (1992a) The development of study processes in distance learning students, in I.S. Jung and W.J. Shin (eds) *The Role of Open Universities in Promoting*

Education for All (pp. 331–45). Seoul: Korea Air and Correspondence University (ERIC Document Reproduction Service No. ED 355 402).

Ekins, J.M. (1992b) Study approaches of distance learning students, studying in a second language. Paper presented at the 16th World Conference of the International Council for Distance Education, 'Distance Education for the Twenty-First Century,' Nonthaburi, Thailand, 9–13 November (ERIC Document Reproduction Service No. ED 355 810).

Eklund-Myrskog, G. (1997) The influence of the educational context on student nurses' conceptions of learning and approaches to learning, *British Journal of Educational Psychology*, 67: 371–81.

Eklund-Myrskog, G. (1998) Students' conceptions of learning in different educational contexts, *Higher Education*, 35: 299–316.

Eley, M.G. (1992) Differential adoption of study approaches within individual students, *Higher Education*, 23: 231–54.

Entwistle, N. (1981) *Styles of Learning and Teaching: An Integrated Outline of Educational Psychology for Students, Teachers and Lecturers.* Chichester: Wiley.

Entwistle, N. (1987) A model of the teaching-learning process, in J.T.E. Richardson, M.W. Eysenck and D. Warren Piper (eds) *Student Learning: Research in Education and Cognitive Psychology* (pp. 13–28). Milton Keynes: SRHE and Open University Press.

Entwistle, N. (1988) Motivational factors in students' approaches to learning, in R.R. Schmeck (ed.) *Learning Strategies and Learning Styles* (pp. 21–51). New York: Plenum Press.

Entwistle, N. (1992) Student learning and study strategies, in B.R. Clark and G.R. Neave (eds) *The Encyclopedia of Higher Education: Vol. 3. Analytical Perspectives* (pp. 1730–40). Oxford: Pergamon Press.

Entwistle, N. (1997a) Contrasting perspectives on learning, in F. Marton, D. Hounsell and N. Entwistle (eds) *The Experience of Learning: Implications for Teaching and Studying in Higher Education*, 2nd edn (pp. 3–22). Edinburgh: Scottish Academic Press.

Entwistle, N. (1997b) Reconstituting approaches to learning: a response to Webb, *Higher Education*, 33: 213–18.

Entwistle, N.J. and Entwistle, D. (1970) The relationships between personality, study methods and academic performance, *British Journal of Educational Psychology*, 40: 132–43.

Entwistle, N., Hanley, M. and Hounsell, D. (1979) Identifying distinctive approaches to studying, *Higher Education*, 8: 365–80.

Entwistle, N. and Marton, F. (1984) Changing conceptions of learning and research, in F. Marton, D. Hounsell and N. Entwistle (eds) *The Experience of Learning: Implications for Teaching and Studing in Higher Education* (pp. 211–36). Edinburgh: Scottish Academic Press.

Entwistle, N. and Marton, F. (1994) Knowledge objects: understandings constituted through intensive academic study, *British Journal of Educational Psychology*, 64: 161–78.

Entwistle, N.J., Meyer, J.H.F. and Tait, H. (1991) Student failure: disintegrated perceptions of studying and the learning environment, *Higher Education*, 21: 249–61.

Entwistle, N.J., Nisbet, J., Entwistle, D. and Cowell, M.D. (1971) The academic performance of students: 1. Prediction from scales of motivation and study methods, *British Journal of Educational Psychology*, 41: 258–67.

Entwistle, N.J. and Ramsden, P. (1983) *Understanding Student Learning.* London: Croom Helm.

Entwistle, N. and Tait, H. (1990) Approaches to learning, evaluations of teaching and preferences for contrasting academic environments, *Higher Education*, 19: 169–94.

Entwistle, N.J., Thompson, J. and Wilson, J.D. (1974) Motivation and study habits, *Higher Education*, 3: 379–95.

Entwistle, N. and Waterston, S. (1988) Approaches to studying and levels of processing in university students, *British Journal of Educational Psychology*, 58: 258–65.

Entwistle, N.J. and Wilson, J.D. (1970) Personality, study methods and academic performance, *Universities Quarterly*, 24: 147–56.

Entwistle, N.J. and Wilson, J.D. (1977) *Degrees of Excellence: The Academic Achievement Game.* London: Hodder and Stoughton.

Ericsson, K.A. and Simon, H.A. (1980) Verbal reports as data, *Psychological Review*, 87: 215–51.

Ericsson, K.A. and Simon, H.A. (1984) *Protocol Analysis: Verbal Reports as Data.* Cambridge, MA: MIT Press.

Ericsson, K.A. and Simon, H.A. (1993) *Protocol Analysis: Verbal Reports as Data*, rev. edn. Cambridge, MA: MIT Press.

Escotet, M.A. (1980) Adverse factors in the development of an open university in Latin America, *Programmed Learning and Educational Technology*, 17: 262–70.

Eysenck, H.J. and Eysenck, S.B.G. (1964) *Manual of the Eysenck Personality Inventory.* London: University of London Press.

Eysenck, M.W. (1978) Levels of processing: a critique, *British Journal of Psychology*, 69: 157–69.

Eysenck, M.W. and Keane, M.T. (1990) *Cognitive Psychology: A Student's Handbook.* Hove: Erlbaum.

Farnes, N. (1975) Student-centred learning, *Teaching at a Distance*, No. 3, pp. 2–6.

Ferrell, B.G. (1983) A factor analytic comparison of four learning-styles instruments, *Journal of Educational Psychology*, 75: 33–9.

Figueroa, M.L. (1992) Understanding students' approaches to learning in university traditional and distance education courses, *Journal of Distance Education*, 7(3): 15–26.

Fleming, D. (1993) A gradualist model for the development of a flexible learning framework, *Educational and Training Technology International*, 30: 319–26.

Fogarty, G.J. and Taylor, J.A. (1997) Learning styles among mature-age students: some comments on the *Approaches to Studying Inventory* (ASI-S), *Higher Education Research and Development*, 16: 321–30.

Ford, N. (1980) Teaching study skills to teachers: a reappraisal, *British Journal of Teacher Education*, 6: 71–8.

Ford, N. (1985) Learning styles and strategies of postgraduate students, *British Journal of Educational Technology*, 16: 65–79.

Francis, H. (1993) Advancing phenomenography: questions of method, *Nordisk Pedagogik*, 13: 68–75. Reprinted (1996) in G. Dall'Alba and B. Hasselgren (eds) *Reflections on Phenomenography: Toward a Methodology?* (pp. 35–47). Göteborg: Acta Universitatis Gothoburgensis.

Fransson, A. (1977) On qualitative differences in learning: IV. Effects of intrinsic motivation and extrinsic test anxiety on process and outcome, *British Journal of Educational Psychology*, 47: 244–57.

Freedman, R.D. and Stumpf, S.A. (1978) What can one learn from the Learning Style Inventory? *Academy of Management Journal*, 21: 275–82.

Gadzella, B.M., Ginther, D.W. and Williamson, J.D. (1987) Study skills, learning processes and academic achievement, *Psychological Reports*, 61: 167–72.

Garrison, D.R. and Shale, D. (1987) Mapping the boundaries of distance education: problems in defining the field, *American Journal of Distance Education*, 1(1): 7–13.

Gatz, F.A. (1986) Personal, instructional and environmental factors associated with completion and attrition in correspondence study and distance education, *Dissertation Abstracts International*, 46: 3655A–6A.

Geiger, M.A., Boyle, E.J. and Pinto, J. (1992) A factor analysis of Kolb's revised Learning Style Inventory, *Educational and Psychological Measurement*, 52: 753–9.

Geiger, M.A., Boyle, E.J. and Pinto, J.K. (1993) An examination of ipsative and normative versions of Kolb's revised Learning Style Inventory, *Educational and Psychological Measurement*, 53: 717–26.

Geiger, M.A. and Pinto, J.K. (1991) Changes in learning style preference during a three-year longitudinal study, *Psychological Reports*, 69: 755–62.

Geller, L.M. (1979) Reliability of the Learning Style Inventory, *Psychological Reports*, 44: 555–61.

Gergen, K.J. (1994) *Realities and Relationships: Soundings in Social Construction*. Cambridge, MA: Harvard University Press.

Gibbs, G. (1981) *Teaching Students to Learn: A Student-Centred Approach*. Milton Keynes: Open University Press.

Gibbs, G. (1992) *Improving the Quality of Student Learning*. Bristol: Technical and Educational Services.

Gibbs, G. (ed.) (1994) *Improving Student Learning: Theory and Practice*. Oxford: Oxford Centre for Staff Development.

Gibbs, G. (ed.) (1995) *Improving Student Learning: Through Assessment and Evaluation*. Oxford: Oxford Centre for Staff Development.

Gibbs, G., Habeshaw, S. and Habeshaw, T. (1988) *53 Interesting Ways to Appraise Your Teaching*. Bristol: Technical and Educational Services.

Gibbs, G., Lockwood, F., Morgan, A. and Taylor, E. (1982a) *Student Learning and Course Design: 1. In-text Teaching Devices in Open University Texts* (Study Methods Group Report No. 12). Milton Keynes: The Open University, Institute of Educational Technology.

Gibbs, G., Morgan, A. and Taylor, E. (1980) Why students don't learn, in *Institutional Research Review*, No. 1 (pp. 9–32). Milton Keynes: The Open University.

Gibbs, G., Morgan, A. and Taylor, E. (1982b) A review of the research of Ference Marton and the Goteborg group: a phenomenological research perspective on learning, *Higher Education*, 11: 123–45.

Gibbs, G., Morgan, A. and Taylor, E. (1984) The world of the learner, in F. Marton, D. Hounsell and N. Entwistle (eds) *The Experience of Learning* (pp. 165–88). Edinburgh: Scottish Academic Press.

Gibson, C.C. (1990) Questions and research strategies: one researcher's perspective, *American Journal of Distance Education*, 4: 69–81.

Gibson, C.C. and Graff, A.O. (1992) Impact of adults' preferred learning styles and perception of barriers on completion of external baccalaureate degree programs, *Journal of Distance Education*, 7(1): 39–51.

Gilligan, C. (1982) *In a Different Voice: Psychological Theory and Women's Development*. Cambridge, MA: Harvard University Press.

Gilligan, C., Ward, J.V. and Taylor J.M. (with Bardige, B.) (1988) *Mapping the Moral Domain: A Contribution of Women's Thinking to Psychological Theory and Education.* Cambridge, MA: Harvard University Graduate School of Education, Center for the Study of Gender, Education and Human Development.

Glaser, B.G. and Strauss, A.L. (1967) *The Discovery of Grounded Theory: Strategies for Qualitative Research.* Chicago, IL: Aldine.

Goldstein, M.B. and Bokoros, M.A. (1992) Tilting at windmills: comparing the Learning Style Inventory and the Learning Style Questionnaire, *Educational and Psychological Measurement*, 52: 701–8.

Goodyear, M. (1976) *OU Student Motivation* (P. Davey and J. Field, eds). Milton Keynes: The Open University, Institute of Educational Technology.

Gow, L. and Kember, D. (1990) Does higher education promote independent learning? *Higher Education*, 19: 307–22.

Gow, L. and Kember, D. (1993) Conceptions of teaching and their relationship to student learning, *British Journal of Educational Psychology*, 63, 20–33.

Hambleton, I.R., Foster, W.H. and Richardson, J.T.E. (1998) Improving student learning using the personalised system of instruction, *Higher Education*, 35: 187–203.

Hammersley, M. (1996) The relationship between qualitative and quantitative research: paradigm loyalty versus methodological eclecticism, in J.T.E. Richardson (ed.) *Handbook of Qualitative Research Methods for Psychology and the Social Sciences* (pp. 159–74). Leicester: BPS Books.

Harper, G. and Kember, D. (1986) Approaches to study of distance education students, *British Journal of Educational Technology*, 17: 212–22.

Harper, G. and Kember, D. (1989) Interpretation of factor analyses from the Approaches to Studying Inventory, *British Journal of Educational Psychology*, 59: 66–74.

Harris, D. (1987) *Openness and Closure in Distance Education.* Lewes: Falmer Press.

Harris, D. and Holmes, J. (1976) Open-ness and control in higher education: towards a critique of the Open University, in R. Dale, G. Esland and M. MacDonald (eds) *Schooling and Capitalism: A Sociological Reader* (pp. 78–87). London: Routledge and Kegan Paul.

Hattie, J., Biggs, J. and Purdie, N. (1996) Effects of learning skills interventions on student learning: a meta-analysis, *Review of Educational Research*, 66: 99–136.

Hattie, J. and Watkins, D. (1981) Australian and Filipino investigations of the internal structure of Biggs' new Study Process Questionnaire, *British Journal of Educational Psychology*, 51: 241–4.

Hayes, K., King, E. and Richardson, J.T.E. (1997) Mature students in higher education: III. Approaches to studying in Access students, *Studies in Higher Education*, 22: 19–31.

Hayes, K. and Richardson, J.T.E. (1995) Gender, subject and context as determinants of approaches to studying in higher education, *Studies in Higher Education*, 20: 215–21.

Hazemi, R., Hailes, S. and Wilbury, S. (eds) (1998) *The Digital University: Reinventing the Academy.* Berlin: Springer-Verlag.

Hedges, L.V. and Olkin, I. (1985) *Statistical Methods for Meta-Analysis.* Orlando, FL: Academic Press.

Henson, M. and Schmeck, R.R. (1993) Learning styles of community college versus university students, *Perceptual and Motor Skills*, 76: 118.

Hezel, R.T. and Dirr, P.J. (1990) *Understanding Distance Education: Identifying Barriers to College Attendance* (Report from the Annenberg/CPB Project). Syracuse, NY: Hezel Associates (ERIC Document Reproduction Service No. ED 340 335).

Hipp, H. (1997) Women studying at a distance: what do they need to succeed? *Open Learning*, 12(2): 41–9.

Hoc, J.M. and Leplat, J. (1983) Evaluation of different modalities of verbalization in a sorting task, *International Journal of Man–Machine Studies*, 18: 283–306.

Holmberg, B. (1981) *Status and Trends of Distance Education*. London: Kogan Page.

Holmberg, B. (1993) Key issues in distance education: an academic viewpoint, in K. Harry, M. John and D. Keegan (eds) *Distance Education: New Perspectives* (pp. 330–41). London: Routledge.

Honey, P. and Mumford, A. (1982) *The Manual of Learning Styles*. Maidenhead: Honey.

Hounsell, D. (1984a) Learning and essay-writing, in F. Marton, D. Hounsell and N. Entwistle (eds), *The Experience of Learning* (pp. 103–23). Edinburgh: Scottish Academic Press.

Hounsell, D.J. (1984b) Students' conceptions of essay-writing. Unpublished doctoral dissertation, University of Lancaster, UK (British Theses Index No. DX54364/85AX).

Hounsell, D. (1987) Essay writing and the quality of feedback, in J.T.E. Richardson, M.W. Eysenck and D. Warren Piper (eds) *Student Learning: Research in Education and Cognitive Psychology* (pp. 109–19). Milton Keynes: SRHE and Open University Press.

Hudson, L. (1968) *Frames of Mind: Ability, Perception and Self-Perception in the Arts and Sciences*. London: Methuen.

Hudson, R., Maslin-Prothero, S. and Oates, L. (1997) *Flexible Learning in Action: Case Studies in Higher Education*. London: Kogan Page.

Johnson, T., Ainley, J. and Long, M. (1996) *The 1995 Course Experience Questionnaire: A report prepared for the Graduate Careers Council of Australia*. Parkville, Victoria: Graduate Careers Council of Australia.

Jonassen, D.H. and Grabowski, B.L. (1993) *Handbook of Individual Differences, Learning and Instruction*. Hillsdale, NJ: Erlbaum.

Joughin, G., Lai, T. and Cottman, C. (1992) Distance learners' approaches to studying: the nature of 'deep' and 'surface' approaches reconsidered. Paper presented at the 16th World Conference of the International Council for Distance Education, 'Distance Education for the Twenty-First Century', Nonthaburi, Thailand, 9–13 November.

Kahl, T.N. and Cropley, A.J. (1986) Face-to-face versus distance learning: psychological consequences and practical implications, *Distance Education*, 7: 38–48.

Katz, N. (1986) Construct validity of Kolb's Learning Style Inventory, using factor analysis and Guttman's smallest space analysis, *Perceptual and Motor Skills*, 63: 1323–6.

Kaye, A.R. and Rumble, G.W.S.V. (1982) Analysing distance learning systems, in M.W. Neil (ed.), *Education of Adults at a Distance* (pp. 227–46). London: Kogan Page.

Keegan, D.J. (1980) On defining distance education, *Distance Education*, 1: 13–36.

Keegan, D.J. (1988) Problems in defining the field of distance education, *American Journal of Distance Education*, 2(2): 4–11.

Keegan, D. (1990) A theory for distance education, in M. Moore (ed.) *Contemporary Issues in American Distance Education* (pp. 327–32). Oxford: Pergamon Press.

Keegan, D. (1996) *Foundations of Distance Education*, 3rd edn. London: Routledge.

Keegan, D. and Rumble, G. (1982) Distance teaching at university level, in G. Rumble and K. Harry (eds) *The Distance Teaching Universities* (pp. 15–31). London: Croom Helm.

Kember, D. (1981) Some factors affecting attrition and performance in a distance education course at the University of Papua New Guinea, *Distance Education*, 2: 164–88.

Kember, D. (1989a) An illustration, with case studies, of a linear-process model of drop-out from distance education, *Distance Education*, 10: 196–211.

Kember, D. (1989b) A longitudinal-process model of drop-out from distance education, *Journal of Higher Education*, 60: 278–301.

Kember, D. (1990) The use of a model to derive interventions which might reduce drop-out from distance education courses, *Higher Education*, 20: 11–24.

Kember, D. (1995) *Open Learning Courses for Adults: A Model of Student Progress*. Englewood Cliffs, NJ: Educational Technology Publications.

Kember, D. (1996) The intention to both memorise and understand: another approach to learning? *Higher Education*, 31: 341–54.

Kember, D. (1997) A reconceptualisation of the research into university academics' conceptions of teaching, *Learning and Instruction*, 7: 255–75.

Kember, D. and Gow, L. (1989) A model of student approaches to learning encompassing ways to influence and change approaches, *Instructional Science*, 18: 263–88.

Kember, D. and Gow, L. (1990) Cultural specificity of approaches to study, *British Journal of Educational Psychology*, 60: 356–63.

Kember, D. and Gow, L. (1991) A challenge to the anecdotal stereotype of the Asian student, *Studies in Higher Education*, 16: 117–28.

Kember, D. and Gow, L. (1994) Orientations to teaching and their effect on the quality of student learning, *Journal of Higher Education*, 65, 58–74.

Kember, D. and Harper, G. (1987a) Approaches to studying research and its implications for the quality of learning from distance education, *Journal of Distance Education*, 2(2): 15–30.

Kember, D. and Harper, G. (1987b) Implications for instruction arising from the relationship between approaches to studying and academic outcomes, *Instructional Science*, 16: 35–46.

Kember, D., Lai, T., Murphy, D., Siaw, I., Wong, J. and Yuen, K.S. (1990) Naturalistic evaluation of distance learning courses, *Journal of Distance Education*, 5(1): 38–52.

Kember, D., Lai, T., Murphy, D., Siaw, I. and Yuen, K.S. (1992) Student progress in distance education: identification of explanatory constructs, *British Journal of Educational Psychology*, 62: 285–98.

Kember, D., Lai, T., Murphy, D., Siaw, I. and Yuen, K.S. (1994) Student progress in distance education courses: a replication study, *Adult Education Quarterly*, 45: 286–301.

Kember, D. and Leung, D.Y.P. (1998) The dimensionality of approaches to learning: an investigation with confirmatory factor analysis on the structure of the SPQ and LPQ, *British Journal of Educational Psychology*, 68: 395–407.

Kember, D. and Murphy, D. (1990) A synthesis of open, distance and student centred learning, *Open Learning*, 5(2): 3–8.

Kember, D., Murphy, D., Siaw, I. and Yuen, K.S. (1991) Towards a causal model of student progress in distance education: research in Hong Kong, *American Journal of Distance Education*, 5(2): 3–15.

Kennedy, D. and Powell, R. (1976) Student progress and withdrawal in the Open University, *Teaching at a Distance*, No. 7, pp. 61–75.

Kirkpatrick, D. (1997) Becoming flexible: contested territory, *Studies in Continuing Education*, 19: 160–73.

Kolb, D.A. (1981) Experiential learning theory and the Learning Style Inventory: a reply to Freedman and Stumpf, *Academy of Management Review*, 6: 289–96.

Kolb, D.A. (1984) *Experiential Learning: Experience as the Source of Learning and Development*. Englewood Cliffs, NJ: Prentice-Hall.

Kolb, D.A. and Fry, R. (1975) Towards an applied theory of experiential learning, in C.L. Cooper (ed.) *Theories of Group Processes* (pp. 33–57). London: Wiley.

Kolb, D.A., Rubin, I.M. and McIntyre, J.M. (1971) *Organizational Psychology: An Experiential Approach*. Englewood Cliffs, NJ: Prentice-Hall.

Kolb, D.A., Rubin, I.M. and Osland, J. (1991) *Organizational Behavior: An Experiential Approach*. Englewood Cliffs, NJ: Prentice-Hall.

Köymen, U.S. (1992) Comparison of learning and study strategies of traditional and open-learning-system students in Turkey, *Distance Education*, 13: 108–17.

Krippendorff, K. (1980) *Content Analysis: An Introduction to its Methodology*. Beverly Hills, CA: Sage.

Lamb, S.W. and Certo, S.C. (1978) The Learning Styles Inventory (LSI) and instrument bias, in J.C. Susbauer (ed.) *Proceedings of the 38th Annual Meeting of the Academy of Management* (pp. 28–32). San Francisco: Academy of Management.

Landbeck, R. and Mugler, F. (1994) *Approaches to Study and Conceptions of Learning of Students at the USP*. Suva, Fiji: University of the South Pacific, Centre for the Enhancement of Learning and Teaching.

Laurillard, D.M. (1978) A study of the relationship between some of the cognitive and contextual factors in student learning. Unpublished doctoral dissertation, University of Surrey, UK (British Theses Index No. DX5755/9AX).

Laurillard, D. (1979) The processes of student learning, *Higher Education*, 8: 395–409.

Laurillard, D. (1984) Learning from problem-solving, in F. Marton, D. Hounsell and N. Entwistle (eds) *The Experience of Learning* (pp. 124–43). Edinburgh: Scottish Academic Press. Reprinted (1997) as Styles and approaches in problem-solving, in F. Marton, D. Hounsell and N. Entwistle (eds) *The Experience of Learning: Implications for Teaching and Studying in Higher Education*, 2nd edn (pp. 126–44). Edinburgh: Scottish Academic Press.

Laurillard, D. (1993) *Rethinking University Teaching: A Framework for the Effective Use of Educational Technology*. London: Routledge.

Lennon, K. and Whitford, M. (eds) (1994) *Knowing the Difference: Feminist Perspectives in Epistemology*. London: Routledge.

Lewis, R. (1986) What is open learning? *Open Learning*, 1(2): 5–10.

Lewis, R. and Spencer, D. (1986) *What is Open Learning? An Introduction to the Series* (Open Learning Guide 4). London: Council for Educational Technology.

Lockhart, D. and Schmeck, R.R. (1984) Learning styles and classroom evaluation methods: different strokes for different folks, *College Student Journal*, 17: 94–100.

Lonka, K. and Lindblom-Ylänne, S. (1996) Epistemologies, conceptions of learning and study practices in medicine and psychology, *Higher Education*, 31: 5–24.

Loo, R. (1996) Construct validity and classification stability of the revised Learning Style Inventory (LSI-1985), *Educational and Psychological Measurement*, 56: 529–36.

Loo, R. (1999) Confirmatory factor analyses of Kolb's Learning Style Inventory (LSI-1985), *British Journal of Educational Psychology*, 69: 213–19.

MacKenzie, N., Postgate, R. and Scupham, J. (1975) *Open Learning: Systems and Problems in Post-secondary Education.* Paris: Unesco Press.

Markowitz, H., Jr. (1983) Independent study by correspondence in American universities, *Distance Education,* 4: 149–70.

Marland, P. (1989) An approach to research on distance learning, *British Journal of Educational Technology,* 20: 173–82.

Marland, P., Patching, W. and Putt, I. (1992) Thinking while studying: a process tracing study of distance learners, *Distance Education,* 13: 193–217.

Marland, P., Patching, W., Putt, I. and Putt, R. (1990) Distance learners' interactions with text while studying, *Distance Education,* 11: 71–91.

Marland, P., Patching, W., Putt, I. and Store, R. (1984) Learning from distance-teaching materials: A study of students' mediating responses, *Distance Education,* 5: 215–36.

Marshall, H. and Nicolson, P. (1991) Why choose psychology? Mature and other students' accounts at graduation, in J. Radford (ed.) *The Choice of Psychology,* Group of Teachers of Psychology Occasional Paper No. 12 (pp. 22–9). Leicester: British Psychological Society.

Marshall, J.C. and Merritt, S.L. (1985) Reliability and construct validity of alternate forms of the Learning Style Inventory, *Educational and Psychological Measurement,* 45: 931–7.

Marshall, J.C. and Merritt, S.L. (1986) Reliability and construct validity of the Learning Style Questionnaire, *Educational and Psychological Measurement,* 46: 257–62.

Mårtenson, D.F. (1986) Students' approaches to studying in four medical schools, *Medical Education,* 20: 532–4.

Martin, E. and Ramsden, P. (1987) Learning skills, or skill in learning? in J.T.E. Richardson, M.W. Eysenck and D. Warren Piper (eds) *Student Learning: Research in Education and Cognitive Psychology* (pp. 155–67). Milton Keynes: Society for Research into Higher Education and Open University Press.

Marton, F. (1970) *Structural Dynamics of Learning,* Göteborg Studies in Educational Sciences, No. 5. Stockholm: Almqvist and Wiksell.

Marton, F. (1975) On non-verbatim learning: I. Level of processing and level of outcome, *Scandinavian Journal of Psychology,* 16: 273–9.

Marton, F. (1976a) On non-verbatim learning: III. The erosion effect of a task-induced learning algorithm. *Scandinavian Journal of Psychology,* 17: 41–8.

Marton, F. (1976b) On non-verbatim learning: IV. Some theoretical and methodological notes, *Scandinavian Journal of Psychology,* 17: 125–8.

Marton, F. (1976c) What does it take to learn? Some implications of an alternative view of learning, in N. Entwistle (ed.) *Strategies for Research and Development in Higher Education* (pp. 32–42). Amsterdam: Swets and Zeitlinger.

Marton, F. (1978) *Describing Conceptions of the World Around Us,* Report No. 66. Mölndal, Sweden: University of Göteborg, Institute of Education (ERIC Document Reproduction Service No. ED 169 074).

Marton, F. (1979) Skill as an aspect of knowledge, *Journal of Higher Education,* 50: 602–14.

Marton, F. (1981) Phenomenography: describing conceptions of the world around us, *Instructional Science,* 10: 177–200.

Marton, F. (1986) Phenomenography: a research approach to investigating different understandings of reality, *Journal of Thought,* 21(3): 28–49. Reprinted (1988) in R.R. Sherman and W.B. Webb (eds) *Qualitative Research in Education: Focus and Methods* (pp. 141–61). London: Falmer Press.

Marton, F. (1988) Phenomenography: exploring different conceptions of reality, in D.M. Fetterman (ed.) *Qualitative Approaches to Evaluation in Education: The Silent Scientific Revolution* (pp. 176–205). New York: Praeger.

Marton, F. (1994) Phenomenography, in T. Husén and T.N. Postlethwaite (eds) *The International Encyclopedia of Education*, 2nd edn (Vol. 8, pp. 4424–9). Oxford: Pergamon Press.

Marton, F. and Booth, S. (1997) *Learning and Awareness*. Mahwah, NJ: Erlbaum.

Marton, F., Carlsson, M.A. and Halász, L. (1992) Differences in understanding and the use of reflective variation in reading, *British Journal of Educational Psychology*, 62: 1–16.

Marton, F. and Dahlgren, L.O. (1976) On non-verbatim learning: III. The outcome space of some basic concepts in economics, *Scandinavian Journal of Psychology*, 17: 49–55.

Marton, F., Dall'Alba, G. and Beaty, E. (1993) Conceptions of learning, *International Journal of Educational Research*, 19: 277–300.

Marton, F., Dall'Alba, G. and Tse, L.K. (1996) Memorizing and understanding: the keys to the paradox? in D.A. Watkins and J.B. Biggs (eds) *The Chinese Learner: Cultural, Psychological and Contextual Influences* (pp. 71–83). Hong Kong: University of Hong Kong, Comparative Education Research Centre. Melbourne: Australian Council for Educational Research.

Marton, F., Hounsell, D. and Entwistle, N. (eds) (1997) *The Experience of Learning: Implications for Teaching and Studying in Higher Education*, 2nd edn. Edinburgh: Scottish Academic Press.

Marton, F. and Säljö, R. (1976a) On qualitative differences in learning: I. Outcome and process, *British Journal of Educational Psychology*, 46: 4–11.

Marton, F. and Säljö, R. (1976b) On qualitative differences in learning: II. Outcome as a function of the learner's conception of the task, *British Journal of Educational Psychology*, 46: 115–27.

Marton, F. and Säljö, R. (1984) Approaches to learning, in F. Marton, D. Hounsell and N. Entwistle (eds) *The Experience of Learning* (pp. 36–55). Edinburgh: Scottish Academic Press.

Marton, F. and Svensson, L. (1979) Conceptions of research in student learning, *Higher Education*, 8: 471–86.

Marton, F. and Wenestam, C.-G. (1978) Qualitative differences in the understanding and retention of the main point in some texts based on the principle-example structure, in M.M. Gruneberg, P.E. Morris and R.N. Sykes (eds) *Practical Aspects of Memory* (pp. 633–43). London: Academic Press.

McClelland, D.C. (1961) *The Achieving Society*. Princeton, NJ: Van Nostrand.

McKay, J. and Kember, D. (1997) Spoon feeding leads to regurgitation: a better diet can result in more digestible learning outcomes, *Higher Education Research and Development*, 16, 55–67.

Merritt, S.L. and Marshall, J.C. (1984) Reliability and construct validity of ipsative and normative forms of the Learning Style Inventory, *Educational and Psychological Measurement*, 44: 463–72.

Meyer, J.H.F. (1988) Student perceptions of learning context and approaches to studying, *South African Journal of Higher Education*, 2: 73–82.

Meyer, J.H.F. (1991) Study orchestration: the manifestation, interpretation and consequences of contextualised approaches to studying, *Higher Education*, 22: 297–316.

Meyer, J.H.F. (1995) Gender-group differences in the learning behaviour of entering first-year university students, *Higher Education*, 29: 201–15.

Meyer, J.H.F. and Dunne, T.T. (1991) Study approaches of nursing students: effects of an extended clinical context, *Medical Education*, 25: 497–516.

Meyer, J.H.F., Dunne, T.T. and Richardson, J.T.E. (1994) A gender comparison of contextualised study behaviour in higher education, *Higher Education*, 27: 469–85.

Meyer, J.H.F., Dunne, T.T. and Sass, A.R. (1992) Impressions of disadvantage: I. School versus university study orchestration and consequences for academic support, *Higher Education*, 24: 291–316.

Meyer, J.H.F. and Muller, M.W. (1990a) Evaluating the quality of student learning: I. An unfolding analysis of the association between perceptions of learning context and approaches to studying at an individual level, *Studies in Higher Education*, 15: 131–54.

Meyer, J.H.F. and Muller, M.W. (1990b) An unfolding analysis of the association between perceptions of learning context and approaches to studying, *South African Journal of Higher Education*, 4: 46–58.

Meyer, J.H.F. and Parsons, P. (1989a) Approaches to studying and course perceptions using the Lancaster Inventory: a comparative study, *Studies in Higher Education*, 14: 137–53.

Meyer, J.H.F. and Parsons, P. (1989b) An empirical study of English- and Afrikaans-speaking students' approaches to studying, *South African Journal of Higher Education*, 3: 109–14.

Meyer, J.H.F., Parsons, P. and Dunne, T.T. (1990a) Individual study orchestrations and their association with learning outcome, *Higher Education*, 20: 67–89.

Meyer, J.H.F., Parsons, P. and Dunne, T.T. (1990b) Study orchestration and learning outcome: evidence of association over time among disadvantaged students, *Higher Education*, 20: 245–69.

Meyer, J.H.F. and Watson, R.M. (1991) Evaluating the quality of student learning: II. Study orchestration and the curriculum, *Studies in Higher Education*, 16: 251–75.

Miller, C.D., Alway, M. and McKinley, D.L. (1987) Effects of learning styles and strategies on academic success, *Journal of College Student Personnel*, 28: 399–404.

Miller, C.D., Finley, J. and McKinley, D.L. (1990) Learning approaches and motives: male and female differences and implications for learning assistance programs, *Journal of College Student Development*, 31: 147–54.

Miller, C.M.L. and Parlett, M. (1974) *Up to the Mark: A Study of the Examination Game.* London: Society for Research into Higher Education.

Moore, M.G. (1972) Learner autonomy: the second dimension of independent learning, *Convergence*, 5: 76–88.

Moore, M.G. (1973) Toward a theory of independent learning and teaching, *Journal of Higher Education*, 44: 661–79.

Moore, M.G. (1980) Independent study, in R.D. Boyd, J.W. Apps and Associates, *Redefining the Discipline of Adult Education* (pp. 16–31). San Francisco: Jossey-Bass.

Moore, M.G. (1983) The individual adult learner, in M. Tight (ed.) *Education for Adults: Vol. 1. Adult Learning and Education* (pp. 153–68). London: Croom Helm.

Moore, M.G. (1985) Some observations on current research in distance education, *Epistolodidaktika*, No. 1, pp. 35–62.

Moore, M.G. (1986) Self-directed learning and distance education, *Journal of Distance Education*, 1(1): 7–24.

Moore, M.G. (1989) Editorial: three types of interaction, *American Journal of Distance Education*, 3(2): 1–6.

Moore, M.G. (1994) Trends and needs in distance education research. Paper presented at the First Conference on Distance Education in Russia, Moscow, 5–8 July.

Morgan, A. (1984) A report on qualitative methodologies in research in distance education, *Distance Education*, 5: 252–67.

Morgan, A. (1991) *Research into Student Learning in Distance Education.* Geelong, Victoria: Deakin University. Underdale, South Australia: University of South Australia (ERIC Document Reproduction Service No. ED 342 371).

Morgan, A. and Beaty, L. (1997) The world of the learner, in F. Marton, D. Hounsell and N. Entwistle (eds) *The Experience of Learning: Implications for Teaching and Studying in Higher Education*, 2nd edn (pp. 217–37). Edinburgh: Scottish Academic Press.

Morgan, A., Gibbs, G. and Taylor, E. (1980) *Students' Approaches to Studying the Social Science and Technology Foundation Courses: Preliminary Studies.* Study Methods Group Report No. 4. Milton Keynes: The Open University, Institute of Educational Technology (ERIC Document Reproduction Service No. ED 197 639).

Morgan, A., Gibbs, G. and Taylor, E. (1981) *What Do Open University Students Initially Understand about Learning?* Study Methods Group Report No. 8. Milton Keynes: The Open University, Institute of Educational Technology (ERIC Document Reproduction Service No. ED 203 748).

Morgan, A., Taylor, E. and Gibbs, G. (1982) Variations in students' approaches to studying, *British Journal of Educational Technology*, 13: 107–13.

Morgan, A., Taylor, E. and Gibbs, G. (1983) Students' experiences of learning: orientations to learning, perceptions of gains and development as learners. Paper presented at the Annual Meeting of the American Educational Research Association, Montreal, Canada, 11–15 April (ERIC Document Reproduction Service No. ED 237 048).

Moss, C.J. (1982) Academic achievement and individual differences in the learning processes of basic skills students in the university, *Applied Psychological Measurement*, 6: 291–6.

Mugridge, I. (ed.) (1992) *Perspectives on Distance Education: Distance Education in Single and Dual Mode Universities.* Vancouver: Commonwealth of Learning.

Mumford, A. (1993) Putting learning styles to work: an integrated approach, *Journal of European Industrial Training*, 17(10): 3–9.

Murray-Harvey, R. (1994) Learning styles and approaches to learning: distinguishing between concepts and instruments, *British Journal of Educational Psychology*, 64: 373–88.

Newble, D.I. and Clarke, R.M. (1986) The approaches to learning of students in a traditional and in an innovative problem-based medical school, *Medical Education*, 20: 267–73.

Newble, D. and Clarke, R. (1987) Approaches to learning in a traditional and an innovative medical school, in J.T.E. Richardson, M.W. Eysenck and D. Warren Piper (eds) *Student Learning: Research in Education and Cognitive Psychology* (pp. 39–46). Milton Keynes: SRHE and Open University Press.

Newble, D.I. and Entwistle, N.J. (1986) Learning styles and approaches: implications for medical education, *Medical Education*, 20: 162–75.

Newble, D.I., Hejka, E.J. and Whelan, G. (1990) The approaches to learning of specialist physicians, *Medical Education*, 24: 101–9.

Newstead, S.E. (1992) A study of two 'quick-and-easy' methods of assessing individual differences in student learning, *British Journal of Educational Psychology*, 62: 299–312.

Nielsen, H.D., Moos, R.H. and Lee, E.A. (1978) Response bias in follow-up studies of college students, *Research in Higher Education*, 9: 97–113.

Nisbett, R.E. and Wilson, T.D. (1977) Telling more than we can know: verbal reports on mental processes, *Psychological Review*, 84: 231–59.

Olgren, C.H. (1993) Adults' learning strategies and outcomes in an independent study course, *Dissertation Abstracts International*, 54: 403A.

Olgren, C.H. (1996) Cognitive strategies in independent learning, in C.C. Gibson (ed.) *Distance Education Symposium 3: Learners and Learning*, Research Monograph No. 13 (pp. 4–16). University Park, PA: Pennsylvania State University, American Center for the Study of Distance Education.

O'Neil, M.J. and Child, D. (1984) Biggs' SPQ: a British study of its internal structure, *British Journal of Educational Psychology*, 54: 228–34.

Parer, M.S. (1988) *Textual Design and Student Learning*. Churchill, Victoria: Gippsland Institute, Centre for Distance Learning.

Parer, M. and Benson, R. (1989) *Professional Training by Distance Education. Perspectives from Psychology Majors: A Student Diary Report*. Churchill, Victoria: Gippsland Institute, Centre for Distance Learning.

Parlett, M.R. (1970) The syllabus-bound student, in L. Hudson (ed.) *The Ecology of Human Intelligence* (pp. 272–83). Harmondsworth: Penguin Books.

Parsons, P.G. (1988) The Lancaster Approaches to Studying Inventory and Course Perceptions Questionnaire: a replicated study at the Cape Technikon, *South African Journal of Higher Education*, 2: 103–11.

Pascarella, E.T. and Terenzini, P.T. (1991) *How College Affects Students*. San Francisco: Jossey-Bass.

Pask, G. (1976) Styles and strategies of learning, *British Journal of Educational Psychology*, 46: 128–48.

Pask, G. (1988) Learning strategies, teaching strategies and conceptual or learning style, in R.R. Schmeck (ed.) *Learning Strategies and Learning Styles* (pp. 83–100). New York: Plenum Press.

Pask, G. and Scott, B.C.E. (1972) Learning strategies and individual competence, *International Journal of Man–Machine Studies*, 4: 217–53.

Perry, R.P. (1991) Perceived control in college students: implications for instruction in higher education, in J.C. Smart (ed.) *Higher Education: Handbook of Theory and Research* (Vol. VII, pp. 1–56). New York: Agathon Press.

Perry, W.G., Jr (1970) *Forms of Intellectual and Ethical Development in the College Years: A Scheme*. New York: Holt, Rinehart and Winston.

Perry, W.G., Jr, Sprinthall, N.A. and Wideman, J.M. (1968) Notes on *The Checklist of Educational Views*, in W.G. Perry, Jr, *Patterns of Development in Thought and Values of Students in a Liberal Arts College: A Validation of a Scheme* (pp. 99–119). Cambridge, MA: Harvard University, Bureau of Study Counsel (ERIC Document Reproduction Service No. ED 024 315).

Phipps, R. and Merisotis, J. (1999) *What's the Difference? A Review of Contemporary Research on the Effectiveness of Distance Learning in Higher Education*. Washington, DC: Institute for Higher Education Policy.

Price, G.E., Dunn, R. and Dunn, K. (1991) *Productivity Environmental Preference Survey (PEPS Manual)*. Lawrence, KS: Price Systems.

Prosser, M. and Trigwell, K. (1999) *Understanding Learning and Teaching: The Experience in Higher Education*. Buckingham: SRHE and Open University Press.

Provost, S.C. and Bond, N.W. (1997) Approaches to studying and academic performance in a traditional psychology course, *Higher Education Research and Development*, 16: 309–20.

Pugliese, R.R. (1994) Telecourse persistence and psychological variables, *American Journal of Distance Education*, 8(3): 22–39.

Pugliese, R. (1996) The loneliness of the long distance learner, in C.C. Gibson (ed.) *Distance Education Symposium 3: Learners and Learning*, Research Monograph No. 13 (pp. 30–41). University Park, PA: Pennsylvania State University, American Center for the Study of Distance Education.

Race, P. (1994) *The Open Learning Handbook: Promoting Quality in Designing and Delivering Flexible Learning*, 2nd edn. London: Kogan Page.

Ramsden, P. (1979) Student learning and perceptions of the academic environment, *Higher Education*, 8: 411–27.

Ramsden, P. (1981) A study of the relationship between student learning and its academic context. Unpublished doctoral dissertation, University of Lancaster, UK (British Theses Index No. DX42179/82AX).

Ramsden, P. (1984) The context of learning, in F. Marton, D. Hounsell and N. Entwistle (eds) *The Experience of Learning* (pp. 144–64). Edinburgh: Scottish Academic Press. Reprinted (1997) as The context of learning in academic departments, in F. Marton, D. Hounsell and N. Entwistle (eds) *The Experience of Learning: Implications for Teaching and Studying in Higher Education*, 2nd edn (pp. 198–216). Edinburgh: Scottish Academic Press.

Ramsden, P. (1988) Context and strategy: situational influences on learning, in R.R. Schmeck (ed.) *Learning Strategies and Learning Styles* (pp. 159–84). New York: Plenum Press.

Ramsden, P., Beswick, D.G. and Bowden, J.A. (1986) Effects of learning skills interventions on first year university students' learning, *Human Learning*, 5: 151–64.

Ramsden, P., Beswick, D.G. and Bowden, J.A. (1987) Learning processes and learning skills, in J.T.E. Richardson, M.W. Eysenck and D. Warren Piper (eds) *Student Learning: Research in Education and Cognitive Psychology* (pp. 168–76). Milton Keynes: SRHE and Open University Press.

Ramsden, P. and Entwistle, N.J. (1981) Effects of academic departments on students' approaches to studying, *British Journal of Educational Psychology*, 51: 368–83.

Rasch, G. (1960) *Probabilistic Models for Some Intelligence and Attainment Tests*. Copenhagen: Denmarks paedagogiske Institut.

Rekkedal, T. (1983) Enhancing student progress in Norway, *Teaching at a Distance*, No. 23, pp. 19–24.

Rekkedal, T. ([1973] 1984) The written assignments in correspondence education. Effects of reducing turn-around time. An experimental study (S. Turner, trans.), *Distance Education*, 4: 231–52.

Relf, S. and Geddes, T. (1992) A method for assessing student use of study notes, in T. Evans and P. Juler (eds) *Research in Distance Education 2* (pp. 105–11). Geelong, Victoria: Deakin University, Institute of Distance Education.

Ribich, F.D. and Schmeck, R.R. (1979) Multivariate relationships between measures of learning style and memory, *Journal of Research in Personality*, 13: 515–29.

Richardson, J.T.E. (1978) A factor analysis of self-reported handedness, *Neuropsychologia*, 16: 747–8.

Richardson, J.T.E. (1983) Student learning in higher education, *Educational Psychology*, 3: 305–31.

Richardson, J.T.E. (1990) Reliability and replicability of the Approaches to Studying Questionnaire, *Studies in Higher Education*, 15: 155–68.

Richardson, J.T.E. (1992) A critical evaluation of a short form of the Approaches to Studying Inventory, *Psychology Teaching Review*, 1: 34–45.

Richardson, J.T.E. (1993) Gender differences in responses to the Approaches to Studying Inventory, *Studies in Higher Education*, 18: 3–13.

Richardson, J.T.E. (1994a) Cultural specificity of approaches to studying in higher education: a literature survey, *Higher Education*, 27: 449–68.

Richardson, J.T.E. (1994b) Mature students in higher education: I. A literature survey on approaches to studying, *Studies in Higher Education*, 19: 309–25.

Richardson, J.T.E. (1995a) Cultural specificity of approaches to studying in higher education: a comparative investigation using the Approaches to Studying Inventory, *Educational and Psychological Measurement*, 55: 300–8.

Richardson, J.T.E. (1995b) Mature students in higher education: II. An investigation of approaches to studying and academic performance, *Studies in Higher Education*, 20: 5–17.

Richardson, J.T.E. (1996) Measures of effect size, *Behavior Research Methods, Instruments and Computers*, 28: 12–22.

Richardson, J.T.E. (1998) Approaches to studying in undergraduate and postgraduate students, *Studies in Higher Education*, 23: 217–20.

Richardson, J.T.E. (1999) The concepts and methods of phenomenographic research, *Review of Educational Research*, 69: 53–82.

Richardson, J.T.E., Eysenck, M.W. and Warren Piper, D. (eds) (1987) *Student Learning: Research in Education and Cognitive Psychology*. Milton Keynes: SRHE and Open University Press.

Richardson, J.T.E. and King, E. (1991) Gender differences in the experience of higher education: quantitative and qualitative approaches, *Educational Psychology*, 11: 363–82.

Richardson, J.T.E. and King, E. (1998) Adult students in higher education: burden or boon? *Journal of Higher Education*, 69: 65–88.

Richardson, J.T.E., Landbeck, R. and Mugler, F. (1995) Approaches to studying in higher education: a comparative study in the South Pacific, *Educational Psychology*, 15: 417–32.

Richardson, J.T.E., MacLeod-Gallinger, J., McKee, B.G. and Long, G.L. (2000) Approaches to studying in deaf and hearing students in higher education, *Journal of Deaf Studies and Deaf Education*, 5: 156–73.

Richardson, J.T.E., Morgan, A. and Woodley, A. (1999) Approaches to studying in distance education, *Higher Education*, 37: 23–55.

Richardson, J.T.E. and Woodley, A. (1999) Approaches to studying in people with hearing loss. *British Journal of Educational Psychology*, 69: 533–46.

Riding, R. and Rayner, S. (1998) *Cognitive Styles and Learning Strategies: Understanding Style Differences in Learning and Behaviour*. London: David Fulton.

Roberts, D., Boyton, B., Buete, S. and Dawson, D. (1991) Applying Kember's linear-process model to distance education at Charles Sturt University-Riverina, *Distance Education*, 12: 54–84.

Ross, M. (1989) Relation of implicit theories to the construction of personal histories, *Psychological Review*, 96: 341–57.

Ruble, T.L. and Stout, D.E. (1990) Reliability, construct validity and response-set bias of the revised Learning Style Inventory (LSI-1985), *Educational and Psychological Measurement*, 50: 619–29.

Ruble, T.L. and Stout, D.E. (1991) Reliability, classification stability and response-set bias of alternate forms of the Learning Style Inventory (LSI-1985), *Educational and Psychological Measurement*, 51: 481–9.

Rumble, G. (1989) 'Open learning,' 'distance learning,' and the misuse of language, *Open Learning*, 4(2): 28–36.

Rumble, G. and Keegan, D. (1982) Introduction, in G. Rumble and K. Harry (eds) *The Distance Teaching Universities* (pp. 9–14). London: Croom Helm.

Russell, T.L. (1999) *The No Significant Difference Phenomenon as Reported in 355 Research Reports, Summaries and Papers: A Comparative Research Annotated Bibliography on Technology for Distance Education.* Raleigh, NC: North Carolina State University, Office of Instructional Telecommunications.

Ryan, M.P. (1984) Monitoring text comprehension: Individual differences in epistemological standards, *Journal of Educational Psychology*, 76: 248–58.

Saba, F. (1988) Integrated telecommunications systems and instructional transaction, *American Journal of Distance Education*, 2(3): 17–24. Reprinted (1990) in M.G. Moore (ed.) *Contemporary Issues in American Distance Education* (pp. 344–52). Oxford: Pergamon Press.

Sadler-Smith, E. (1996) Approaches to studying: age, gender and academic performance, *Educational Studies*, 22: 367–79.

Sadler-Smith, E. (1997) 'Learning style': frameworks and instruments, *Educational Psychology*, 17: 51–63.

Sadler-Smith, E. and Tsang, F. (1998) A comparative study of approaches to studying in Hong Kong and the United Kingdom, *British Journal of Educational Psychology*, 68: 81–93.

Saga, H. (1992) Students' and tutors' perceptions of learning at Allama Iqbal Open University. Paper presented at the 16th World Conference of the International Council for Distance Education, 'Distance Education for the Twenty-First Century', Nonthaburi, Thailand, 9–13 November (ERIC Document Reproduction Service No. ED 357 736).

Säljö, R. (1975) *Qualitative Differences in Learning as a Function of the Learner's Conception of the Task.* Göteborg: Acta Universitatis Gothoburgensis.

Säljö, R. (1979a) Learning about learning, *Higher Education*, 8: 443–51.

Säljö, R. (1979b) *Learning in the Learner's Perspective: I. Some Common-Sense Assumptions*, Report No. 76. Göteborg: University of Göteborg, Institute of Education.

Säljö, R. (1982) *Learning and Understanding: A Study of Differences in Constructing Meaning from a Text*, Göteborg Studies in Educational Sciences, No. 41. Göteborg: Acta Universitatis Gothoburgensis.

Säljö, R. (1984) Learning from reading, in F. Marton, D. Hounsell and N. Entwistle (eds) *The Experience of Learning* (pp. 71–89). Edinburgh: Scottish Academic Press.

Säljö, R. (1988) Learning in educational settings: methods of inquiry, in P. Ramsden (ed.) *Improving Learning: New Perspectives* (pp. 32–48). London: Kogan Page.

Saussure, F. de ([1916] 1955) *Cours de Linguistique Générale*, 5th edn. Paris: Payot.

Saussure, F. de ([1916] 1959) *Course in General Linguistics* (W. Baskin, trans.). New York: Philosophical Library.

Schmeck, R.R. (1980) Relationships between measures of learning style and reading comprehension, *Perceptual and Motor Skills*, 50: 461–2.

Schmeck, R.R. (1983) Learning styles of college students, in R.F. Dillon and R.R. Schmeck (eds) *Individual Differences in Cognition, Vol. 1* (pp. 233–79). New York: Academic Press.

Schmeck, R.R. (1988) Individual differences and learning strategies, in C.E. Weinstein, E.T. Goetz and P.A. Alexander (eds) *Learning and Study Strategies: Issues in Assessment, Instruction and Evaluation* (pp. 171–91). San Diego, CA: Academic Press.

Schmeck, R.R. and Geisler-Brenstein, E. (1989) Individual differences that affect the way students approach learning, *Learning and Individual Differences*, 1: 85–124.

Schmeck, R.R., Geisler-Brenstein, E. and Cercy, S.P. (1991) Self-concept and learning: the Revised Inventory of Learning Processes, *Educational Psychology*, 11: 343–62.

Schmeck, R.R. and Grove, E. (1979) Academic achievement and individual differences in learning processes, *Applied Psychological Measurement*, 3: 43–9.

Schmeck, R.R., Ribich, F. and Ramanaiah, N. (1977) Development of a self-report inventory for assessing individual differences in learning processes, *Applied Psychological Measurement*, 1: 413–31.

Schooler, J.W., Ohlsson, S. and Brooks, K. (1993) Thoughts beyond words: when language overshadows insight, *Journal of Experimental Psychology: General*, 122: 166–83.

Schuemer, R. (1993) *Some Psychological Aspects of Distance Education*. Hagen, Germany: FernUniversität, Zentrales Institut für Fernstudienforschung.

Scouller, K. (1998) The influence of assessment method on students' learning approaches: multiple choice question examination versus assignment essay, *Higher Education*, 35: 453–72.

Severiens, S.E. and ten Dam, G.T.M. (1994) Gender differences in learning styles: a narrative review and quantitative meta-analysis, *Higher Education*, 27: 487–501.

Severiens, S. and ten Dam, G. (1997) Gender and gender identity differences in learning styles, *Educational Psychology*, 17: 79–93.

Severiens, S. and ten Dam, G. (1998) Gender and learning: comparing two theories, *Higher Education*, 35: 329–50.

Shaw, B. and Taylor, J.C. (1984) Instructional design: distance education and academic tradition, *Distance Education*, 5: 277–85.

Sims, R.R., Veres, J.G., III and Shake, L.G. (1989) An exploratory examination of the convergence between the Learning Styles Questionnaire and the Learning Style Inventory II, *Educational and Psychological Measurement*, 49: 227–33.

Sims, R.R., Veres, J.G., III, Watson, P. and Buckner, K.E. (1986) The reliability and classification stability of the Learning Style Inventory, *Educational and Psychological Measurement*, 46: 753–60.

Siqueira de Freitas, K. and Lynch, P. (1986) Factors affecting student success at the National Open University of Venezuela, *Distance Education*, 7: 191–200.

Smith, D.M. and Kolb, D.A. (1986) *Learning Style Inventory: User's Guide*. Boston, MA: McBer.

Spady, W.G. (1970) Dropouts from higher education: an interdisciplinary review and synthesis, *Interchange*, 1(1): 64–85.

Spady, W.G. (1971) Dropouts from higher education: toward an empirical model, *Interchange*, 2(3): 38–62.

Speth, C. and Brown, R. (1988) Study approaches, processes and strategies: are three perspectives better than one? *British Journal of Educational Psychology*, 58: 247–57.

Strack, F. and Schwarz, N. (1992) Communicative influences in standardized question situations: the case of implicit collaboration, in G.R. Semin and K. Fiedler (eds) *Language, Interaction and Social Cognition* (pp. 173–193). London: Sage.

Strauss, A. and Corbin, J. (1990) *Basics of Qualitative Research: Grounded Theory Procedures and Techniques*. Newbury Park, CA: Sage.

Strauss, A. and Corbin, J. (1994) Grounded theory methodology: an overview, in N.K. Denzin and Y.S. Lincoln (eds) *Handbook of Qualitative Research* (pp. 273–85). Thousand Oaks, CA: Sage.

Suen, H.K. and Stevens, R.J. (1993) Analytic considerations in distance education research, *American Journal of Distance Education*, 7(3): 61–9.

Svensson, L. (1976) *Study Skill and Learning*. Göteborg: Acta Universitatis Gothoburgensis.

Svensson, L. (1977) On qualitative differences in learning: III. Study skill and learning, *British Journal of Educational Psychology*, 47: 233–43.

Sweet, R. (1986) Student dropout in distance education: an application of Tinto's model, *Distance Education*, 7: 201–13.

Tait, H. and Entwistle, N. (1996) Identifying students at risk through ineffective study strategies, *Higher Education*, 31: 97–116.

Tan, C, (1994) Effects of modes of assessment on students' preparation strategies, in G. Gibbs (ed.) *Improving Student Learning: Theory and Practice* (pp. 151–70). Oxford: Oxford Centre for Staff Development.

Taylor, E.M. (1983) Orientation to study: a longitudinal investigation of two degree courses in one university. Unpublished doctoral dissertation, University of Surrey, UK (British Theses Index No. DX48285/84AX).

Taylor, E., Gibbs, G. and Morgan, A. (1980) *The Orientations of Students Studying the Social Science Foundation Course*, Study Methods Group Report No. 7. Milton Keynes: The Open University, Institute of Educational Technology.

Taylor, E., Gibbs, G. and Morgan, A. (1981a) *The Outcomes of Learning from the Social Science Foundation Course: Students' Understandings of Price Control, Power and Oligopoly*, Study Methods Group Report No. 9. Milton Keynes: The Open University, Institute of Educational Technology.

Taylor, E., Morgan, A. and Gibbs, G. (1981b) *Students' Understandings of the Concept of Social Class*, Study Methods Group Report No. 10. Milton Keynes: The Open University, Institute of Educational Technology.

Taylor, E., Morgan, A. and Gibbs, G. (1983) Students' perceptions of gains from studying D101, in *Institutional Research Review*, No. 2 (pp. 133–47). Milton Keynes: The Open University.

Taylor, I. and Burgess, H. (1995) Orientation to self-directed learning: paradox or paradigm? *Studies in Higher Education*, 20: 87–98.

Taylor, J.C. *et al.* (1986) Student persistence in distance education: a cross-cultural multi-institutional perspective, *Distance Education*, 7: 68–91.

Taylor, L., Morgan, A. and Gibbs, G. (1981c) The 'orientation' of Open University foundation students to their studies, *Teaching at a Distance*, No. 20, pp. 3–12.

Teather, D.C.B. (1987) Academics teaching externally in Australian universities. Unpublished thesis for the degree of Master of Educational Administration, University of New England, Armidale, Australia.

Thomas, K. (1988) Gender and the arts/science divide in higher education, *Studies in Higher Education*, 13: 123–37.

Thomas, K. (1990) *Gender and Subject in Higher Education*. Buckingham: SRHE and Open University Press.

Thompson, E. (1999) Can the Distance Education Student Progress (DESP) inventory be used as a tool to predict attrition in distance education? *Higher Education Research and Development*, 18: 77–84.

Thorpe, M. and Grugeon, D. (1987) Moving into open learning, in M. Thorpe and D. Grugeon (eds) *Open Learning for Adults* (pp. 1–11). Harlow: Longman.

Threlkeld, R. and Brzoska, K. (1994) Research in distance education, in B. Willis (ed.) *Distance Education: Strategies and Tools* (pp. 41–66). Englewood Cliffs, NJ: Educational Technology Publications.

Tierney, W.G. (1992) An anthropological analysis of student participation in college, *Journal of Higher Education*, 63: 603–18.

Tinto, V. (1975) Dropout from higher education: a theoretical synthesis of recent research, *Review of Educational Research*, 45: 89–125.

Tinto, V. (1982) Limits of theory and practice in student attrition, *Journal of Higher Education*, 53: 687–700.

Tinto, V. (1987) *Leaving College: Rethinking the Causes and Cures of Student Attrition.* Chicago, IL: University of Chicago Press.

Tooth, D., Tonge, K. and McManus, I.C. (1989) Anxiety and study methods in preclinical students: causal relation to examination performance, *Medical Education*, 23: 416–21.

Trigwell, K. and Prosser, M. (1991a) Improving the quality of student learning: the influence of learning context and student approaches to learning on learning outcomes, *Higher Education*, 22: 251–66.

Trigwell, K. and Prosser, M. (1991b) Relating approaches to study and quality of learning outcomes at the course level, *British Journal of Educational Psychology*, 61: 265–75.

Trigwell, K. and Prosser, M. (1996a) Changing approaches to teaching: a relational perspective, *Studies in Higher Education*, 21, 275–84.

Trigwell, K. and Prosser, M. (1996b) Congruence between intention and strategy in university science teachers' approach to teaching, *Higher Education*, 32, 77–87.

Trigwell, K., Prosser, M. and Taylor, P. (1994) Qualitative differences in approaches to teaching first year university science, *Higher Education*, 27, 75–84.

Trigwell, K., Prosser, M. and Waterhouse, F. (1999) Relations between teachers' approaches to teaching and students' approaches to learning, *Higher Education*, 37, 57–70.

Trueman, M. and Hartley, J. (1996) A comparison between the time-management skills and academic performance of mature and traditional-entry university students, *Higher Education*, 32: 199–215.

Tulving, E. (1962) Subjective organization in free recall of 'unrelated' words, *Psychological Review*, 69: 344–54.

Van den Brande, L. (1993) *Flexible and Distance Learning.* Chichester: Wiley.

Van de Vijver, F. and Hambleton, R.K. (1996) Translating tests: some practical guidelines, *European Psychologist*, 1: 89–99.

Van Gannep, A. ([1908] 1960) *The Rites of Passage* (M.B. Vizedom and G.L. Caffee, trans.). Chicago: University of Chicago Press.

Van Rossum, E.J., Deijkers, R. and Hamer, R. (1985) Students' learning conceptions and their interpretation of significant educational concepts, *Higher Education*, 14: 617–41.

Van Rossum, E.J. and Schenk, S.M. (1984) The relationship between learning conception, study strategy and learning outcome, *British Journal of Educational Psychology*, 54: 73–83.

Van Rossum, E.J. and Taylor, I.P. (1987) The relationship between conceptions of learning and good teaching: A scheme of cognitive development. Paper presented at the Annual Meeting of the American Educational Research Association, Washington, DC, 20–4 April.

Veres, J.G., III, Sims, R.R. and Locklear, T.S. (1991) Improving the reliability of Kolb's revised Learning Style Inventory, *Educational and Psychological Measurement*, 51: 143–50.

Veres, J.G., III, Sims, R.R. and Shake, L.G. (1987) The reliability and classification stability of the Learning Style Inventory in corporate settings, *Educational and Psychological Measurement*, 47: 1127–33.

Vermetten, Y.J., Lodewijks, H.G. and Vermunt, J.D. (1999a) Consistency and variability of learning strategies in different university courses, *Higher Education*, 37: 1–21.

Vermetten, Y.J., Vermunt, J.D. and Lodewijks, H.G. (1999b) A longitudinal perspective on learning strategies in higher education: different viewpoints towards development, *British Journal of Educational Psychology*, 69: 221–42.

Vermunt, J.D. (1995) Process-oriented instruction in learning and thinking strategies, *European Journal of Psychology of Education*, 10: 325–49.

Vermunt, J.D. (1996) Metacognitive, cognitive and affective aspects of learning styles and strategies: a phenomenographic analysis, *Higher Education*, 31: 25–50.

Vermunt, J.D. (1998) The regulation of constructive learning processes, *British Journal of Educational Psychology*, 68: 149–71.

Vermunt, J.D.H.M. and van Rijswijk, F.A.W.M. (1988) Analysis and development of students' skill in selfregulated learning, *Higher Education*, 17: 647–82.

Villegas Grijalba, J.J. (1995) Scope and limitations of research in distance education, in *Globalized and Cooperative Distance Learning*, Proceedings of the IXth Annual Conference of the Asian Association of Open Universities, pp. 416–25. Taiwan: National Open University.

Volet, S.E., Renshaw, P.D. and Tietzel, K. (1994) A short-term longitudinal investigation of cross-cultural differences in study approaches using Biggs' SPQ questionnaire, *British Journal of Educational Psychology*, 64: 301–18.

Von Prümmer, C. (1990) Study motivation of distance students: a report on some results from a survey done at the FernUniversität in 1987/88, *Research in Distance Education*, 2(2): 2–6.

Wade, W. (1994) Introduction, in W. Wade, K. Hodgkinson, A. Smith and J. Arfield (eds) *Flexible Learning in Higher Education* (pp. 12–16). London: Kogan Page.

Wade, W., Hodgkinson, K., Smith, A. and Arfield, J. (eds) (1994) *Flexible Learning in Higher Education*. London: Kogan Page.

Watkins, D. (1982) Identifying the study process dimensions of Australian university students, *Australian Journal of Education*, 26: 76–85.

Watkins, D. (1983) Assessing tertiary study processes, *Human Learning*, 2: 29–37.

Watkins, D. (1984) Student learning processes: an exploratory study in the Philippines, *Human Learning*, 3: 33–42.

Watkins, D. (1996) Hong Kong secondary school leavers: a developmental perspective, in D.A. Watkins and J.B. Biggs (eds) *The Chinese Learner: Cultural, Psychological and Contextual Influences* (pp. 107–19). Hong Kong: University of Hong Kong, Comparative Education Research Centre. Melbourne: Australian Council for Educational Research.

Watkins, D. and Akande, A. (1992) Assessing the approaches to learning of Nigerian students, *Assessment and Evaluation in Higher Education*, 17: 11–20.

Watkins, D. and Hattie, J. (1980) An investigation of the internal structure of the Biggs Study Process Questionnaire, *Educational and Psychological Measurement*, 40: 1125–30.

Watkins, D. and Hattie, J. (1981a) The internal structure and predictive validity of the Inventory of Learning Processes: some Australian and Filipino data, *Educational and Psychological Measurement*, 41: 511–14.

Watkins, D. and Hattie, J. (1981b) The learning processes of Australian university students: investigations of contextual and personological factors, *British Journal of Educational Psychology*, 51: 384–93.

Watkins, D. and Hattie, J. (1985) A longitudinal study of the approaches to learning of Australian tertiary students, *Human Learning*, 4, 127–41.

Watkins, D., Hattie, J. and Astilla, E. (1983) The validity of the four subscales of the Inventory of Learning Processes for a sample of Filipino freshman college students, *Educational and Psychological Measurement*, 43: 531–6.

Watkins, D., Hattie, J. and Astilla, E. (1986) Approaches to studying by Filipino students: a longitudinal investigation, *British Journal of Educational Psychology*, 56: 357–62.

Watkins, D. and Regmi, M. (1990) An investigation of the approach to learning of Nepalese tertiary students, *Higher Education*, 20: 459–69.

Watkins, D. and Regmi, M. (1992) How universal are student conceptions of learning? A Nepalese investigation, *Psychologia*, 35: 101–10.

Watkins, D. and Regmi, M. (1996) Towards the cross-cultural validation of a Western model of student approaches to learning, *Journal of Cross-Cultural Psychology*, 27: 547–60.

Waugh, R.F. (1999) Approaches to studying for students in higher education: a Rasch measurement model analysis, *British Journal of Educational Psychology*, 69: 63–79.

Waugh, R.F. and Addison, P.A. (1998) A Rasch measurement model analysis of the Revised Approaches to Studying Inventory, *British Journal of Educational Psychology*, 68: 95–112.

Webb, G. (1996) *Understanding Staff Development*. Buckingham: SRHE and Open University Press.

Webb, G. (1997) Deconstructing deep and surface: towards a critique of phenomenography, *Higher Education*, 33: 195–212.

Wedemeyer, C.A. (1971) Independent study: 1. Overview, in L.C. Deighton (ed.) *The Encyclopedia of Education* (Vol. 4, pp. 548–57). New York: Macmillan.

Weinstein, C.E., Underwood, V.L., Wicker, F.W. and Cubberley, W.E. (1979) Cognitive learning strategies: verbal and imaginal elaboration, in H.F. O'Neil, Jr and C.D. Spielberger (eds) *Cognitive and Affective Learning Strategies* (pp. 45–75). New York: Academic Press.

Weinstein, C.E., Zimmermann, S.A. and Palmer, D.R. (1988) Assessing learning strategies: the design and development of the LASSI, in C.E. Weinstein, E.T. Goetz and P.A. Alexander (eds) *Learning and Study Strategies: Issues in Assessment, Instruction and Evaluation* (pp. 25–40). San Diego, CA: Academic Press.

White, P.A. (1989) Evidence for the use of information about internal events to improve the accuracy of causal reports, *British Journal of Psychology*, 80: 375–82.

Wilding, J. and Hayes, S. (1992) Relations between approaches to studying and note-taking behaviour in lectures, *Applied Cognitive Psychology*, 6: 233–46.

Wilding, J. and Valentine, E. (1992) Factors predicting success and failure in the first-year examinations of medical and dental courses, *Applied Cognitive Psychology*, 6: 247–61.

Wilson, K L., Smart, R.M. and Watson, R.J. (1996) Gender differences in approaches to learning in first year psychology students, *British Journal of Educational Psychology*, 66: 59–71.

Wong, S.-L. (1992) Approaches to study of distance education students, *Research in Distance Education*, 4(3): 11–17.

Woodley, A. and Parlett, M. (1983) Student drop-out, *Teaching at a Distance*, 24: 2–23.

Wright, B.D. and Stone, M.H. (1979) *Best Test Design*. Chicago: MESA Press.

Yellen, R.E. (1998) Distant learning students: a comparison with traditional studies, *Journal of Educational Technology Systems*, 26: 215–24.

Author Index

Subject Index

The Society for Research into Higher Education

The Society for Research into Higher Education (SRHE) exists to stimulate and coordinate research into all aspects of higher education. It aims to improve the quality of higher education through the encouragement of debate and publication on issues of policy, on the organization and management of higher education institutions, and on the curriculum, teaching and learning methods.

The Society is entirely independent and receives no subsidies, although individual events often receive sponsorship from business or industry. The Society is financed through corporate and individual subscriptions and has members from many parts of the world.

Under the imprint *SRHE & Open University Press*, the Society is a specialist publisher of research, having over 80 titles in print. In addition to *SRHE News*, the Society's newsletter, the Society publishes three journals: *Studies in Higher Education* (three issues a year), *Higher Education Quarterly* and *Research into Higher Education Abstracts* (three issues a year).

The Society runs frequent conferences, consultations, seminars and other events. The annual conference in December is organized at and with a higher education institution. There are a growing number of networks which focus on particular areas of interest, including:

Access	Learning Environment
Assessment	Legal Education
Consultants	Managing Innovation
Curriculum Development	New Technology for Learning
Eastern European	Postgraduate Issues
Educational Development Research	Quantitative Studies
FE/HE	Student Development
Funding	Vocational Qualifications
Graduate Employment	

Benefits to members

Individual

- The opportunity to participate in the Society's networks
- Reduced rates for the annual conferences

- Free copies of *Research into Higher Education Abstracts*
- Reduced rates for *Studies in Higher Education*
- Reduced rates for *Higher Education Quarterly*
- Free copy of *Register of Members' Research Interests* – includes valuable reference material on research being pursued by the Society's members
- Free copy of occasional in-house publications, e.g. *The Thirtieth Anniversary Seminars Presented by the Vice-Presidents*
- Free copies of *SRHE News* which informs members of the Society's activities and provides a calendar of events, with additional material provided in regular mailings
- A 35 per cent discount on all SRHE/Open University Press books
- Access to HESA statistics for student members
- The opportunity for you to apply for the annual research grants
- Inclusion of your research in the *Register of Members' Research Interests*

Corporate

- Reduced rates for the annual conferences
- The opportunity for members of the Institution to attend SRHE's network events at reduced rates
- Free copies of *Research into Higher Education Abstracts*
- Free copies of *Studies in Higher Education*
- Free copies of *Register of Members' Research Interests* – includes valuable reference material on research being pursued by the Society's members
- Free copy of occasional in-house publications
- Free copies of *SRHE News*
- A 35 per cent discount on all SRHE/Open University Press books
- Access to HESA statistics for research for students of the Institution
- The opportunity for members of the Institution to submit applications for the Society's research grants
- The opportunity to work with the Society and co-host conferences
- The opportunity to include in the *Register of Members' Research Interests* your Institution's research into aspects of higher education

Membership details: SRHE, 3 Devonshire Street, London
W1N 2BA, UK. Tel: 020 7 637 2766. Fax: 020 7 637 2781.
email: srhe@mailbox.ulcc.ac.uk
world wide web: http://www.srhe.ac.uk./srhe/
Catalogue: SRHE & Open University Press, Celtic Court,
22 Ballmoor, Buckingham MK18 1XW. Tel: 01280 823388.
Fax: 01280 823233. email: enquiries@openup.co.uk

TEACHING FOR QUALITY LEARNING AT UNIVERSITY

John Biggs

... full of downright good advice for every academic who wants to do something practical to improve his or her students' learning ... there are very few writers on the subject of university teaching who can engage a reader so personally, express things so clearly, relate research findings so eloquently to personal experience.

Paul Ramsden

John Biggs tackles how academics can improve their teaching in today's circumstances of large classes and diverse student populations. His approach is practical but not prescriptive. Teachers need to make decisions on teaching and assessment methods to suit their own circumstances. In order to do that they need a conceptual framework to inform their decision-making. Such a framework is clearly described and exemplified by this book. University teachers can readily adapt the ideas here to their own subjects and teaching conditions. Particular foci in *Teaching for Quality Learning at University* include:

- making the large lecture a more exciting and productive learning experience
- using assessment methods that reveal the complexity and relevance of student learning and that are manageable in large classes
- teaching international students
- helping teachers to reflect on and improve their own practice.

This is an accessible, jargon-free guide for all university teachers interested in enhancing their teaching and their students' learning.

Contents

Changing university teaching – Constructing learning by aligning teaching: constructive alignment – Formulating and clarifying curriculum objectives – Setting the stage for effective teaching – Good teaching: principles and practice – Enriching large-class teaching – Teaching international students – Assessing for learning quality: I. Principles – Assessing for learning quality: II. Practice – Some examples of aligned teaching – On implementation – References – Index – The Society for Research into Higher Education.

272pp   0 335 20171 7 (Paperback)   0 335 20172 5 (hardback)

ON BECOMING AN INNOVATIVE UNIVERSITY TEACHER
REFLECTION IN ACTION

John Cowan

This is one of the most interesting texts I have read for many years . . . It is authoritative and clearly written. It provides a rich set of examples of teaching, and a reflective discourse.

Professor George Brown

. . . succeeds in inspiring the reader by making the process of reflective learning interesting and thought provoking . . . has a narrative drive which makes it a book too good to put down.

Dr Mary Thorpe

What comes through very strongly and is an admirable feature is so much of the author's own personal experience, what it felt like to take risks and how his own practice developed as a result of taking risks, exploring uncharted territory . . . The book has the potential to become the reflective practitioner's 'bible'.

Dr Lorraine Stefani

This unusual, accessible and significant book begins each chapter by posing a question with which college and university teachers can be expected to identify; and then goes on to answer the question by presenting a series of examples; finally, each chapter closes with 'second thoughts', presenting a viewpoint somewhat distinct from that taken by John Cowan. This book will assist university teachers to plan and run innovative activities to enable their students to engage in effective reflective learning; it will help them adapt other teachers' work for use with their own students; and will give them a rationale for the place of reflective teaching and learning in higher education.

Contents
Introduction – What is meant in education by 'reflecting'? – What does reflection have to offer in education – Is there a methodology you can and should follow – What can you do to encourage students to reflect? – What is involved for students in analytical reflection? – What is involved in evaluative reflection? – How can you adapt ideas from my teaching, for yours? – How should you get started? – How can such innovations be evaluated? – Where should you read about other work in this field? – A Postscript: final reflections – References – Index – The Society for Research into Higher Education.

192pp   0 335 19993 3 (Paperback)   0 335 19994 1 (Hardback)

UNDERSTANDING LEARNING AND TEACHING
THE EXPERIENCE IN HIGHER EDUCATION

Michael Prosser and Keith Trigwell

How can university teachers improve the quality of student learning? Prosser and Trigwell argue that the answer lies in determining how students perceive their unique learning situations. In doing so they draw upon the considerable body of educational research into student learning in higher education which has been developed and published over the past three decades; *and* they enable university teachers to research and improve their own teaching.

This book outlines the key principles underlying successful teaching and learning in higher education, and is a key resource for all university teachers.

Contents

Learning and teaching in higher education – A model for understanding learning and teaching in higher education – Students' prior experiences of learning – Students' perceptions of their learning situation – Students' approaches to learning – Students' learning outcomes – Experiences of teaching in higher education – Understanding learning and teaching – Appendix: Approaches to teaching inventory – References – Index – The Society for Research into Higher Education.

208pp   0 335 19831 7 (Paperback)   0 335 19832 5 (Hardback)